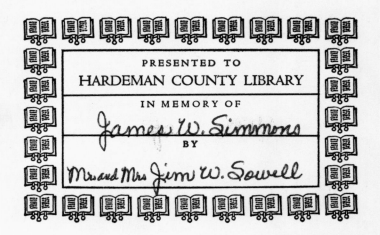

BAD MEDICINE & GOOD

Tales of the Kiowas

Bac

With drawings by
NICK EGGENHOFER

Medicine & Good
Tales of the Kiowas

By *Wilbur Sturtevant Nye*

Norman ✦ University of Oklahoma Press

By Wilbur Sturtevant Nye

Carbine and Lance: The Story of Old Fort Sill (Norman, 1937)

(with Jason Betzinez) *I Fought with Geronimo* (Harrisburg, 1959)

(with Edward J. Stackpole) *The Battle of Gettysburg:* A Guided Tour (Harrisburg, 1960)

Bad Medicine & Good: Tales of the Kiowas (Norman, 1962)

Library of Congress Catalog Card Number: 62-10770

Copyright 1962 by the University of Oklahoma Press,
Publishing Division of the University.
Composed and printed at Norman, Oklahoma, U.S.A.,
by the University of Oklahoma Press. First edition.

To my daughter Helene

We Put That Road Aside

This account of Kiowa history gives a background for the stories that follow. It is a composite of material furnished by Zir-a-cuny, Iseeo, George Hunt, Ay-tah, Hunting Horse, Peah-to-mah, and many others.

☼ We Kiowas first lived north of the great rock that rose out of the plain, pushing up the Boys. In that land was also the magic lake where the medicine man first saw the ten Grandmother gods. We also lived in a country where hot water shot up out of the ground, high in the air. When we first saw this at a distance, we did not know what it was, but when we got nearer, we found that it was boiling water. That was a very dangerous place. We grew up in that hot-water country.[1]

---

[1] An old woman named Zir-a-cuny (Water Monster), who about 1890 gave this account of tribal origins to Captain H. L. Scott, has reversed the chronology. The earliest known home country of the Kiowas was not near the rock she mentions but was in the "hot-water country," that is, the area along and north of the Yellowstone. About 1690, they began to drift eastward toward the Black Hills, settling near Devil's Tower, in Wyoming, which was the rock that pushed up the Boys. These were twin hero-gods, sons of the sun, one of whom gave his body in ten portions to the Kiowas as their tribal medicine. The other disappeared into the magic lake which she mentioned. This is discussed in detail in the story "Tribal Medicine."

From there we went eastward to the land of the Crows. Here we learned about the Cheyennes and Arapahoes, who were southeast of the Crows and who began fighting us. We did not see any Sioux, but we heard of them as being far to the east.

In those days we had no horses, only dogs to pack our things. Each man would have eight or ten dogs. We had few lodges then. Even a man with two wives did not always have a separate tipi for his family. Several families lived together in a good-sized lodge which was supported by twenty poles. Those poles were as long and heavy as the ones we had later when we owned horses, but they were made of spruce instead of cedar. Four dogs were required to drag the supports of a single lodge. The hide cover, too bulky and heavy to pack on a dog's back, was rolled up and carried on a travois dragged behind the dog. In this manner we also carried rawhide parfleche, the bags which contained our camp things and food. We couldn't carry much dried meat because of its weight. Therefore, we made only short moves and camped for a long time in each place.

We killed buffalo in those days by surrounding them and driving them over a cliff. We had men concealed all around them who would rise up and shake robes at the buffalo until they ran out on a high point and plunged over the cliff, those behind pushing those in front. When the Kiowas came and looked over the cliff, it was wonderful! The buffalo were all piled up at the bottom, some with broken legs, others with broken backs. The Kiowas then would be full of meat.

After we got horses, we put that road aside. We surrounded the buffalo on horseback and shot them with arrows.

While we were living near the Black Hills, we fought the Comanches and drove them south until, after long years, we made peace with them. We didn't get many horses at first, only two or three each time we would raid the Comanches. After the Comanches became our friends, and we moved farther south, we got plenty of horses. Before then we wandered mostly north of the Arkansas River and along the eastern slopes of the Rocky Mountains. After the Comanches let us come into their country, we drifted southward until by the Year the Stars Fell[2] our home camps were generally

[2] The Kiowa-Comanche accord was consummated about 1790, according to James Mooney in his *Calendar History of the Kiowas*, Seventeenth Annual Report,

along the Washita River or just north of the Wichita Mountains. In those days our men sometimes rode west through the Rocky Mountains to fight the Utes and Navahos. We were also at war with the Cheyennes and Arapahoes to the north, and the Pawnees, Sah-kee-bo [Sac and Foxes], and Osages to the northeast. Like the Comanches, we traded with the Wichitas to the south along Red River and with the Mescalero Apaches and New Mexicans to the southwest. But with the Texans and the people of Old Mexico there was always trouble.

From the upper waters of the North Fork of Red River our great war trail ran south along the edge of the Staked Plains, crossed the Pecos at a ford which the whites called Horsehead Crossing, and continued through the Big Bend country to a deep canyon of the Rio Grande. Here we crossed into Mexico near Presidio de San Vicente and headed through the no-water country toward Chihuahua and farther southwest to take horses and captives from the red-coated people.[3] Sometimes our men would be gone on these expeditions for two years. A few Kiowa war parties even rode through the valley of the lower Rio Grande into the Timbered Country, where they saw little men in the trees who would not reply to them in any language, not even the sign language.[4]

We saw no Americans in the Kiowa-Comanche country until about ten years before the Year the Stars Fell, when a few traders came with oxcarts to the upper Arkansas where Bent's Fort was later built.

A dreadful tragedy came upon us in the summer of the Year the Stars Fell. Our various bands had separated to hunt buffalo and wild horses, and many of the warriors had gone west to fight the Utes or some other enemy. One village, camped in a mountain gap on a branch of Otter Creek, was attacked early one morning by a strong

Bureau of American Ethnology. The Night the Stars Fell, which places the Year the Stars Fell, refers to a notable meteoric display which occurred early on the morning of November 13, 1833.

[3] Mexicans of Sonora and Chihuahua were probably called "the red-coated people" because of the scarlet jackets of the lancers or the red serapes worn by many peons. The presidio of San Vicente was abandoned about 1800 because of incessant Indian raids.

[4] The Timbered Country refers to the jungles of Tamaulipas, where the Indians saw monkeys in the trees.

party of Osages. Since the young men were away, it was a massacre of the old people and women and children. The Osages cut the throats of their victims and left the heads in the brass camp buckets, from which the affair has since been known as the Cutthroat Massacre. The enemy also carried away two children and our sun dance gods, the *Tai-mes*.

The following year several hundred American soldiers, the first we had ever seen, came from the northeast and visited a Wichita village on the North Fork of Red River near Sheep Mountain.[5] We went there to see what it was all about. At first our men wanted to fight, because there were some Osages with the troops. But when the officer in charge gave back to us the little girl whom the Osages had captured, we cried and shook hands with everyone. We even agreed to make peace with the Osages, in order to get back our *Tai-me*. They gave it to Chief Do-hauson the next year when he visited their camp on the Arkansas. Some of our chiefs also had a council on the Canadian River with the Americans. We agreed to allow white people in wagons to pass westward through our country and to let traders visit us. We were glad to see the traders, for they had many things which we liked. But we were sorry later that we permitted the travelers to go through the plains. They brought us two horrible diseases, smallpox and cholera, which killed half our people. Some of us thought that they gave us these sicknesses on purpose to wipe us out.

During the next few years we had more and more trouble with the Cheyennes, who kept pushing into our country. Three years after the Year the Stars Fell they attacked one of our villages that was traveling north to visit and trade with our old friends the Crows. This occurred about where the city of Denver now stands. The Cheyennes would have killed many of us had it not been for the women, who dug pits in the sand from which the men successfully stood off the enemy. The following summer a Cheyenne war party tried to raid our camp on the upper Washita, where it crosses the present state line. Our men saw several of their scouts spying out the village. Satank led a large party after them, managed to corner the whole

[5] This was Colonel Henry Dodge's Dragoon Expedition.

group, and killed and scalped every one of them. Years later, Stumbling Bear, while on his way west to attack the Utes, saw the forty-eight Cheyenne skeletons still stretched out in a row. This was also where Custer attacked Black Kettle's village.[6]

Satank's defeat of the Cheyennes brought their whole tribe down upon us in a revenge raid the following year. Expecting something like this, all our bands, with some Comanches, were camped together for protection. The Cheyennes struck our village on Wolf Creek, at the site of the Fort Supply reservoir, early one foggy morning. As they rode in, they killed thirty women and children who were skinning buffalo on the prairie and twelve more who were digging roots. Then the fighting swirled through the tipis. After a battle that lasted nearly all day, the enemy withdrew to the north.[7] Many had been killed on both sides, including several prominent war chiefs. One of the latter was Gui-ka-te [Wolf Lying Down], who fifty years before had arranged our peace with the Comanches.

But that was the last fight we had with the Cheyennes. A year or two later an Arapaho chief got both sides together near Bent's Fort. The leaders smoked the pipe and agreed to stop fighting. That agreement was never broken. After that we had a friendly visit from some of the Sioux, with whom we used to fight, but that was so long ago that we had forgotten what started the trouble. The Sioux looked just like the Cheyennes.

Now, our only enemies to the north were the Pawnees and the Sah-kee-bo, Eastern Indians who were coming into the plains to kill our buffalo. After several fights with these people, Mow-way, a big war chief of the Comanches, asked us to help him wipe out the intruders. Many Cheyennes, Arapahoes, Kiowa Apaches, and Osages also accepted the pipe,[8] making a party of several hundred warriors. Our leader was Satank and that of the Cheyennes was their best fighter, Whirlwind. We found a hundred Sah-kee-bo killing buffalo on the Smoky Hill River, in Kansas. When our men started making their charges, the Sah-kee-bo took position behind the bank of a

[6] This refers to the Battle of the Washita, November 27, 1868.
[7] This was called the Battle of Wolf Creek, fought in 1838.
[8] "Accepting the pipe" signified willingness to join a war party.

stream and began picking us off with their rifles. We had only bows and arrows and couldn't get close enough to hurt them. Finally, after losing a number of good men, we gave up the fight. It was a disgrace.[9]

About this time we began to see more and more Americans going west across the plains, especially in Kansas. Also buffalo hunters and farmers breaking up the prairie were coming into our land. The Cheyennes raided them, and sometimes we did too. Washington sent officials out to make treaties with the Plains Indians. Usually we were glad to go to these councils, even though it meant long trips for us, for the officers distributed food, clothing, guns, and other things we liked. But when they told us that we would have to move onto a reservation and give up our captives and stop stealing horses in Texas, we got mad. "Where else can we get horses and mules?" asked our chief, old Do-hauson.

Sometimes the people in Washington got mad too and promised to send soldiers against us if we didn't stop raiding. Our old men laughed. They had been looking and looking, but had yet to see these troops with which we were threatened. Fort Arbuckle had been built in the southeastern part of the plains, and two or three posts in Kansas and Texas. But that was all. There were only a few soldiers at each, who never got together. The Penateka Comanches now and then went to Fort Arbuckle to beg food and sell captives and horses, but we Kiowas and the wild Comanches never did. We preferred to visit the posts in Kansas, such as Fort Larned, where we were sure of receiving a good price for our captives and where food, clothing, and presents were given to us to stop raiding. Once in a while they would give us guns, too, but not much ammunition. We had to attack settlers, travelers, or small troop detachments to get that.

We could never see why the whites made such a fuss over these small fights. Fighting was a man's business—that was the way he earned the respect of his people and was honored by the women. Besides, there never would have been any trouble if the white men

[9] Nearly all prominent Kiowa warriors of that day were in this fight, which occurred in 1854.

had stayed out of our country and left us alone. We were happy before they came.

Another thing we could never understand was why Washington[10] used to scold us for fighting the Texans. They themselves made war against Texas for four years.

That war between the white men was a relief to us and gave us freedom to whip up more raids into Texas and Mexico. Not everything went our way however. Soon after the war started, some Texas troops came north of Red River and took over Fort Arbuckle and Fort Cobb, the latter being an agency on the Washita, north of Medicine Bluff Creek. They even reoccupied Camp Radziminski, a base they had established on Otter Creek three years earlier, then had abandoned. The Texans had with them some Tonkawas and Caddoes. We hated the Tonkawas because they ate people. The Caddoes caused some trouble, too, which you ought to know about.

The summer before the beginning of the white men's war, we were hunting buffalo up toward the Arkansas River, together with some Kotsoteka Comanches. We were met by a band of Penateka Comanches, with whom none of us, not even the other Comanches, were friendly at that time because they were helping the Texans. So we had a little argument, during which some of our young men killed a Caddo boy who was skulking behind a hill. The Caddoes got mad over that and persuaded the Penatekas and some Texas soldiers to come up from Fort Arbuckle and punish us. They did attack our village on the Arkansas, killing several people, including a popular young leader named Bird Appearing.

The next year Tone-tsain (Stray Horse) led a few Kiowas south on a revenge raid. But instead of killing a Caddo, they all were killed themselves, except for one young man who got away, a few miles north of where Fort Sill now stands. So we had another revenge raid, which met the Caddoes this time just west of Rainy Mountain Creek. Once more they killed our men, having good guns and being good shots. We have not cared much for Caddoes since then.

[10] "Washington" is the United States government personified, that is, the Great White Father.

In 1864, Satanta did a lot of raiding in northern Texas, capturing a number of white women and children. Later in the summer we were camped outside Fort Larned, Kansas, celebrating Satanta's victories. Some of the chiefs went to the post to see the commanding officer. One of these was Satank, who was stopped at the gate by a soldier on guard. Satank thought that the soldier was going to shoot him, so he quickly shot several arrows into the man, then ran. This started a stampede. We at once packed up and cleared out, but we circled around to drive off the soldiers' horse herd and to attack a wagon train camped nearby. We had a lot of fun, but soon got scared, so we went down to the Canadian and camped with the Comanches.

While we were there, a Comanche chief named Little Buffalo organized a very large party to raid Texas. Many of our men went along. This has become known as the Elm Creek Raid, in which many settlers were killed and a number of women and children captured. For years afterward, the Indian agent was trying to recover those captives. One of them was never turned over to the whites, a girl who grew up to be Mrs. Goombi but whose real name turned out to be Millie Durgan. We had quite a few captive members in our tribe, as did the Comanches. Most of them were Mexicans, but a few were white. If taken early enough, they learned to like the Indian way of life, or as we say, "liked to eat raw liver." Usually they were adopted by some old couple who had no children. The older ones, especially the women, we made do the hard camp work, and later we either threw them away or sold them at some agency.[11]

In 1864 and 1865, the government of the North was not too concerned about raids in Texas, but those made by the Cheyennes in Kansas and Colorado caused so much excitement and outcry from the settlers on the border that the army sent troop columns against the plains Indians from several directions. One under Chivington massacred Black Kettle's Cheyennes on Sand Creek. Another force from New Mexico under Kit Carson struck at us while we were camped on a creek a little east of Adobe Walls. Carson's Navaho scouts got into our village and killed several old people who were

[11] Though not always readily apparent, quite a few Kiowas have Mexican or white blood, a result of intermarrying with captives.

too feeble or blind to get away. Then Chiefs Do-hauson and Stumbling Bear rallied the warriors, who began charging the troops. Everyone, including Carson, admits that we won that fight. Many of our older people remember it well.

After this, the whites again began to make treaties with us. That was their favorite way of trying to stop a war, but it never worked. When, right after a peace council, we started raiding again, they got mad and acted like spoiled children. When the white man gets mad he wants to kill everyone. He is treacherous too. But at other times he can be so kind that we are ashamed. We never knew what to expect.

Each year, sometimes twice a year, the Great White Father sent out on the plains several very hairy men, dressed in long black coats and wearing high silk hats, to have a council with the Indian chiefs. Our old men liked to go to these smokes, for it made them feel big in the eyes of the tribe. They were given large silver medals, which we call Washington Medals, as well as officer's coats and pants, and blankets. The women and children and the ordinary men liked to sit on the ground in a circle outside the tent fly under which the powwow was going on and watch the council. They understood little of what was said, except when some chief like Satanta stood up, beat his chest, and told what a big fighter he was. Some other war chiefs, such as Big Bow, Woman's Heart, and Satank, said nothing. They did as much raiding as Satanta, but kept quiet about it.

After the meeting, big boxes of presents were opened, and the chiefs distributed these to everyone. That is why we came to the treaty councils. Washington likes to give away presents. If he needs more money, he only has to print it. Several of our chiefs went to Washington in those days and saw the government making money.

The pieces of treaty paper on which the chiefs made their marks always said that we were to stop raiding, give up our captives, and stay on a reservation that the Great White Father was going to give us. It made no difference to Washington that the land he was giving us, and much more besides, was already ours and always had been. We soon began to notice that each time we made a treaty, we lost a little more land, although each time we were told that the new reservation was to be ours "forever." We never fully understood that by "forever" the white man meant "until we want it for ourselves."

On the other hand, we Indians never appreciated that what our chiefs said was regarded by the government as binding on us all. A chief actually spoke only for his little band, not for the tribe as a whole. Furthermore, the people paid attention to him only when they thought that what he said was good for them. Mostly they did as they pleased. That is one reason why we liked the Indian road best.

The whites never understood that we didn't want to be like them. Today we know that some white people wish they were old-time Indians, for they often say so. The Indian never went to school. Or to the office or factory. He could lie abed as long as he liked. And he could go hunting every day.

The Medicine Lodge Treaty was the biggest council we ever saw, and even today it is the basis for our agreements and disagreements with the government. It took place on Medicine Lodge Creek in south central Kansas in 1868. Afterward, we moved down to Fort Cobb, our new agency, and waited to be issued some rations.

In the meantime, General Sheridan and General Custer were marching against the Cheyennes, who were supposed to be on the warpath, but actually were in their winter camps on the upper Washita. After Custer destroyed Black Kettle's village, he moved on Fort Cobb, meeting and taking prisoner our head chief, Lone Wolf, and Satanta. A few weeks later, General Sheridan turned these two men loose, after they promised to stop raiding. Meanwhile, he moved us all down to Medicine Bluff Creek, where he was going to build a new post called Fort Sill and establish our agency there.

As soon as the winter was over, we started raiding again in Texas. At first the troops at Fort Sill did not bother us much, for they were busy building their post, but after we had raided near the post and had stolen all their mules out of the quartermaster corral, they got mad at us. If it had not been for our new agent, we might have had another war. But he kept the post commander from fighting us. The next year, 1871, Satanta, Big Tree, Satank, and a large party of our warriors went to northern Texas, where they made an attack on

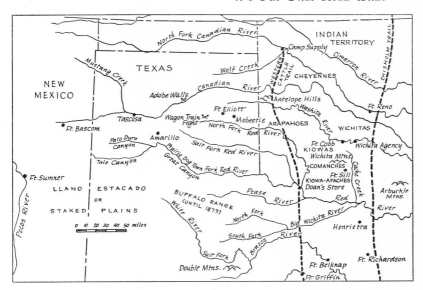

The Red River Area in the 1870's

Warren's wagon train and killed a number of teamsters. General Sherman, in command of the whole army, was nearby. He came to Fort Sill and had Satanta, Satank, and Big Tree put in chains and sent to Texas for trial for murder. Satank was killed trying to get away from the guard, but the other two went to prison. We spent the next two years begging Washington to give them back to us.

At this time we had a young chief named Kicking Bird, who favored peace. He was a stronger man than Lone Wolf and had much power in the tribe. Lone Wolf headed those of the tribe who favored war. Finally, Lone Wolf's son was killed while on a raid in Texas. Lone Wolf felt so bad about that that he got up a big revenge raid. About the same time the Comanches started an attack in the Staked Plains against buffalo hunters at Adobe Walls. The troops began to get up an expedition against all Indians who were off the reservation. Those who were thought to be friendly were registered and given pieces of paper for their protection.

In September there was a flurry at the agency, now at Anadarko, and a little fight, which caused many of the Indians who were not in Kicking Bird's band to leave the reservation and flee to the North Fork of Red River. The troops came out against us from several directions. We were finally driven in to Fort Sill, where we surrendered and were disarmed. The next spring the principal chiefs were sent to prison in Florida. That ended for all times the Indian wars in the southern plains.

It also ended our old free way of life. The next fifty years were hard ones for us. The white man killed off all the game, but did not issue us enough rations to keep us from nearly starving. He made us give up the sun dance and some of our other old customs. He took our children away from us and sent them to school. He tried to make us learn farming, but we weren't much good at it. Then, finally, in 1901, he tricked us into opening up our reservation to white settlement. We were paid seven dollars an acre for our land, but we weren't given the money; it was held for us in Washington. It has been hard to get it when we need it.

Each Indian was given a quarter section of land. That was not enough for cattle-raising, and we didn't have success with farming, for we had never been farmers like the Wichitas. Mostly we rented the land to sharecroppers, who didn't make a go of it either. Since we were landowners, we couldn't get much relief money during the Depression. We didn't have clear title to our land either. During the New Deal days, the Indian commissioner tried to persuade us to go in for communal or co-operative farming. Maybe that would have solved our problem, but we weren't ready to give up our individual ownership of the land. Therefore, we refused, and hence didn't get very sympathetic treatment, during those difficult years, from the Great White Father.

Today, though we have put aside the old road, we are not moving forward as fast as we would like to. Some of our young people are getting good jobs, as a result of education, and some are doing well in the army. The old people, the few who are left, still like to sit in the sun and tell stories of the free days when the wind blew through the grass on the prairie, unhampered by fences and dusty furrows. ☼

xviii

With the exception of a few stories told by Iseeo and one by Quanah, identified as such, which were told to Captain Hugh L. Scott at Fort Sill in the 1890's, and are contained in his manuscript on the sign language in the Library of Congress, the material in this book was communicated to me, through an interpreter and, occasionally, through sign language, in interviews during the period 1933–37.

Thus, the wording in these stories is, in many cases, my own, though I have followed the Indian manner of expression as far as possible without resorting to artificialities and have not distorted the content. The ideas and attitudes presented in the stories belong entirely to the Indians. I have chosen therefore, on the advice of my publishers, the University of Oklahoma Press, to set off the interview material from my own remarks by indicating the opening and closing limits of the stories with a Caslon typographic ornament. This is in clear contradistinction to the use of widely spaced French quotation marks to indicate literal translations or verbatim material, a scheme devised some years ago by the University of Oklahoma Press for some of its books in the field of anthropology.

My chief informant and interpreter was the late George Hunt, originally named Set-maunte after a warrior of that name. His father was Jimmy Gui-tone (Que-tone), whose grandfather An-zah-te was a survivor of the Cutthroat Massacre in 1833. Mr. Hunt's uncle, with whom he lived throughout his youth, was Tah-bone-mah, who later took the name of Iseeo. This man, a participant in many of the adventures related in this book, served his entire life, subsequent to the Indian wars, as a member of Troop L, Seventh Cavalry, the Indian scout troop at Fort Sill. Sitting night after night in Iseeo's tipi, George Hunt listened to just about every story told by the old-time warriors. He learned English by playing with the children of the post and attended their school. Thus, though still a boy, he was perhaps the only Kiowa then able to interpret properly for James Mooney, the Smithsonian ethnologist who studied the Kiowas during the 1890's. Throughout the remainder of his life, Mr. Hunt continued to gather the history of his people. His family clan included some of the most noted Kiowa warriors; he knew still others, such as Big Tree and Gotebo, who became members of his church. I am sure that no one could have rivaled George Hunt as a source of Kiowa history.

I wish to pay tribute also to another old friend, Hunting Horse, who died at Saddle Mountain in July, 1953, at the age of 107. He was a very fine and enthusiastic storyteller and one who had much personal knowledge of the events which he described.

My informants related their tales in simple, straightforward language, in no wise resembling the fanciful pidgin English which fiction and the films credit them with employing. Like the rest of us, their spoken language is largely free of fine figures of speech or other literary adornment. I am furnishing below a sample story which was written for me by an Indian who had had a little schooling. I am under the impression that it represents closely, less its obvious English errors, the way in which the older Kiowas expressed themselves in their own tongue.

Here is the story exactly as written by Sam Ahton:

Gui-kau-da [Wolf Lying Down] kill at Fort Sill in the summer of the measels sundance [1877].

In the summer of this year we was camping on the south side of the little creek now call Sitting Bear creek. The Kiowa tribe are gone out west on north fork of Red River.

A small group of us camping at the spot. A man by the [name of] Sau-Beah-to [or Quiver] family and his second wife by the name of A-mah-ty.

Po-do-say a Mexican Kiowa, his wife, his step son Bootle [Botalye] and Bootle's two sister.

Hoyu-ke-ta, a mother in law of James To-done, Quo-kau-da his wife and a small child.

Polee, a single woman.

My father, name Quo-yote-ta.

And myself Sam Ahton. And man by the name Sanae [which] mean Old Man Snake.

At this time we get our weekly ration. So when the time came for our beef ration my father and a man named Sau-Beah-a [Quiver] went after the beef at the issue corral which located east of where Lawton now.

The man Gui-kau-da is a very popular man, and the way it happen the man who name is Sana or Snake had gun loaded and it was very near noon. We saw the men coming with two head of beef coming toward our camp. Gui-kau-da ask Sana to give him the gun that he wanted to shoot the beef. Sana refuse to let him have the gun. Kept on demanding for the gun it is a misloading [muzzle-loading] gun. Guo-kau-da said let me have the gun I want to shoot the beef. Sana say no I cant let you have it for I want it for myself. After refusing to let him have the gun he walk off toward another tee pee. Guo-kau-da say I go and [take] the gun away from him anyway.

I follow him. And as we [?] he ask for the gun again. Gui-kau-da [said] if you dont want me to have, you keep old gun, for it favor you, anyway.

Guo-kau-da walk away, and went by Bootle mother who is rosting her coffee. Sana said spoke to Guo-kau-da in low voice and said something of him being a one eye mean thing. he [Gui-kau-da] overheard it and want to make sure of what he said to him, so he ask the woman if she heard of what Sana said to him. But woman said she didnt hear of what he said to him. So he said I wish I knew what [he] said to [me]. Sana said if I said anything to you I wouldnt tell you of what I said to you. Guo-kau-da knew of what he said of him being one eyed. He said that one thing I cant stand for any person to call me one eyed. So he turn back and grab the gun away from him.

About this time the two men driving the beef were very near the camp. About the time the trouble started. After he took the gun away from him he started to hold of the barrel of gun to use it for a club. He chase the man around the arbor. The arbor was facing north. Sana start running around the arbor from the open part of the arbor running around the arbor around the south to north. Guo-kau-da run around the other side to meet him facing. He started to [hit] him over the head. Sana make a quick dodge. The bout of the gun hit him on the right shoulder, the gun slide down to the ground, which cause the explotion of the gun went off and shot through the heart of Guo-kau-da instantly kill him.

The man fell dead. The excitement started. Sana hurryly in the tee pee and grabbed a few of his belonging and dash for the timber. My father came up with his pistol and started for Sana, but we call him not to shoot him, for Guo-kau-da shoot himself.

After the matter was explain to these two men Sau-Beah-ty rush to the agency office near where the rock quarries are now. After the report was made to the soldiers a large number of soldiers galloping down to the timber, searching for the murder, but fail to find, but was finly caught above the Medicine Bluff and was put in the guard house. Upon the investigation he came clear, and Guo-kau-da body was taken to old saw mill on Cash creek where the Indian Hospital now stand, and must have been buried.

I am very grateful to my wife Elleane for many helpful suggestions and for typing the manuscript, and to Mr. Robert H. Fowler, editor in chief of *The Civil War Times*, for a critical reading of the book.

Wilbur Sturtevant Nye

Wormleysburg, Pennsylvania
February 7, 1962

Contents

MAPS

BAD MEDICINE & GOOD

Tales of the Kiowas

The Stories

I ❀ THE MEDICINE OF KINDNESS

Two HUNDRED YEARS AGO the Kiowas and the Comanches were almost continually at war. Nevertheless, on several occasions the Comanches were hospitable and kind to individual Kiowas who fell into their hands. The Kiowas were deeply impressed by these acts, one of which in particular they still hold close to their hearts. The Kiowa involved was a tribal hero who bore the hereditary name Pago-to-goodle, which means Lone Young Man, or One Young Man. He was a member of the Ko-eet-senko, a warrior order composed of the ten bravest men of the tribe. Even many enemy warriors either knew Pago-to-goodle by sight or had heard of him.

The following story, told to me by Mary Buffalo, daughter of Chief Poor Buffalo, who was one of the war chiefs to surrender his band at Fort Sill in 1875, has been handed down substantially unchanged for over 175 years. It is a fragment of some of the earliest Kiowa history, as differentiated from legend.

❀ In about the year 1788, as reckoned back from the Year the Stars Fell, the Kiowa young men went on an expedition against the Utes. While they were away, their village on the upper Arkansas River was raided by some Comanches, who killed several of the camp defenders and carried away three or four women and children. One of the latter was Pago-to-goodle's only child, a daughter.

3

Upon their return to the village, and after being informed of the Comanche foray, the warriors at once organized a pursuit. Pago-to-goodle, who was determined to recover his daughter, was in charge. They rapidly rode south into the Comanche country and early the next day sighted a strong Comanche band. This was not the band that had raided their village, but the Kiowas either did not know this or did not take it into account. Although outnumbered, they immediately dashed to attack.

After a battle that lasted until sunset, all the Kiowas except Pago-to-goodle had been killed. He was lying senseless beneath a heap of his dead friends. For some unknown reason he had not been scalped. Late in the evening, he recovered sufficiently to crawl clear of the pile of dead. He staggered off across the prairie in search of water, but in the darkness he suddenly saw the Comanche tipis looming up against the starlit sky. A voice called out sharply in Comanche, which, like many Plains Indians, he understood.

Pago-to-goodle realized that he was too weak to try to flee, so he walked boldly up to the camp sentry and demanded to be taken to the chief.

Word was passed to the head of the village that a wounded Kiowa had entered the camp and wished to speak to him.

"All right," said the chief, "let him come."

They met outside the chief's lodge and shook hands. "What do you want here?" asked the Comanche, staring at the Kiowa's awful condition, for Pago-to-goodle was covered with caked blood and dirt and was almost naked.

Pago-to-goodle said, "My daughter has been captured. I understand that you Comanches have her. She is my only daughter, and I think a lot of her. I wish to see her. After that you may kill me."

The chief was silent for a few moments. Then he said, "Let us go inside and smoke the pipe." He conducted the Kiowa into his lodge and had his women bring water, that the Kiowa might cleanse himself, and a robe for a covering. Food was placed before him.

When Pago-to-goodle had eaten, he thanked his host. The Comanche filled a pipe with chopped tobacco and sumac. The two men smoked reflectively.

4

At length the chief said, "I am the head of this village. I will not kill you. I will not permit it to be done. But I want you to kill four fat buffalo for me. If you do this, you may have your daughter, who is with another band. Afterward, I'll send you both home."

Pago-to-goodle was quite overcome at such kindness and generosity at the hands of an enemy. He was unaware that it was a Comanche characteristic to show mercy to a stranger, even an enemy, who came to them in distress and that the laws of hospitality to one who came peaceably to a Comanche lodge were rarely broken. He readily agreed to go on a buffalo chase and to kill as many buffalo as the chief should require. Then the Comanche explained that by "four fat buffalo" he had meant that he wanted Pago-to-goodle to assist them in four war expeditions. Pago-to-goodle said that he would do it.

First they went against the Utes. Pago-to-goodle was the hero of that fight. He charged straight at the leading Ute and knocked him off his horse with a lance. Then he killed three other Utes in quick succession and brought their scalps and mounts to the Comanche chief.

Pago-to-goodle also took part in expeditions against the Navahos, Mescalero Apaches, and finally, far down in Sonora, against the Yaquis. On each of these raids he greatly distinguished himself and won high praise from the Comanches.

On their return from the fourth raid the Comanche chief said, "Friend, there are four horses awaiting you outside my lodge. Two are pack horses, and there is one riding horse apiece for you and your daughter. I have sent for her, and she will arrive soon. Then the two of you may go home to your people."

Shortly afterward, the young girl was seen approaching in company with an old Comanche, who proved to be the man who with his wife had adopted the captive. Pago-to-goodle hastened to meet his daughter, embraced and kissed her. After they had cried together, the Kiowa said to the chief, "Now I am satisfied. You may kill me if you wish."

But the Comanche answered, "No. I do not care to do so. Your four brave fights have not been surpassed in the history of our tribe.

We are thankful to you for your strong help against our enemies. Now you may take your daughter and start back to your home."

Pago-to-goodle was scarcely able to thank the chief. Then he suggested that the girl remain with the Comanches for safekeeping while he returned to his tribe and brought back two or three friends as an escort. He explained that if he and the child went back together, they might encounter enemies. Burdened with the care of the girl, he could not properly defend himself and could not escape. But alone he might manage it.

"If my wife is still alive, I'll bring her back, too, so that she may be with our daughter during the long trip home," he added.

The Comanche chief agreed to this. The daughter asked Pago-to-goodle to take her first to the Comanche camp from which she had come. She wanted to see her foster mother once more. Pago-to-goodle said that he would take her there and leave her with the old couple who had been taking care of her. She would remain with them until he returned from the Kiowa village.

The Comanches dressed the girl in a rich doeskin garment and

gave her and her father several rawhide bags filled with dried meat. The chief also sent several presents for the chief of the other village. Laden with these articles, they set forth.

The journey was made safely, and Pago-to-goodle placed his daughter in the care of the old Comanches. Then he started out on his lonely and dangerous trip northward.

When Pago-to-goodle was near the Canadian River, he was seen by a party of four Arapahoes, who rode up cautiously. Seeing that he was alone, they charged him confidently. They were met by a flight of swiftly discharged arrows which wounded one of them and caused the others to veer off. The Arapahoes continued to circle the lone Kiowa, who had dismounted and taken cover behind a low bank. The fighting continued at long range until near sunset, when the Arapahoes stopped for a council among themselves.

"I think I have seen that man before in a fight," said one of them. "He is a very dangerous fighter. Already two of us have been hit. We are liable to lose a man, or maybe two, if we keep on. I think we ought to pull out." The others agreed.

Soon, Pago-to-goodle saw his enemies ride off in the gathering dusk, headed northeast. He did not see them again.

A day or so later, Pago-to-goodle saw the Kiowa village strung out along the banks of a big stream. From the number of tipis, he realized that the bands had gathered for the annual medicine dance. He rode up a hill overlooking the river valley. On the crest was a single brush arbor, under which a woman was sitting with bowed head. As he came nearer, he saw that it was his mother. She was weeping. He thought he knew why. He had been gone so long that his people must have decided that he was dead. None of his war party had ever returned to tell what had happened.

He called to her, and she looked up. "I am your son, Pago-to-goodle," he said. But she only stared at him. "Don't you know me? I am not a spirit. I am alive. All my friends were wiped out, but I came through safely. I have been with the Comanches during the last two years. They finally let me come home. Stop crying."

They embraced and kissed.

"I had given you up for dead," the old woman said. "I cried for you for two years. But today I am crying because they are appointing a chief to take your place. And the warriors of the Ko-eet-senko are initiating your successor. You wait here. I am going down to tell your father and other relatives that you have come back."

"Good," said Pago-to-goodle. "And bring me some other clothing, so I won't be taken for a Comanche."

She went to the village and stopped outside the Ko-eet-senko lodge, where a dance was in progress. Her husband came out after she had called to him.

"Today I am glad!" she said.

"Yes, I notice that you have changed," he replied.

"Our son, Pago-to-goodle, has come back and is waiting for us on the hill."

The old man started to cry. They assembled the other relatives. While the old man was giving them the good news, she ran to get some clothing for her son. They sent word to the Ko-eet-senko that their son had returned. At once the man who had been selected to take Pago-to-goodle's place slipped out the back of the lodge and went off with Pago-to-goodle's wife, whom he recently had appropriated.

On the hill there was a very happy reunion. Later there was much joyful shouting and celebration in the village, for Pago-to-goodle was popular. That night a big dance was held in his honor. The drums throbbed, the singers chanted. Pago-to-goodle danced with the others. Then he went to his lodge. He was tired after his long trip. After he had eaten, and rested for a time, he wanted to return to the dance.

"This is your day!" said his father. "They had given you up for dead and were putting the sash on your successor. But now you will be restored to your place!"

"Yes," said Pago-to-goodle, "after two years it was right that they pick someone else to have my sash. Now I am rested and would like to meet my warrior society. Also, I want to shake hands with the man they chose to take my place."

8

They went to the Ko-eet-senko lodge, where the members were still dancing. After they had all taken his hand and hugged him, Pago-to-goodle said, "Sing my favorite song. I want to dance." After he had danced a little, they all sat down and listened while he told his story. He finished by saying that he was glad to be back and that he had no hard feelings toward his successor.

The members said that there would be no successor, now that he was back. The other man was a big war chief, but he wasn't in the same class with Pago-to-goodle.

"Just the same," said Pago-to-goodle, "I would like to shake his hand."

It was noticed that the other man's place in the circle was still vacant. They looked all over the village for him, but he could not be found. He never came back, and Pago-to-goodle never saw his wife again. The Kiowas restored him to his position in the tribe and in the Ko-eet-senko and presented him with a new sash. The other man's medicine had been strong, but Pago-to-goodle's was stronger. ✿

The Kiowas do not remember whether Pago-to-goodle went back to get his daughter. However, since the Kiowas and the Comanches made a permanent peace a year or two later, it is likely that the two were reunited. It is also probable that Pago-to-goodle's report of the kindness he had received from the Comanches had much to do with the willingness of the tribe to make that everlasting peace with their former enemies. That good medicine has endured to this day.

2 ⚜ THE MEDICINE OF PEACE

DURING THE LAST HALF of the eighteenth century, the incessant fighting between the Kiowas and Comanches had nearly exhausted both tribes. The Kiowas for ten years or more had been pushing farther and farther south in search of better hunting and to secure more plunder from the settlements in Colorado, the latter being widely scattered ranchos owned by Mexicans. In penetrating this arid region they came into conflict with Utes, Navahos, and, above all, with Comanches. By this time the Comanches had become widely recognized as being the "Lords of the Southwest Plains," and they were fully conscious of their own strength. Nevertheless, there was no overwhelming reason for their hostility to the Kiowas, there being buffalo and plunder enough for both tribes. It was simply that no one on either side was able or willing to take the first step toward establishment of friendly relations. The story of how peace was finally made was told to James Mooney in 1890, mainly by Kiowas whose grandparents had personal knowledge of that happy event. I discussed it with Comanches and Kiowas many years later, but by that time the Comanches had no recollection of when they were not allies of the Kiowas. The latter, however, retained essentially the same remembrances which they had communicated to Mooney. The following story is drawn from these sources and Mooney's report.

❂ Not long after the Kiowas had settled in the land of the Crows, in the area west of the Black Hills, they were visited by traders from southwestern Colorado and northeastern New Mexico, then part of the domain of New Spain. These Mexicans came with pack trains laden with blankets, cloth, silver ornaments, and other articles attractive to the Indians, which they exchanged for beaver pelts and buffalo hides. The Kiowas also received from this source their first metal knives and bits of iron with which to fashion arrow points. It is thought, too, that from such traders they may have obtained their first horses. This trading led to a friendly relationship between certain New Mexicans and the wild Indians. A few hardy Kiowas even ventured into the hostile country south of the Platte and Arkansas to return these visits and to conduct further trading. There seems to have been, on occasion, an armed truce between warring tribes while they were engaged in trading with New Mexicans and later with whites in the vicinity of where Bent's Fort was later established on the upper Arkansas.

Early in the spring of 1790, as estimated by Mooney, a young Kiowa war chief named Gui-ka-te (Wolf Lying Down) led a few men south from the Kiowa villages which were then on the headwaters of the South Platte near the site of Denver. They following the trail east of the mountains, approximately the route of the present U.S. 85 and 87, passing the site of Colorado Springs, crossing the Arkansas about where Pueblo is now, on through Raton Pass, and finally coming to the area near the present Las Vegas, New Mexico. They must have made this trip on at least one previous occasion, for they went straight to the home of a ranchero who came to the door and embraced them as old friends.

But as soon as the Kiowas entered the front of the *casa*, they heard Comanche being spoken in the next room. Instantly they fitted arrows into their bowstrings and prepared for the desperate fight which they knew would occur as soon as the enemy discovered their presence. Their Mexican host, not wishing to have his home torn apart, urged them to wait until he could make a truce between them and the Comanches. It was high time, he said, that the Kiowas and Comanches became friends.

After a brief conversation in the sign language, the Kiowas agreed. The Mexican went into the next room and informed the astonished Comanches that several Kiowas were in the front of the house but that they wished to talk peace. There would be no treachery—they had his word for that.

The Comanches, by nature an unsuspicious people who were willing to meet friendly gestures halfway, responded favorably. After talking over the situation briefly among themselves, they stalked into the front room where the Kiowas were silently waiting. Negotiations proceeded formally at first, both sides speaking a little Spanish, using the sign language, and with the aid of a Comanche captive of the Kiowas who had been adopted into that tribe when a boy. Gradually the atmosphere thawed, until finally the Indians sat down and smoked amicably together. The Comanches invited the Kiowas to have one of their men accompany them back to the Comanche base camp in order to arrange a meeting between the two tribes for the purpose of making a lasting peace. It was further suggested that such a meeting be held somewhere along the upper Canadian, one day's good ride east of where they were then.

A long silence followed this proposal. The Comanches inwardly fidgeted. They were accustomed to reaching decisions quickly, but acting slowly. The Kiowas always considered things at length, but when their minds were made up, they took action at once. On this occasion they were still suspicious, most of them feeling that a Kiowa who went alone with the Comanches would not be seen again.

At length Gui-ka-te spoke. "I will go. I am a chief. I am not afraid."

His companions objected strenuously, but Gui-ka-te insisted. He said further that he would take the captive Comanche with him, to act as interpreter and to be returned to his own people, if he so desired, in proof of the good intentions of the Kiowas. The Mexican also volunteered to go along to assist in arranging the peace council. His offer was accepted. Gui-ka-te said that he would invite all the Comanches to meet the Kiowas at the selected site, at which time the final agreement would be made.

"Return when the leaves are beginning to turn yellow," he said to his men. "The Comanches say that the home camps of their band are on the Double Mountain Fork of the Brazos[1] less than ten day's ride southeast of here. But it will take most of the summer to get word to all the other Comanche bands and for them to travel to the council grounds. Bring all the Kiowa bands with you and all the chiefs. Each band must be prepared to smoke the pipe with the Comanches."

In parting with his friends, Gui-ka-te said to them, "If, when you come, I am not here, you will know that I am dead. Then you must avenge me. But I feel sure that I will be here. I remember the good way in which Pago-to-goodle was received by the Comanches when he was in their hands several years ago."

The Comanches belonged to the Nokoni, or Wanderer, band. Like the Quahadi Comanches, they wandered mostly on the Staked Plains, and along the upper waters of the Brazos and the branches of Red River. Their head chief received Gui-ka-te and the Mexican hospitably and listened to the plans for making peace between the two tribes.

"Good!" he said. "We make peace. I will send out to all Comanches to come here to listen."

These preliminary arrangements took much time, for the dozen or more divisions of the Comanche tribe were scattered over a vast area and had little contact with one another. The Penateka Comanches, who were in eastern Texas and generally out of touch with the others, were not even contacted. But the other divisions sent representatives to this first council of Comanches, where a general approval of making peace with the Kiowas was expressed. They all said that they would move their villages to the meeting place late in the summer.

Since there were still several weeks intervening before it was time

[1] The Indians, of course, do not use this name in referring to the Brazos and its tributaries. Indeed, their names for nearly all the rivers and other terrain features were, in the early days, different from those now in use. But, in general, the Indians with whom I talked were able to identify rivers and mountains by their present names on the maps. This is probably the result of much discussion among themselves, with the aid of younger members of the tribes who have been to school and studied geography.

13

for the Nokonis to pack up their village and move to the Canadian River, the rest of the summer was spent enjoyably in entertaining Gui-ka-te and the Mexican. Buffalo hunts, horse races, feasts, and dances were held in their honor. The guests had a very pleasant time, and the basis for the intertribal accord was laid.

Gui-ka-te and the Comanches arrived at the rendezvous just as the cottonwoods were beginning to show color. Soon afterward, they saw a long line of horsemen approaching in the distance. It was the Kiowa warriors, riding ahead of their moving villages. When they came within three bowshot lengths of the Comanches, several chiefs rode forward and met the Comanche chiefs between the two villages, the rest of the people sitting on their horses and watching to see what would happen. The chiefs shook hands, dismounted, and sat down on the prairie for a talk. Plans were made for the big council to be held when all bands were present. Arrangements were made as to which camping places would be allotted the several villages.

The council, when it took place, was not a long one. After the pipe had been passed among the head chiefs, a simple promise was made that the Kiowas and Comanches would be friends and allies thenceforth and that the Kiowas might freely come into the Comanche range to hunt and to camp. For their part, the Kiowas said that they would help the Comanches against their enemies at any time there was danger. The peace made at that time has never been broken, and despite some unfortunate incidents involving a few individuals, the friendship between the two tribes has deepened through the years. It has been good medicine. ❁

3 ✣ PIPE MEN

THE TO-YOP-KE, or leader of a war expedition, was known as a "pipe man," or "has the pipe," or "holds the pipe." This expression originated with an Indian custom in which a war chief carried a ceremonial pipe. If you see a photograph of an old-time Indian holding a long-stemmed pipe, you will know that he was a leader, and probably a chief. Iseeo explained the custom in the following account.

✣ A leader's road is hard. Some men are good leaders. Everyone knows who they are, and for that reason such men have little trouble in raising a large war party. This is the way a *to-yop-ke* recruits followers for a particular raid:

One day he meets another man in the village, to whom he says, "I am going to war. Will you go with me?" Then he asks another man. And another. When he has three members, he calls a big council, at which he announces that he is going against an enemy tribe such as the Utes or Pawnees, or that he is going to Texas or Mexico to steal horses and mules. He fills his pipe and offers it to each man there. If a man accepts and smokes the pipe, he has said, "Yes, I will go with you to war." Of course, he may refuse the pipe if he wishes.

The night before the start of a raid, the men who have smoked the pipe go into a big lodge, where there are a number of men and women singing while one man beats time with a stick against a lodge pole. After a short time—to allow all the members of the war party to enter and seat themselves—the musicians hold up by its edges a stiff, hard rawhide. They drum on this and sing until midnight, when they stop.

A war party usually goes out a little before the full of the moon, to have moonlight for their journey. They ride at night and camp in the brush or timber by day. The time of departure is set by the leader, who usually plans so that they arrive at the raiding place when the moon is brightest.

When they are ready to start from the home village, the leader mounts his horse, holding the pipe, together with his reins, in his left hand. The stem is always pointed down. He never ties the pipe to his saddle, but continues to hold it in that manner whenever they are traveling. He does not lay it down until they have returned to the village.

If any member of the group becomes tired during the journey, they all stop to rest and smoke. They always halt just below the crest of a hill or ridge so that some of them can peer over and out through the grass to see that no enemy is approaching.

The leader always rides at the head of the party. When they are some distance from their camping place, he goes ahead to make sure there is no danger. He gets there before first light, looks around, and if the area is safe, makes his camp. Then he listens for the approach of his men. He can hear them coming a long way off, for they are singing as they ride in single file. They always sing as they approach a rendezvous at night, usually the Kiowa Journey Song, so that they won't be mistaken for enemies.

When all have arrived at the end of the first night's ride, the leader calls them together and says, "When we were home in the village and I decided to go to war, everyone knew of it—men, women, and children. Now that I see you here I feel glad that we are going to war with such a big party. I want three assistant leaders." These men are also called pipe men, but only the leader actually carries a pipe.

No one speaks out, but they talk it over among themselves, which is the custom.

16

Then the leader, as if scolding them, says, "That man is a good man. And that one. And that one."

The first man chosen says he will go with the leader, whereupon the latter says, "Aho, Aho—thank you, thank you!" The other two men whom he has named say that they also will assist him, and they are likewise thanked by the leader.

During the second night's journey, these lieutenants follow in single file right behind the leader. In a fight their roads are the strongest.

When the men arrive near the place where they are going to attack, they remain in hiding for a day or so while they study the lay of the land and scout out the best routes of approach. If there is a hill or a mountain nearby, they climb that and observe from the hillside, concealed in the timber. They watch to see if there are soldiers in the nearest towns.

If the Indians have a large, strong war party, they attack boldly just at daybreak. Otherwise, they rely on stealth and approach at night, allowing time to make their getaway before dawn.

When the men are getting ready to attack, the leader puts the pipe in his quiver, to have his hands free for fighting. After the

battle, he takes it out and continues to carry it in his hand until the raid is over.

Just before the party makes its charge, the leader rides out alone toward the enemy. He rides back and forth along the front of his line to encourage his young men and "hold them." During the battle if an Indian's horse is killed, the leader takes the rider up behind him and carries the man out of the fight. If a man is killed and the enemy approaches his body, the leader takes it up across his own horse and saves it from the enemy.

If all the young men retreat, the leaders stay behind to ward off pursuit.

The leader's road is the hardest of all. He is ashamed to be afraid. He would rather die. He has no commands for advancing, firing, or retiring, as soldier chiefs have. He just calls out, "Take courage, take courage! Do not be frightened." Or he shouts, "Charge! Ah-Ko!" And continues to encourage his men.

The leader never abuses anyone. He would be ashamed to do that, for he loves all his men, and they love him. If he should be killed, the young men all dash towards the enemy to drive them back and to bring away the leader's body. Otherwise the enemy would strike it and cut it. If the enemy gets the leader's body, the people in the village would hear of it and everybody would be ashamed.

A long time ago, four of us went on a raid to Mexico. One night we saw a distant campfire. On creeping up to observe it, we saw a lot of mules and a Mexican walking around them on guard.

Our leader said, "Get ready! Take courage now. When he comes around again we will rush in and shoot him with arrows, then drive off the stock."

When the Mexican again came around his circle, and was closest to where we were peering at him through the bushes, we ran silently towards him. When we were within three leaps of him, we all let fly arrows. He fell but managed to cry out and give the alarm. In a few moments, as we were cutting loose the mules, a crowd of Mexicans charged us out of the darkness and began firing.

We ran back into the night. In a moment we stopped. Our leader wasn't with us. None of us had seen him fall.

Just then he called, softly, "I am shot! My die day has come! Tell about it when you get home!"

We called back, "Where are you hit?"

"In the leg," he answered. "It is broken. Go on! Don't try to pick me up. Run!"

Then we heard the enemy catch him. There were many shots. Everything was quiet for a minute. Then we heard them talking among themselves. We saw them make a big fire, and we knew what that was for. We found our horses and rode away, crying for our leader.

The next morning as we watched from our hiding place on the hillside, we realized that we had come upon a large force of Mexican soldiers who had camped for the night. We could see them packing their mules and getting ready to move. After we were sure that all of them were gone, we went down to look for some sign of our leader. We found a big clot of blood on the ground where they had caught and shot him. We saw the embers of the big fire on which they had thrown his body. But we did not find even one small piece of him. He was all burned up.

We went back to the Kiowa village ashamed.

Everybody is afraid of losing a leader. That is when we know our medicine has failed. ✸

4 ✣ BLACK BEAR BECOMES A CHIEF

THE FOLLOWING STORY is based on an account obtained from Peah-to-mah, wife of Hunting Horse.

✣ In the winter of 1867–68, several war parties were recruited for raids against the Navahos, who were on a reservation in eastern New Mexico. Because of the freezing weather, many of the Kiowas had bad colds with running noses. As they rode along through the burned-off prairie, the wind stirred up clouds of soot and dust which turned their faces and nostrils black. For this reason the raid was called, quite inelegantly, the Black-Snot Raid.

One group of about twenty men and boys, led by a warrior whose name is forgotten, contained the famous war chief Big Bow, who was to be one of the last hostile chiefs to surrender at Fort Sill, and a young inexperienced brave named Sait-kone-kia, or Black Bear. They made their raid headquarters near the Pecos River and, before crossing, left their horses and heavy camping equipment there under the charge of two boys. Using a single pack mule to carry their food and blankets, they went west on foot. They crossed the river at a ford known to the older men, noticing with some apprehension that the river was rising and would soon be unfordable.

Several days' journey west of the Pecos brought them to the foot-hills of the mountains. They knew they were in enemy country, but for some unexplained reason the leader failed to provide a rear guard or camp sentinels at night. As was learned much later, several Navahos had crossed their trail and were following them.

One night they camped in a large canyon, making their bivouac under an overhanging cliff and staking out the mule to graze some distance back down the canyon. All unsuspected by the Kiowas, the enemy arrived just at dusk and were waiting in the brush to make a dawn attack.

Black Bear, an industrious fellow and habitual early riser, got up before daylight and nudged two sleeping boys. "You boys go up that little side canyon to a spring and carry back a couple of buckets of water. I'll go down and bring back the animal."

When he returned with the pack mule, Black Bear began shaking the other members of the party. "Wake up," he said softly. "Every-one ought to be up and wide awake. Something is going to happen! The mule was snorting in fright a minute ago, but it is still too dark to see anything."

At that moment, the two boys who had gone after water came dashing back, followed suddenly by a burst of gunfire. Immediately the camp was thrown into confusion. Most of the men snatched up their weapons and scattered up the sides of the canyon, abandoning their bedding and food supply.

A few had pistols, but Big Bow was the only man who had a rifle. In their fright they abandoned the mule, which was caught by the enemy.

Only Big Bow and Black Bear stood fast, and somehow the two boys remained with them. They took refuge behind some large cottonwoods, peering through the darkness and trying to see the enemy. Red flashes came closer, but slowly. They could tell that the enemy, uncertain of the lay of the land and not knowing how many were left to defend the campsite, were approaching cautiously.

As the sky gradually lightened and the shadows in the canyon shortened, Big Bow was able to fire occasional shots at figures of the enemy flitting from rock to rock. But from the hillsides came no supporting fire, no encouraging yells. At length the Navahos mounted up and began to circle the four Kiowas who were still defending the camp. Occasional shots were fired, but no one was hit on either side. This kept up intermittently during most of the day. The enemy made no charge, evidently preferring to wait until the Kiowas had exhausted their ammunition. They seemed quite sure of the final outcome.

About midafternoon, Big Bow was knocked down by a bullet that passed entirely through his body. After a few minutes he pulled himself to his feet and began dragging along behind the others who were dodging around trees and behind boulders trying to keep such shelter between themselves and the circling Navahos. He could still carry his war shield, but had to lean his old muzzle-loader against a rock. He was unable to hold it to his shoulder.

Now only Black Bear was left to do the fighting. He was in a great state of excitement and anxiety, very much afraid and almost on the verge of panic. The two boys had no weapons. Everything depended on him.

Big Bow understood Black Bear's feelings. He called, "Black Bear! Don't give up! Try your best. Keep fighting back!" Then he said to the boys, who were cowering behind the other man, "Come here, boys. One of you take my gun. Help me to lie down. I'm badly hit."

About that time, Black Bear came out of his fright and mental confusion. All of a sudden he became calm. His mind was absolutely clear. His hands were steady.

"Load the gun," he shouted to the older boy. "Shoot at the enemy horses. You can hit them more easily than the men!"

The boy fired a few times, eventually killing one horse and stampeding the others, so that the Navahos were swiftly carried out of good rifle range. Since the short winter day was drawing to a close and the Kiowas still seemed to be resisting strongly, the enemy apparently decided to suspend fighting until next day. Black Bear could see them riding slowly back down the canyon.

Soon the four Kiowas began walking in the opposite direction. Big Bow, bleeding and in great pain, was helped along by the others.

After a few minutes the rest of the band, who had been concealed on the ridges during the day and who had not even shouted encouragement, began calling to them. The whole party assembled once more at the bottom of the canyon. For a time they sat on the ground behind some boulders, discussing what they should do next. The leader had no ideas, no suggestions to offer. Yet he was responsible for their safety. The situation was desperate. They had no food, no blankets, and no horses. It would be very cold after the sun went down. Worse yet, a strong breeze was stirring the tops of the cottonwoods. A norther was coming, which meant that within a few hours, maybe only one or two, the temperature would drop to zero. Most of them could keep alive by walking, but Big Bow could hardly move. Before morning he would be dead, frozen.

Finally Black Bear spoke up. "I'm going back to our campsite to see if any blankets are left. We need them most of all. The rest of you men move on up the trail until you find a safe place for us to spend the night. It will be dark soon, and we can't do anything more until morning. But *don't leave this wounded man here!* I might not be able to find him if I am late coming back."

When he got back to the overhanging cliff, Black Bear found only smoldering ashes. Everything was burned. There were no blankets.

Black Bear was shivering as he started up the trail—as much from worry as from the chill air. But it was still light enough to see the path clearly, which crossed and recrossed a dry stream bed. In the sand he saw the tracks of horses leading off to the right into a side canyon. Black Bear followed them with a quickened pace. Around a bend he saw that the draw ended in a high cliff which reflected the light of the full moon. Across the bottom of the canyon was a rail fence which, with the cliffs, made a large corral. An old white horse was staring at him with its head over the fence rails. As he went up to the animal, it whinnied softly. It was tame and glad to see a human being. He unwound from his waist a lariat, such as he and his friends always took on raids. He had expected to use it to catch the horses they had hoped to steal. And now the rope was to be a lifesaver. With it he tied the gentle horse to the fence. Then with his flint he lit a bundle of dried grass and held it up. The light shone on

23

several other horses standing at the far end of the corral. With his bow he shot one, which proved to be a two-year-old mare. He built a small, sheltered fire near the slain animal, in the light of which he skinned and butchered the carcass. He packed some of the meat in the hide and tied it on the back of the horse he had caught. Then he mounted up and rode to join the rest of the Kiowas.

Soon he thought that he should be overtaking them, so he called out, "Where are you men?" There was no answer. He called again. Big Bow, lying half-conscious beside the trail, roused himself enough to make a feeble reply. Then the others came down out of the brush where they had concealed themselves when they heard the horse approaching.

Black Bear built another small fire between two boulders where there was soft sand. He dragged Big Bow to the side of the fire and brought him a drink of water in a skin bag. Then he started to cook the horse meat. "I'm sorry," he said. "There were no blankets."

After giving the injured man some hot meat, Black Bear hollowed out a bed for him in the sand, which he lined with dry grass. He lowered Big Bow gently into this bed and piled more grass over him. Then he lay down beside the chief and pulled the horsehide over them. Every other member of the party wanted to crowd into the bed also, for they had allowed the fire to die down lest the enemy who might be lurking in the vicinity spot its glow. But Black Bear thrust them aside angrily. Let them dig their own holes, tear up their own grass, he growled.

It was a miserable night, but daybreak came at last, with a chill, gray sky. The smell of snow was in the air. Big Bow was still alive, but stiff from his wounds and the cold. A brief look around convinced Black Bear that there would be no renewal of the attack. The enemy had gone. So he permitted the boys to build another small fire over which the Indians warmed themselves and cooked more horse meat. Then Black Bear called a conference. No one protested his leadership of the party.

"The Navahos will be backtracking along our trail west from the river," he said. "They will expect to ambush us on our return journey. Also they will decide that we may move upstream, where there are easier fording places. So, we will fool them by going southeast and hit the river far below where we crossed before. It may be hard to get across, but we will find a way. We'll avoid our raid head-quarters."

After some dissension, the others agreed to Black Bear's plan. He had them fasten the horsehide between two poles to make a litter for Big Bow. Then taking turns carrying him, they set out along a ridge leading in the direction they wished to travel, staying up high where they could spy any enemy trying to cut them off.

When they camped that night, Black Bear cooked most of the horse meat for Big Bow. Several of the men asked him to kill the horse which he had caught and use it for food. "We will get too weak to travel if we don't eat soon," they said.

Black Bear refused. "Everyone gather here," he called. "Hear my announcement. Some of you want me to slaughter this horse. I know you are hungry. I'm hungry too. But I am not going to do it. I hereby pledge this horse to the *Tai-me*. If we get back safely, it will be offered as a sacrifice at the next sun dance."

Though most of the men didn't care for that decision, they dared not go against the *Tai-me*. But they could, and did, grumble.

One of the men, Kau-goo, moaned all night, keeping them awake much of the time. He claimed to have been shot in the forehead when the enemy had made their last attack just about dark. Big Bow made no sound at all. He did not grumble or complain. And he was silent about his wound. Black Bear was skeptical about Kau-goo's alleged head wound. But he had no proof the man was faking, so he said nothing, especially since Kau-goo did have a bleeding cut on his forehead.

The next morning, Black Bear was up before dawn. He washed Big Bow's wound and greased it with tallow. Then he roused the rest of the Kiowas, saying, "I'm going on ahead. I'll take Big Bow's rifle. Maybe I can kill a deer or something. When you hear a shot or two, follow in the same direction. But don't leave this wounded man behind!"

After he had gone less than a mile, Black Bear was lucky in kill-ing two does. He had skinned them and was preparing to roast the meat when he saw several of his party approaching.

"Where is Big Bow?" he cried, anxiously.

"They're bringing him along at the rear," Set-toi-yoi-te (Many Bears) answered. "We are taking turns carrying him."

In a few moments, the rest of the party appeared, bringing Big Bow, who seemed to be stronger. After they had made the old chief comfortable, two of the younger men helped Black Bear cook the meat. Each of the men got a good-sized chunk.

While they were eating breakfast, Black Bear stared hard at Kau-goo, who was still complaining. Presently he noticed a little stick of wood protruding from the man's scalp.

"While you are finishing your meal, I will scout out the country ahead. Four of you young men come with me. We may find more horses, so bring those straps which I have just cut from the deerskin. We'll make several bridles."

After they had gone far enough that their voices could not be heard by the main group, Black Bear stopped. "Kau-goo was not shot," he explained. "I think he ran into a dead branch during his flight up the mountain side, and he has a splinter stuck in his scalp. You grab him and hold him down while I operate."

In a few minutes the other Kiowas joined them. "For some time I have heard a little puppy whimpering," said Black Bear. "I think it is about time to put him out of his misery!"

At his signal the four young men seized and held Kau-goo. The latter gave a surprised yelp. "I'm a poor man," he wailed. "I've had a hard, hard time! What are you going to do? Kill me?"

Making no reply, Black Bear quickly took out his awl, opened Kau-goo's superficial wound, and extracted a small stick about half an inch long.

He held it up for all to see. "This poor fellow was shot, sure enough," he said sarcastically. "Here is the bullet!"

The others held their sides in merriment.

During the day Black Bear killed several more deer, which he skinned and butchered. Now there were enough hides so that the men could pair up at night, and each pair would have a blanket. He also found a small herd of hobbled horses grazing in an upland meadow. They easily caught these, so that there were enough mounts for everyone, riding double.

26

Though he was glad to have the horses, Black Bear was secretly worried. He realized that their owners would not be far away and that the disappearance of the animals would stimulate a search for the raiders. He was also afraid that the firing he had done in getting the venison had aroused either the enemy or the white settlers. The latter would certainly notify the commander of any military post in the area. An organized pursuit, in addition to the possibility of encountering Navahos, would be a severe threat, at least until they could cross the Pecos. There was scant possibility of increasing their speed, because of being burdened with the wounded Big Bow and having mounts for only half their number. Of course they could scatter and attempt to get home in every-man-for-himself style, but Black Bear was not yet ready to resort to such a measure.

That evening, as they made camp, Black Bear's fears were shown to be well founded. The two scouts whom he had appointed to travel far to the rear of their column reported that some kind of enemy was trailing them. It seemed to be cavalry with Navaho scouts or trackers out in advance.

Black Bear called a council. "They won't follow us during darkness," he said. "The mountains are too rough for night travel, and the Navahos can't see our trail. But we must move out early, or they will catch up with us before we reach the Pecos."

By midmorning the next day they saw the river in the distance. But the rear guard signaled that the enemy were in sight, circling to pick up their trail. Black Bear decided they should head straight for the river, not losing time trying to conceal their tracks. He knew it was going to be a close race.

The river was seventy-five yards wide, running strong, and filled with chunks of ice and snow. Black Bear quickly instructed two of the men to make a pontoon by wrapping deer skin around a pile of brush and bent willow branches. "Tie Big Bow on top and get the raft, with him on it, floating in the water as soon as you can. I'll be back in a few minutes to tow him across."

He ran back to fire a few shots at the leading pursuers in an effort to make them stop and deploy. He hoped that they would not grasp the fact that he was the only Kiowa who had a serviceable gun.

His plan worked! As soon as he saw the enemy stop and take cover behind rocks on both sides of the trail, he hurried to the river, placed his rifle on the raft with Big Bow, and began to ferry the craft across, wading and finally swimming. On reaching the shore, he at once gathered some driftwood and built a fire. The enemy were shooting at them now, but from too great a distance to be effective.

"The rest of you men drive those horses into the river and swim them across," he shouted. "Hang onto their tails!"

Every man made it safely, but several were half dead from cold and fatigue. He allowed them to warm themselves at the fire for only a short time. Already some of the enemy were creeping closer to the river. Their bullets glanced across the water.

"That's enough," cried Black Bear. "We've got to get moving!"

"No! No! Let us stay by the fire just a minute longer," the men pleaded.

But Black Bear drove them ruthlessly beyond the sand dunes and kept them moving into the chaparral. Then he let them stop to catch their breath in a mesquite thicket. It was not a moment too soon. The enemy had reached the river and were ranging up and down the bank shooting in the direction in which the Kiowas had disappeared.

As Black Bear peered stealthily from the thicket, it seemed to him that the enemy battle lust was not strong enough to force them into the swift and icy river. But he did not voice this hope. He ordered the Kiowas to continue their flight. "We've got to get as far ahead of them as we can," he explained. "We are not yet in our country. We are not safe. One of you go upstream to our raid headquarters and tell the boys there to join us at Muchaque with the spare horses."

There was much grumbling. "We are wet," they said. "We'll freeze to death. Let us stop and build another fire."

But Black Bear would not hear of it. "You can get warm and dry by walking and running," he said. "We will lead the horses. Big Bow must ride, however. I'll wrap him up good. He is still wet."

The complaining grew louder. It began to look as though Black Bear had a mutiny on his hands. At this juncture, Big Bow came to his support.

28

"Now all you men listen to me!" he said. "You have whined enough. Black Bear is not to blame for your troubles. Instead, he is saving your lives. So stop this homesick complaining and quarreling. Don't get cranky just because we are having a little trouble. I say that this young man is going to get us all home safely. So straighten up! Be men!"

The men stood silent, ashamed. At length the warrior who had recruited the party and who had been its leader at the beginning spoke. "You are right. I have not filled my job. I have not cared for my men. I hereby resign as *to-yop-ke* in favor of Black Bear!"

And thus the young, unrecognized Black Bear became the *to-yop-ke*, the leader of a war party. When they reached their main camp near Rainy Mountain, north of the Wichita Mountains, there was a victory dance, even though they had brought home no scalps and only a few horses. At that celebration it was announced that Black Bear was now a war chief!

Maybe it was good medicine to pledge that horse to the *Tai-me*. ☼

5 ✿ THE DEATH OF NAH-GOEY

THE KIOWA TRIBE was divided into six divisions or subtribes, of which the most prominent and the largest was the Kata. Another popular subdivision was the Kogui, or Elks. Jimmy Gui-tone's grandfather, An-zah-te, had married into the Kogui band, and sometimes went on raids with them. He told Jimmy a story of a disastrous raid into the Southwest, illustrating the fact that some Indians, even chiefs, were often skeptics when it came to heeding the warnings of their medicine or the strong tribal taboos. The year of this raid was not given, though there is a slight indication on the Hau-vah-te calendar that it took place in 1829. The story as set down here substantially follows the account furnished by Gui-tone.

✿ One winter the Kogui band was moving north with the entire tribe. The Koguis decided to separate temporarily from the main tribe and turn back to the south. After they had settled down in a winter camp on the upper Washita, a man named Nah-goey recruited a war party to make a raid in the direction of the Pecos River, in southwest Texas. Some twenty warriors accepted the pipe, all of them being Koguis except for one or two Comanches and two Kiowas who had married into the Kogui band. The latter were An-zah-te [Buffalo Udder] and another young man named Tau-kan-ta-le, or

30

Antelope Boy. He was the medicine man who had charge of the antelope drives.

Elaborate preparations were made for the expedition, which would be a hard and dangerous one and might last for several months. It was essential that the leader, or *to-yop-ke*, be experienced and resourceful and acquainted with all the landmarks and water holes in the arid country where they expected to operate.

The first obstacle was Red River, which, swollen from recent heavy rains, was unfordable. The Kiowas swam their horses across, a feat which they often practiced. Equipment which had to be kept dry was ferried on little pontoons made by wrapping rawhide or canvas around bundles of brush. One of the men was custodian of a Grandmother god, one of ten sacred medicines which the Kiowas had possessed as long as they could remember. One of the rules of this medicine was that it should not be allowed to get wet. But on this occasion the float which carried the god became water-logged, so that the pouch in which the medicine was carried became soaked. All the men except Nah-goey felt that this was a very bad sign. They wanted to build a sweat lodge and offer some earnest prayers to the medicine in order to propitiate it. Nah-goey, evidently an agnostic, deplored the delay, but told them to go ahead. During the ceremony, a robe which was being thrown over the frame of the sweat lodge caught fire and was scorched. This was taken as a warning that they ought to abandon the expedition and turn back.

This did not suit Nah-goey. All these alleged bad luck signs in his view were bad luck for their enemy—good luck for the Koguis. He expressed so much scorn for his companions' fears and talked so long and loudly that they finally agreed to continue the journey. But they were very uneasy.

Their misgivings were increased a hundredfold a day or so later when they encountered a bear on the trail. Owing to a long-standing superstitious awe of the bear, the Kiowas would have avoided this creature, but instead of running from them, he came toward them. This was most unusual and was thought to be another bad omen.

The bear stood on his hind legs, then got down on all fours and came toward them a few steps. He repeated this maneuver. Finally,

31

a fourth time [four is the magic number with the Indians] he stood up, and even appeared to be waving to the Kiowas to turn back. This should have been enough for anyone. But as is so often the case, the man who took a positive stand prevailed. Nah-goey told the men that the bear had given them a sign that they would defeat their enemies.

"See!" he cried, "The bear is running from us. That is the way our enemies will run from us."

The party continued southward, but there was much muttering as they rode along.

The following day a vast flock of crows flew over them. The Indians wondered what this meant. Nah-goey assured them that it was a sign that they would adorn themselves with the black paint of victory when they returned to the village.

A fourth omen visited the group in the form of a great swarm of flies, quite unexplainable because they were in a semidesert, an area where flies were not ordinarily found. Nah-goey was cheerful even about this.

"Even the flies tell us of good luck to come," he predicted. "Soon we will be seeing the flies feasting on the bodies of our victims."

Each night the young medicine man, Antelope Boy, slept apart from the rest of the group, trying to get a vision of what was going to happen. Nah-goey kept telling him that all was well, that he and An-zah-te were safe with the Koguis. Since no warning dream came to him, he finally concluded that Nah-goey was right. No more omens appeared.

The days passed. They had wandered along the edge of the Staked Plains and had moved west until they were nearing the Navaho country beyond the Pecos. It was spring, and the weather was getting warm. As they rode along, Nah-goey said, "I would like to know if any young man will go out ahead of us to build a rock altar so that the hot atmosphere will make the altar appear to be larger?" By this he was calling for a man to act as advance scout.

An-zah-te offered his services. Nah-goey then asked if some other man would be willing to scare the crows away from their old camp-site, which meant that he wanted someone to act as rear scout or rear guard. The other non-Kogui, Antelope Boy, said that he would do it. This was in accordance with custom. The Indians usually detailed for scout duty were very young men, apprentice warriors, or other unrecognized members of the party. The duty was a hard one, because they had to travel farther and faster than the main body, and often were exposed to danger. It was normal for the experienced warriors to save themselves as much as possible, perhaps so that they would be fresh when fighting occurred. So in this case the two members of the party who were not Koguis volunteered for the duty as scouts.

Antelope Boy went back to the old campsite and concealed himself among the rocks at a distance from which he could see whether an enemy was following their trail and would examine the campground in the morning. Toward afternoon he saw two men approaching to scout out the campsite, followed by a very large party who, in the distance, appeared to be Indians. They were too far away for Antelope Boy to identify, but he thought from their action of following the trail of the Koguis that they must be enemies. He went forward, by-passed Nah-goey and the rest of the men, and met Anzah-te at a previously selected rendezvous so that they could discuss what they had seen during the day before making their report to Nah-goey. As he approached, he began, in fun, to chant the Messenger-Announcing Song. He thrust a broomstraw in his hair in the traditional manner of messengers coming to report and told Anzah-te what he had seen.

The two scouts went to the camping place for that evening and reported to Nah-goey. The latter listened impassively, then remarked, "At this time of year people are often fooled by the sight of large herds of elk, which in the distance sometimes look like men on horseback."

Then he gave Antelope Boy an Indian lie detector test, which consisted of pinching the scout. If he cried out, he was not telling the truth. By this action Nah-goey showed doubt and implied criticism of his rear guard. Antelope Boy was indignant, but said nothing further. Therefore, Nah-goey called out to the other men that the rear scout had been fooled by a herd of elk, which brought a laugh.

33

On the following day Nah-goey again called for men to act as advance and rear scouts. The same men volunteered. Nah-goey impressed on them the need for verifying anything unusual which they might see.

Antelope Boy took his post on a hill at a distance from the old camp. After two or three hours he again saw a large party of mounted men approaching. This time he could see clearly the sun glinting on their weapons, and the bright-colored war trappings which they were wearing. That evening he again reported that some hostile party was following them and had examined their old campsite. Nah-goey grabbed his arm and pinched him severely. Antelope Boy resented this. "Perhaps," he said sarcastically, "elks now wear feathers in their hair and carry shields."

Since his reports were not believed, Antelope Boy was inclined to refuse to act as a scout the next day. An-zah-te tried to persuade him to do it once more. He told An-zah-te that trouble would occur that day and that An-zah-te should stay well out to the front so as to avoid being involved in a possible disaster to the main body. Antelope Boy said that he was so sure that they would be attacked that day that it would look bad later if he remained apart from the group. Therefore, he was *not* going to act as rear guard, but would stay with the main body. He informed Nah-goey of this decision, who appointed another man to scout to the rear.

An-zah-te's first position as advance scout was on a high mountain well to the front. From this post he saw the main body attacked by an overwhelming force of some enemy tribe, probably Navaho. It was from his account of this that the tribe later learned what had happened.

The fight lasted only a few minutes. When the enemy first appeared, and Nah-goey saw that he and his men were surrounded and heavily outnumbered, he said, "When a buffalo cow runs all day, then is butchered, the meat is soft and no good. I am not going to run and let my meat get soft and rotten. I want my meat to taste good to the dogs of the enemy. The rest of you may run and save yourselves if you can. I stay here and fight to the last!"

A few of the enemy paused briefly to kill Nah-goey, while the rest of them went after the Koguis who were fleeing. It was a massacre. So far as An-zah-te could see, all his friends were killed, including Antelope Boy, who had stayed with Nah-goey.

The horrified An-zah-te saw the enemy standing around the bodies of the fallen. After a time they withdrew in the direction from which they had come. An-zah-te sadly made his way down the mountainside and came to the awful scene. As he feared, all were dead except Antelope Boy, who was hobbling toward him, using his bow for a crutch. An-zah-te made him sit down while he dressed the young man's deep cuts and slashes. Then they counted the bodies. One man was missing, whom they later found alive though wounded. They stayed on the scene all through the day, piling rocks over the slain. The omens came true. The flies and crows swarmed over the bodies.

Nah-goey was not a prudent leader. Like many others of various times and peoples, he was a war leader who felt it necessary to keep up the spirits of his men by making a show of optimism. But like others, he carried it too far and allowed it to neutralize a caution that might have saved them all. Nevertheless, he was one of the bravest of the brave. The Kiowas mourned for him and for his men. ⚙

6 ❀ THE T'AU

T<small>HIS STORY IS ESSENTIALLY BASED</small> on accounts given me by George Hunt and Hunting Horse.

❀ About 1837, ten Kiowas, led by Guadal-onte, rode south from Rainy Mountain to Paso del Norte, where El Paso was later built. At this time there was in that vicinity no town north of the Río Grande, only a few ranches along the river. But south of the Río Grande was Ciudad Juárez, with its presidio and garrison of Mexican lancers. Do-hauson, principal chief of the Kiowa tribe, was with the expedition as an ordinary member, but so great was his skill and courage that the chances of success for this raid seem assured.

Nevertheless, because of the vigilance of the garrison, the Kiowas decided not to raid the haciendas in that area, but to turn back to their own country, far to the north. That evening as they were riding toward the Hueco Mountains, north of the river, they were spied in the distance by some of the enemy, who at once set out in pursuit. Guadal-onte, looking back, saw the Mexican redcoats coming along in column about a mile behind them. He urged his men to increase their speed so that they could escape into the mountains. Au-tone-a-kee objected. They had come a long way, but had not yet smelled gun powder. What would the tribe think if they returned without something to show for their efforts? After some argument, this point of view prevailed. The Kiowas halted and awaited the Mexican attack.

But when the Mexicans came close, it was seen that they out-numbered the Kiowas at least four to one. The Indians suddenly decided to run for it. The decision was made almost too late, but in their headlong flight the Kiowas passed a rocky depression or arroyo somewhere near Hueco Tanks. They scrambled down into this and took refuge in a cave that ran back under the lip of the canyon. One man tried to take his horse with him, but the delay this caused per-mitted the Mexicans to get within musket range. The volley they delivered killed the horse and wounded the Indian. Both fell into the gulch, from which the others dragged the wounded man back into the cave.

The enemy surrounded the place, keeping so tight a watch both by day and night that the Kiowas had no chance to slip away. At night the Indians crawled from beneath their shelter to drink from a little pool of water caught in the rocks in the middle of the can-yon. This sally failed because the Mexicans had built a big fire on the mesa above, in the light of which they fired at anything they saw moving. Even worse, the putrefying horse was lying half in the water, spoiling it for use. The only unpolluted water the Indians could get was by licking moisture seeping from some of the rocks within the cave.

After a siege lasting six days, the Kiowas were in a pitiable con-dition. They had exhausted their supply of dried meat, yet were unable to eat the flesh of the bloated horse. The wounded man, a brother of Au-tone-a-kee, had died. No one was getting enough water. Because they were hundreds of miles from their home camp, there was no chance of a party coming to their rescue.

Just as they were giving way to despair, a joyful shout came from one of the men who had wormed his way back into the far reaches of the cave. They all scrambled to join him. Looking where he pointed, they saw a little patch of blue sky in a crevice overhead. The whole party took turns helping the discoverer of this escape route to enlarge the hole. When one of them finally came to the surface he saw that the hole emerged on the plain at some distance from the edge of the canyon, and that it was not being watched by the enemy. After a short consultation, the Kiowas agreed to wait until after dark to make the escape attempt. But at the last moment one of the men poked his head out for one last look around. One of the Mexicans, seeing him, fired. As the Kiowas crawled back into the main cave, they heard rocks and earth being thrown into the hole and knew that this path of escape was blocked. The disappointment was almost more than they could bear.

Just when their spirits were lowest, a voice speaking Comanche called to them from the rim of the canyon.

"Don't give up!" cried the stranger, cheerily. "The Mexicans are going to throw some food down to you soon. It will be all right, because they hope to take you alive. I will help you escape later."

The Kiowas discussed this incident, deciding that the stranger was some Comanche boy who had been captured years ago by the Mexicans and now was going to aid them. Their hopes revived.

A few minutes later the Kiowas heard something drop to the floor of the canyon. Their caution dulled by hunger and desperation, they rushed to the cave entrance. There in front of them, slithering in their direction, were five or six fat rattlesnakes. They had to jump back to avoid being bitten and had difficulty finding rocks with which to kill the snakes. A roar of derisive laughter came from the edge of the canyon, followed by bursts of gunfire.

A moment later, Tsone-ai-tah spoke to the leader: "We have lost one man. Another is wounded. We are starving, getting weaker by the hour. We are going to die here like helpless women."

Then he turned to Au-tone-a-kee, who had urged them to fight the Mexicans in the first place. "Au-tone-a-kee," he said, "you are the cause of all our trouble. You are responsible for your own brother lying there all black and bloated." With that he drew his scalping knife and hacked off Au-tone-a-kee's hair, including his small braided scalplock. He stood silent and ashamed, while the others threw the hair on the corpse of his brother.

Tsone-ai-tah then turned to the group. "If you are willing to die like women," he said, "there is no help for us. Let us get out of this

38

foul place and die in the open like men and warriors! Then if any report of this affair reaches our people, it will be that we were killed in battle—not starved like badgers in a hole in the ground."

He began cutting the thongs from his leggings, which he braided into a rope. "Are you willing to make a rush for it after dark, even if every one of us is killed? All right. I want a volunteer to go first along the shadows of that overhanging ledge and help the others up the cliff when he finds a good spot. We will all follow. But you, Shaved Head, will go last!"

After midnight, when the Mexicans were getting drowsy and their camp fires were burning low, Tsone-ai-tah gathered his comrades about him in the cave. He tied their bows to their wrists with the strings so that they would have both hands free to climb and would not lose their weapons if they dropped them in the darkness.

"One last word! If anyone, one man, even, gets through safely, he must carry home to our people the story of how we died. Are you ready?"

The other Kiowas nodded.

"Then if we are going to die, let it be now!" With that the Kiowas slipped silently out of the cave and ran single file down the gulch, keeping under its edge and hoping not to be seen.

But the Mexican sentry saw their shadows. A burst of gunfire lighted the canyon walls. Though two Kiowas fell, the others did not stop to help them. That had been agreed. One of the wounded was Kone-au-beah. He picked himself up and hobbled to catch up. The other wounded man lay still. The survivors continued swiftly down the canyon, the enemy following along the rim, firing at every rustle of a dislodged stone. The lights of the fires no longer illuminated the scene; the Kiowas now had a chance.

In the lead was the mighty Do-hauson. Seeing a stunted cedar growing on the side of the arroyo, he caught hold of the roots and dragged himself up. With his bow he helped the others climb out, one at a time.

Dagoi, severely wounded, was exhausted. He didn't have the strength to grasp the bow extended to him. There was no time to tie the lariat around him. The Mexicans were approaching.

39

"Don't leave me here!" cried Dagoi. "I want to see my father's face again."

"It is our life or yours," replied Do-hauson. "If we stay to help you, no one will get away. Make your heart strong! Die like a Kiowa warrior!"

"Very well. Thank you," said Dagoi more composedly. "I stay. Tell my father to come back and avenge my death." He sat down with his back against the wall and began to chant his death song. In a few moments the Mexicans came along and shot him several times.

The Mexicans found the other Kiowa who, besides Kone-au-beah, had been wounded in the escape lying prostrate in the pit, but still alive. They scalped him and dragged his body to the mesa above. When daylight came, they saw that he was not yet dead. So they tied him to a wild mustang, and by whipping the animal caused it to run, bucking and tossing among the rocks. The Mexicans expected to enjoy seeing the Indian's brains dashed out. But somehow he survived this cruel sport. At length, when the horse was standing drooping in exhaustion, they untied the Kiowa and let him fall to the ground. Too delirious to realize that he was in the hands of his enemies, he asked for food.

One of the grinning Mexicans climbed down into the arroyo and cut a piece of rotten flesh from the dead horse. They handed this to the Indian and howled with mirth to see him retch. They made him repeat this performance again and again. He asked for water. They gave him mud. There was no pity in their hearts. They had seen too many of their own people mutilated by the Indians. At length they tied him over a horse and took him to Juárez to furnish sport for the rest of the garrison.

Several years later the Kiowas were greatly surprised to see this man come riding into their camps on the Arkansas River. He was wearing a fine serape and riding a splendid blooded stallion. On his head, covering the place where he had been scalped, was a silver plate. He said that a kindhearted Mexican gentleman had saved his life, nursed him back to health, and finally sent him to his people, laden with presents. Because of his silver plate, the Kiowa was renamed Hone-geah-tau-te, which means "silver headplate." He lived for many years, the wonder of the tribe, not only because of his remarkable adventure, but also as a living testimony to the kindness of an enemy.

The Kiowas who escaped from the disaster at Hueco Tanks fled across the desert until they came to another canyon. They followed its course until they came to a thick patch of cactus, where they concealed themselves until the following night. That evening they climbed out and went up a hill to the place where they had established their raid headquarters and where their spare horses and extra equipment had been left in charge of two young boys. It was a difficult trip because they were carrying the wounded Kone-au-beah.

On the following day they reached the summit of Sun Mountain, so called because it shines when the sun is upon it, possibly because of certain glistening rocks. Here they stopped at a spring for some rest. It seemed certain that Kone-au-beah could not last much longer. His wounds were festering. He was hot to the touch and scarcely conscious. They decided not to be burdened with him any longer.

So Kone-au-beah was laid on the ground, and rocks were piled around him to keep the coyotes from eating him. He was placed within reach of the spring so that he could ladle up some water in his hands in case he regained consciousness. Then they rode away.

41

When the shadows on the shoulder of the mountain grew longer, the wounded Indian slowly regained his senses. He soon realized that he was alone, abandoned by his companions. There was no sound but the wind sighing in the piñons. He could feel the maggots working in his wounds. He thought then of his home tipi and his family far to the north and felt that he would never see them again. Soon the Kiowas would be gathering for the sun dance. When he did not return, they would kill his horses, burn his property, and his women would begin wailing for him. His name would never be spoken again. Kone-au-beah's eyes filled with tears.

As the desert valley far below turned from gold to purple and the stars began to come out in the deep blue sky, Kone-au-beah heard the soft rustle of wild animals carefully drawing near to him. A wolf howled nearby. In a few minutes the wolf climbed up on the pile of rocks surrounding the man and gazed down at him, its eyes gleaming in the bright desert starlight. Kone-au-beah could see its sharp ears and muzzle silhouetted against the sky. The two creatures of the wild—Indian and beast—stared at each other silently for a few moments. Then the wolf crept down and began to lick the man's wounds. The chill of the desert was settling. The strange new friend lay down beside the Indian and kept him warm through the night. With the first light of morning it was gone.

For three successive nights the wolf cared for Kone-au-beah. But the Kiowa was growing weaker from lack of food. On the fourth night he was lying thinking of home. He heard a faint whistle in the air, steadily growing louder. The wolf sprang up and slunk away. Now it seemed that the whistle came from directly overhead. Kone-au-beah recognized it as the eagle-bone whistle of the *Tai-me*, the great god of the sun dance. He heard in the breeze the Gourd Rattle Song, the song of his warrior society. The voice of the *Tai-me* spoke to him, saying, "I pity you and will care for you. Be of strong heart. I will see to it that you get back to your home."

The next day the *Tai-me* sent a cooling rain which washed Kone-au-beah's wounds and refreshed him. He felt stronger almost at once, but still was unable to sit up. That night the wolf began to bark at something approaching through the darkness on the mountainside. In a moment the wolf was gone. Kone-au-beah heard horses' hoofs clicking against the rocks and the soft whinny of a pony as it sniffed the smell of water at the spring. Several men rode up and began to make camp. The Kiowa listened to their low conversation, trying to determine whether they were friends or enemies. When he heard a few words of Comanche he tried to call to them. But his voice would not come out. All he could manage was a groan.

At once the Comanches stopped what they were doing, and stood with arrows in their bows, ready for instant action. Then their brave leader walked over to the pile of rocks.

"Here is a man almost dead," he said after a moment. The Comanches lighted wisps of grass and stared at Kone-au-beah. They gave him a drink, then lay down to rest until daylight. The next morning they examined Kone-au-beah carefully, after which they stood weeping in pity over his awful condition. They peeled off his filthy clothing, washed him thoroughly, and dressed his wounds with buffalo tallow. Then they made some broth for him from dried buffalo meat, which they fed him sparingly.

For several days the Comanches remained at Sun Mountain, nursing Kone-au-beah. They had intended going on a raid into Mexico, but now after a conference they decided to give this up and take Kone-au-beah back to his people. Though he was a stranger to them, the Comanches followed their custom of taking care of people whom they found in distress in the wilderness. When he was strong enough to stand the journey, they made a travois from two poles, which they fastened to either side of a gentle horse, and on it they built a little arbor for the wounded man. Then they started the long trip north through the waste of sand, rocks, yucca, and mesquite.

After several days of weary travel they reached the buffalo plains where the grass was taller and thicker and there was an occasional stream. By this time Kone-au-beah was well enough to sit on a horse. One day as they rode up a little crest on the rolling prairie, they saw a *Tai-me* idol stuck in the ground.

"It is a medicine idol that one of our Comanches captured from the Crows some years ago," explained the Comanche leader. "But it brought nothing but bad luck to the man who owned it. Finally he was killed on a raid, so his relatives abandoned it here."

Kone-au-beah asked if he might have the *Tai-me*. The Comanches agreed carelessly. Not having a sun dance, they had no use for a sun dance idol. Kone-au-beah felt sure that this was the *Tai-me* he had seen in his vision; the one who had promised to help him get home.

Kone-au-beah was greeted with a mixture of joy and astonishment when he returned to the Kiowa camp. He had been given up for dead. Presents of many fine horses were bestowed on the kind Comanches who had taken so much trouble with him. A big feast and dance was held in their honor. The bond between the two tribes was still further strengthened.

Considerable wonder was expressed over Kone-au-beah's new *Tai-me*. The tribe already possessed two, a male and a female idol which they had obtained many years before and which they regarded with extreme veneration. They were not sure whether this was a real *Tai-me* or an imitation. But they allowed Kone-au-beah to keep it and even to place it beside the other two gods on the altar during the sun dance.

Kone-au-beah now began to have other visions and dreams. The *Tai-me* god appeared to him and commanded him to make, in thanksgiving for his miraculous escape from death, a *T'au*. In compliance with this supernatural demand, Kone-au-beah had an old woman secure for him a stick of well-seasoned chinaberry wood, from which he fashioned a medicine stick, the *T'au*. He carved the head to resemble that of the *Tai-me*. This magic stick was also given a prominent place during the sun dance.

On such occasions Kone-au-beah was an honored participant in the ceremony, carrying the *T'au*. It was about two feet long, with the bark peeled off, a feather tied to its *Tai-me*-like face, and a blue-beaded necklace and skunkskin skirt draped around it. This *T'au*, during the sun dance, was stuck in the ground beside the three *Tai-mes*. Kone-au-beah also had a medicine dance wand, a forked stick of seasoned chinaberry wood. When each dance was over, he put his *Tai-me* and *T'au* away in rawhide cases, just like the *Tai-mes* of old. Several years later he gave the *T'au* to Tay-bodal and the forked medicine stick to his nephew *Co-yante*. This was in 1848. Kone-au-beah died during the awful cholera epidemic of 1849, but Tay-bodal and Co-yante survived.

At the close of the 1857 sun dance, Co-yante thrust his forked medicine stick in the ground on the site of the sun dance lodge and left it there as a special offering to the *Tai-me*. When the Kiowas returned to the spot the following year, the forked stick had sprouted, putting forth green leaves like Aaron's rod! That sun dance year was known as "the Year the Forked Stick Sprouted."

Kone-au-beah's *Tai-me*, on his death, went to Pau-goo-hainte [Dehorned Buffalo]. It was captured by the Utes in 1868, together with one of the other *Tai-mes*.

But Tay-bodal kept the *T'au* until he inherited one of the ten Grandmother gods. Since it was forbidden to keep two different kinds of idols, he gave the *T'au* to Tay-nay-daute, who kept it packed in a medicine pouch with eagle-bone whistles. It has descended to his son or grandson, Oliver Tay-nay-dau, and every year the family has a celebration for it.

A chinaberry tree, the living descendant of the Forked Stick That Sprouted, now grows beside the Tay-nay-dau house in Kiowa County, Oklahoma. ✸

7 ❁ BUFFALO MEDICINE MEN

George Hunt obtained this story from Old Man Humming Bird, in 1937 the sole surviving member of the Buffalo Society, the Pau-ewey.

❁ Two brothers, one ten years old and the other twelve, were orphaned during the time the Kiowas were wandering about over the plains. No one would look after them, not even their uncle and aunt. They managed to exist by going from one lodge to another, begging for food and shelter. Finally an elderly childless couple took pity on them and became their foster parents. The boys had little to do, but were put in charge of their foster parents' two ponies, on which they lavished much care.

After several years one brother was old enough to go on a raid, and he was making preparations to join a small party which was leaving soon. The younger brother wanted to go too, despite the fact that his foster father said that he was still a little too young. But both boys insisted, so the old man gave his consent.

"All right," he said. "You may go. But both of you be sure and bring back some horses."

The raid was successful. The older brother, T'on-zau-te, made a first coup, which entitled him to three horses as his share of the

46

plunder. On their return from the raid, the boys were praised by the old couple, who were delighted to receive the stock.

One night the woman, Pau-tso-hain, said, "I want to give these boys a good story." At one time she had been a captive of the Pawnees, but had escaped and made her way back to the Kiowa tribe. She told of her adventures on this journey and a vision she had:

"During my journey I was overtaken by a terrible storm—black clouds, thunder and lightning, and large hailstones. I was out on the plains. There was no place to hide. Then as a flash of lightning lighted up the prairie around me, I saw in the grass the dried-up carcass of a buffalo. The skin still covered the ribs, so I crawled inside to take refuge from the huge hailstones which were bruising me. After a while I dropped off to sleep.

"During the night the buffalo appeared to me in a vision. It spoke to me, saying, 'I am going to give you a worthwhile present, valuable in time of war. Get the tail feathers of the fastest hawk, the one which has red stripes across his tail. Use three of these feathers as ornaments for a shield, which must be painted half red. It must also have a fringe of smaller feathers. A buffalo-tail wand must be made and the hoofs of a buffalo fashioned into rattles. These rattles are to be used to deaden the pain of a wound suffered in battle and to staunch the flow of blood. Two crow tail-feathers must be trimmed down to a circle at the end, then fastened to the head to represent the eyes of a buffalo. All this is to be worn by a man who thus becomes a buffalo medicine man. One or more such men will go with each war party to doctor those who are hurt.' "

Based on this story, the two young orphans became buffalo medicine men, wearing the costume prescribed by the old woman's vision. They went on every raid, and were very successful. Soon they organized the Buffalo Society, called Pau-ewey.

When members of a war party were wounded, the buffalo men would shake their rattles and their buffalo tails and sing their special song. They also painted their faces with red stripes, running horizontally across the mouth, and painted similar stripes on their horses. They not only claimed great success in healing the wounded, but also became great war chiefs. ✺

47

George Hunt said that the medicine men had several songs, all of which he knew. Sometimes, while they were treating a wounded man and singing their songs, a female voice would be heard singing somewhere. The medicine men said that this was the Buffalo Woman who had had the vision.

8 ✿ TRIBAL MEDICINE

EACH KIOWA HAD HIS OWN PERSONAL MEDICINE, somewhat like a guardian angel or patron saint of the Christian faith. In addition there were a number of tribal medicines which were venerated by all the Kiowas. The guardianship of these sacred objects was hereditary.

The Grandmother Gods
The oldest tribal medicine was in ten separate parts, called the Grandmother gods, or Our Grandmothers. The ethnologist James Mooney gives this medicine two names: *Adalbeahya*, which seems to have something to do with hair or scalps, and *Ta-lyi-da-i*, which is translated in Harrington's Kiowa vocabulary as "Boy Medicine." My informants called it *Tai-li-ope-kau*, which they said means "Our Grandmothers." The history or legend of this medicine does not tell why it is called Our Grandmothers, but the origin of Boy Medicine is clear from Mooney's account, given him about 1890 by an old Kiowa, probably Tay-bodal:

> The Adalbeahya is the eucharistic body of their supernatural hero-teacher, the Sun-boy, and has been known among them from the beginning of their existence as a people. According to the myth, a girl was one day playing with some companions when she discovered a porcupine in the branches of a tree. She climbed up to capture it, but as she climbed the tree it grew, carrying her with it, until it

49

pierced the arch of the sky into the upper world; here the porcupine took on his proper form as the Sun; they were married and had a son. Her husband warned her that in her excursions in search of berries and roots, she must never go near the plant called azon (pomme blanche) if its top had been bitten off by a buffalo. Like Eve or Pandora she longed to test the prohibition, so one day while digging food plants she took hold of a pomme blanche which had been cropped by a buffalo and pulled it up by the root, leaving a hole through which she saw, far below, the earth, which she had forgotten since the day she climbed the tree after the porcupine. Old memories awakened, and full of an intense longing for her former home, she took her child and fastening a rope above the hole began letting herself down to the earth. Her husband, returning from the hunt, discovered her absence and the manner of her escape, and throwing a stone after her through the hole, before she had reached the end of the rope, struck her upon the head and she fell to the ground dead. The child was uninjured, and after staying some time beside the body of his mother he was found and cared for by the Spider Woman, who became a second mother to him. One day in playing he threw upward a gaming wheel, which came down upon his head and cut through his body without killing him, so that instead of one boy there were now twin brothers. After many adventures in the course of which they rid the world of several destructive monsters, one of the brothers walked into a lake and disappeared forever under its waters, after which the other transformed himself into this "medicine" and gave himself in that shape to the Kiowa, who still preserve it as the pledge and guardian of their national existence.

This "Boy-medicine" is in ten portions, in the keeping of as many priests. Its chief priest is T'e-bodal, the oldest man of the tribe, with whom the author once had the opportunity of seeing the pouch in which it is carried, for no man, unless possibly the priest himself, has ever been permitted to open it and look upon its contents. It is kept in a small pouch fringed with numerous scalps, in a special tipi appointed for its residence; it is brought out for use in connection with a sweat-house ceremony as individuals may desire to sacrifice to it, and not, like the *taime*, at tribal gatherings.[1]

[1] James Mooney, "Calendar History of the Kiowa Indians," *Seventeenth Annual Report of the Bureau of American Ethnology* (Washington, D.C., Government Printing Office, 1898), Part I, 238–42.

In 1935, a little more information was given me concerning the contents of the pouch in which a Grandmother medicine was kept. According to George Hunt, it contained little packages of red paint, a mineral pigment obtained from a prominent bank along a creek which flowed from north of Mount Scott into Medicine Bluff Creek, some packets of dried and possibly powdered medicinal herbs or roots, and human scalps on small hoops. The gods themselves were unknown, mysterious objects entirely wrapped in scalps. As a guess, I would venture that these might have been "madstones," obtained from the stomach of a buffalo; or they also might have been dried bear paws, or almost anything considered to have magic qualities. The scalps were offerings that had been made to the god over the years. In former times, when they began to decay, they were replaced or renewed by the keeper of the medicine. I would not care to speculate on what is done about this today.

The keeper of a Grandmother god was not permitted to cast his eyes upon the contents of the pouch. No doubt he was restrained in any curiosity he might feel by a superstitious fear of what might happen to him and his family should he violate the taboo. Therefore when it was necessary to renew the scalps or make other repairs on the medicine, he had to do this in the dark, by sense of touch.

I was given the privilege of seeing two Grandmother god pouches: one kept by An-pay-kau-te, which he had inherited from his father, Satank, and one guarded by Silverhorn, a medicine man who did not go out of favor even in modern times. An-pay-kau-te took out of the pouch and displayed with pride a large silver medal which had been presented to his father on some past occasion, possibly during the Medicine Lodge Treaty gathering. I was informed that besides these two idols or medicines Ah-po-ma had one, Audel-pah-gui-tain had two, Blue Jay, one, and Mrs. Haumpo, several (presumably the remaining four). Today, all these medicines are still in the possession of hereditary guardians.

The Tai-me

Another important tribal medicine of the Kiowas was the *Tai-me*, sometimes called the Grandfather god. It is the medicine of the sun dance, referred to often in the lore and history of the tribe. James Mooney, in his "Calendar History of the Kiowa Indians," gives the following description of the *Tai-me* and the story of its origin.

The great central figure of the sun dance is the taime. This is a small image, less than 2 feet in length, representing a human figure dressed in a robe of white feathers, with a headdress consisting of a single upright feather and pendants of ermine skin, with numerous strands of blue beads around its neck, and painted upon the face, breast, and back designs symbolic of the sun and moon. The image itself is of dark-green stone, in form rudely resembling a human head and bust, probably shaped by art like the stone fetishes of the Pueblo tribes. It is preserved in a rawhide box in charge of the hereditary keeper, and is never under any circumstances exposed to view except at the annual sun dance, when it is fastened to a short upright stick planted within the medicine lodge, near the western side. It was last exposed in 1888. The ancient taime image was of buckskin, with a stalk of Indian tobacco for a headdress. This buckskin image was left in the medicine lodge, with all the other adornments and sacrificial offerings, at the close of each ceremony. The present taime is one of three, two of which came originally from the Crows, through an Arapaho who had married into the Kiowa tribe, while the third came by capture from the Blackfeet.

According to the legend, an Arapaho, who was without horses or other wealth, attended with his tribe the sun dance of the Crows and danced long and earnestly before the medicine, in hopes that it would pity him and make him prosperous. The chief priest of the Crows rewarded him by giving him the taime image, notwithstanding the protest of the Crows, who were angry at seeing such favors shown to a stranger. Fortune now smiled on the Arapaho; he stole many horses and won new blessings for himself by tying numerous ponies to the medicine lodge as a sacrifice to the taime, until at last his herd was one of the largest. Being now grown wealthy, when next his people visited the Crows he collected his horses and started back with them, but the jealous Crows followed secretly, untied the taime bag from the pole in front of his tipi and stole it. On discovering his loss the Arapaho made duplicates, which he took back with him to his own people. He afterwards married a Kiowa woman and went to live with her tribe, bringing with him the taime, which thus became the medicine of the Kiowa. Since that time the taime has been handed down in his family, the keeper consequently being always of part Arapaho blood.

The present [*circa* 1895] guardian is a woman, Emäa, who succeeded to the office at the death of Taimete, "Taime-man," in 1894; she is the ninth successive guardian, the Arapaho being the first. The fifth keeper, Long Foot (or Big Foot) held it forty years —from before the Osage massacre until his death in the winter of 1870–71. . . . The Kiowa must have obtained the taime about 1770. Of the two taime images, both of which were of the same shape and material, one, the "man," was small, only a few inches in length, while the other, the "woman," was much longer. It is believed among the Kiowa that the Crows still have the originals which they stole from the Arapaho.

Long afterwards, after the Kiowa had confederated with the Comanches, the latter had a fight with the Blackfeet, in which they killed a warrior and captured his medicine. The Comanche captor kept the medicine one night in his tipi, but it kept up a strange noise, which so frightened him that the next day he gave it to a Kiowa, who pulled off the long "tooth" attached to it, and thenceforth it was silent. Learning afterwards that it was a part of the taime medicine, he gave it to the taime keeper, who put it with the other images. It is said to have been nearly similar in appearance to the smaller image.

The complete taime medicine thus consisted of three decorated images. They were kept in a rawhide case, shaped somewhat like a kidney and painted with the taime symbols, the larger image being in one end of the case and the two smaller ones in the other. The smaller images, like the ark of the covenant, were sometimes carried to war, the box being slung from the shoulders of the man who carried it, and consequently were captured by the Utes. The large image was never taken from the main home camp.

The taime has been twice captured by enemies, first by the Osage in 1833, and again by the Ute in 1868. In the first instance the Osage surprised the Kiowa and captured all the images with the bag, killing the wife of the taime priest as she was trying to loosen it from its fastenings, but returned it two years later, after peace had been made between the two tribes. In the other case the Kiowa had taken the two smaller images, as a palladium of victory, upon a war ex-

53

pedition, when they were met by a war party of the Ute, who defeated them, killing the bearer of the medicine, and carried off the images, which have never since been recovered. The larger image is still with the tribe.[2]

As nearly as I could determine from an interview with the venerable *Tai-me* keeper, Ay-mah-ah (Mooney's Emäa), the following is a list of the successive guardians of the *Tai-me*:

Period	Keeper
1770–75	The Arapaho.
1775–90	Niece of the Arapaho.
1790–1810	Set-toi-yo-te, or Heap of Bears, husband of the Arapaho's niece. He too was part Arapaho.
1810–30	Heap of Bears, a nephew of the preceding keeper.
1830–70	Anso-gia-ny, or Ansote (Long Foot), sometimes called Old Man Foot.
1871–75	Do-hent (No Moccasins), nephew of the second Heap of Bears.
1876–93	Heap of Bears, nephew of Do-hente.
1894–1939	Ay-mah-ah, granddaughter of the second Heap of Bears.
1940———	Bo-tone, son of Ay-mah-ah.

Note that the story of how the present *Tai-me*, the one not captured by the Utes, was obtained from the Comanches differs in some respects from the version given in the story entitled "The T'au." Similarly, the account given me by Ay-mah-ah is not exactly the same as the one published by Mooney. However, these stories are in substantial agreement, especially on all vital points.

In 1935, Ay-mah-ah was living with her daughter and son-in-law, Benny Thompson, in a house east of Rainy Mountain, the area having been a favorite with the Kiowas since about 1830. She kept the *Tai-me* in the storm cellar, not having the material with which to erect the traditional tipi. The case was wrapped in oilcloth, which

2 Mooney, *loc. cit.*

when unwrapped disclosed a rawhide case about twenty inches long and roughly ovoid in shape. Today it is not easy for the younger Kiowas to maintain a constant watch over the *Tai-me* and the Grandmother gods, for they have other things to do than stay home at all times and guard these ancient religious relics.

Ay-mah-ah was born in 1854, a landmark in Kiowa history, for that was the year of the battle with the Sah-kee-bo. She said that her cousin, from whom she inherited the *Tai-me*, gave her her name, which means "Giving Him the Food." This was in commemoration of an incident which took place during a big raid into Montague County, Texas. During the attack he found a white woman hiding in the brush, who gave him food. In gratitude he spared her life.

According to Ay-mah-ah, the medicine originally was the personal property of a medicine man of the Crow tribe who lived in the far north near the Black Hills. In this man's household was an Arapaho servant. The Crow taught the Arapaho the ritual associated with the medicine and finally presented him with a *Tai-me* image. Soon afterward the Arapaho started south to his own country. The Arapahoes, on his arrival at their camp, jealously thought that the medicine ought to go to a more influential man. They took it from him, whereupon he said, "No matter. I alone of the Arapahoes know the details of the ceremony and the significance of the equipment that goes with the medicine. I shall make a duplicate *Tai-me*." So he did.

Because of the hatred and hostility of his fellow tribesmen, the Arapaho went to live with the Kiowas and married into the tribe. He staged his medicine ceremony, which became so attractive to the Kiowas that they adopted it as their great tribal medicine dance. On his death, the *Tai-me* passed to his niece, and on down through the chain of priests as shown in the foregoing list. When it came to Do-hente, a Mexican captive named Mokeen [Joaquin?], an adopted son of the predecessor of Do-hente, was designated to conduct the ritual. This was said to have happened because Do-hente was embarrassed at having to prance around in front of the entire tribe practically nude, as will be described in the story which deals with the sun dance.

Ay-mah-ah said that the *Tai-me* equipment, also kept in the case, consisted of eagle-bone whistles, crow-feather fans, paint, and other articles. According to Benny Thompson, Mokeen took the *Tai-me* out of its case in 1932 to repair it, being assisted by Moses Bo-tone. The rawhide case has also been repaired from time to time. The *Tai-me* itself could very well be placed on exhibit except for the fact that this can only be done during a sun dance. In 1887, a misguided Indian agent threatened to bring in troops against the Indians if they persisted in holding another sun dance. During the 1890's, Captain H. L. Scott, while at Fort Sill, tried to persuade the Kiowas to resume the dance. But they did not have the facilities, mainly lacking a buffalo. Probably they could obtain one today from the Wild Life Reserve, but apparently there is no general desire to re-establish the ceremony, nearly all of the Kiowas being earnest Christians and feeling, no doubt, that the dance would be a return to paganism.

9 ❀ THE MEDICINE DANCE

EACH OF THE PLAINS TRIBES, except the Comanches, celebrated an annual medicine dance called the sun dance. The Kiowa version differed from the others chiefly in that there was no physical torture endured by the celebrants other than the hardship of having to dance for four days and nights with very little rest or refreshment.

The whole ceremony was described in some detail by the Quaker teacher, Thomas Battey, and more briefly by Mooney, but their books are now out of print and generally unavailable. Therefore, I repeat here an account given to me by George Hunt, who as a boy witnessed several dances. Some details from Battey's description have been inserted, but Hunt's account is more important because he understood the significance of most of what he saw whereas Battey did not.

❀ The sun dance was held in the summer, when the cottonwoods were in down, generally late in June. Well ahead of this time the *Tai-me* keeper assembled a council or committee composed of members of his warrior order and other tribal leaders. They discussed the details and selected the time and place for the dance. Usually it was held near the banks of some familiar stream where there was ample wood, water, and grazing for the horse herds, as well as suitable camping grounds for the entire tribe. These matters having been determined, messengers were sent out to the several bands comprising the tribe, announcing that the dance was to be held and telling when and where the first assemblies were to take place. Such messengers might be men from any of the warrior orders, but this duty was the special responsibility of those men whose war shields were painted red. These were known as "*Tai-me* shields."

When the announcement was received in camp, the people shouted and yelled with joy. At once buffalo hunts were held, and much meat dried, for during the assemblies preceding the dance there might be no buffalo in the vicinity. Therefore it was desirable that ample food supplies be taken. Furthermore, since the gathering was to be a time for family and society feasting and singing, delicacies such as dried fruit, apples, crackers, or other things of this kind were set aside for the happy occasion. As the time approached, the tipis were taken down and everything packed for the move.

The first assembly was for the purpose of gathering the various bands, which might be widely scattered. While they were coming in, the time was utilized for practicing, in and near the *Tai-me* keeper's lodge, the special song that was to be used at that particular sun dance. Such rehearsals were open to all. The Gourd Society would rehearse its Gourd Rattle Song, as would the other orders. There was much feasting, story-telling, and visiting between friends and relatives.

But above all, men who had pledged themselves to make sweat-house sacrifices to Grandmother gods now did so. Such a hut, made of willow branches, was shaped like an igloo. Over this frame was thrown a covering of buffalo robes. The door faced east; to the side of the opening, and about seven feet away, was a firepit in which stones were heated. The man who was making the offering went to the tipi where a Grandmother god was kept and carried it in its case to the sweat house, followed by the medicine man who was its guardian. Several gods might be taken to one hut. The priests entered and lay just inside the door. The man making the sacrifice handed in to them the pouches containing the gods. They placed the medicines in a circle on a platform of sage brush. The heated rocks were pushed into a firepit in the center of the sweat house, then the man making the offering handed in a bucket of water which the priests threw on the rocks. Then fanning the steam about inside the hut with wisps of grass, the priests began to pray for the supplicant. They begged their gods to grant him long life, good health, much luck, success on the warpath, no sickness for his family, or whatever else he had requested. If the steam got unbearable, they opened the door a little. Meantime the supplicant crouched on the outside, covering the door with a robe. After the priests had made their prayers four times, they went out and sat on the west side of the sweat house while the supplicant crawled back in, retrieved the medicine cases, and delivered them back to the tipi where they were kept. The Grandmother gods were covered with scalps so that they could not be seen, and at this time it was appropriate for the man making the sacrifice to offer recently acquired scalps. These gods have been handed down through succeeding generations since before history and have always been greatly respected.

Two more preliminary assemblies were held, each being four or five miles from the preceding one. Activities were the same at each. During the first or second assembly the *Tai-me* priest, accompanied by his committee, went out to select the cottonwood tree which would be the center of the sun dance lodge. It had to be of ample size and height, with a well-shaped fork at the top. At this time the priest also selected the place for the dance. The site had to be large enough to accommodate the entire tribal circle, which was about half a mile in diameter, with an opening to the east. The site was staked out, so that those concerned would know the prospective locations of the medicine lodge and the family and individual tipis. The lodges of the people were in concentric circles around the medicine lodge, the inner circle being about fifty yards from it. Each lodge faced the medicine lodge, rather than the east as was normally the case.

From the beginning of the preliminary assemblies until the sun dance was over, no one was allowed to go out on a raid or other warlike expeditions. Buffalo chases were permitted, however, and while the men were so engaged the young boys were imitating their elders by hunting rabbits, coyotes, and other small game. The boys had their own "military order," something like the Boy Scouts of today, which was called the Rabbits. They lived in their own small tipis during this time and had their own entertainment.

In the evening the "soldier" orders met to enjoy their dances and traditional songs.

At length all the bands and scattered family groups had come in, some of them from a great distance. The time for the final assembly had arrived. When the older men gathered in the evening to smoke the pipe and discuss plans for the sun dance, they decided that on the following morning the formal announcement for the final assembly would be made. At once a crier was sent through the camp notifying the people of this decision. From then till the completion of the announcement the following day, no one was allowed to leave camp.

Early the next morning the sponsor of the dance, carrying in front of him the *Tai-me*, rode slowly around the camp, crying for mercy. After circling the camp four times he returned the *Tai-me* to its tipi.

This was the signal to strike camp and assemble for the final move to the place where the sun dance was to be held. When everyone was packed up and ready, the whole tribe moved out together, the warriors on the flanks singing and beating tom-toms. In the lead was the *Tai-me* priest with his committee, carrying the *Tai-me*. On approaching the site of the sun dance, they circled it once, halted, dismounted, and then smoked the pipe four times while the people sat in a circle and watched. This was repeated, at which time the pipe was smoked thrice. The third time they smoked twice. Because this was the next-to-last time, everyone got excited. At the fourth halt they smoked the pipe once. When the *Tai-me* priest mounted for the last time, he raised his hand.

He was then ready to give the signal for the warriors to charge the stake driven in the ground in the center of the circle where the sun dance lodge was to be erected. This stake, which was the *T'au*, was partly clothed like a scarecrow and represented an enemy. The first man to touch it might count this as a coup, just as though the *T'au* were a live enemy. The second man had to run it down, and he had to be a warrior who had ridden over a real enemy.

Just before the priest gave the signal to start the race, some of the men sneaked out to the edge of the crowd to get a clear, unobstructed start. When the *Tai-me* keeper dropped his arm in the direction of the *T'au,* the race was on!

After the excitement of the charge had subsided, several designated warriors began showing the women where to pitch the tipis, the places having been staked out beforehand. The *Tai-me* lodge, which was painted red, was placed in the center of the encampment. After the tipis were up, the women erected arbors covered on top with brush to serve as sun shades under which the people might sit in front of their tipis during the heat of the day.

While the women were putting up the camp, some of the men went out to get meat. Toward evening, when all work was completed, the soldier orders formed a parade. This parade, like those which followed, was always led by the most prominent war chiefs. In preparation for a parade the men painted themselves and their horses, usually with heraldic designs that identified them in battle and were hereditary. They decorated themselves with all their ornaments, such as hair-pipe breast plates, silver gorgets, strings of beads

tied to their scalp locks, earrings and other pendants, and the like. They wore war bonnets if entitled to do so and carried their shields and other weapons. Red marks were painted on the horses to represent wounds they had received. Occasionally two men would be seen on a single horse, to commemorate an episode in which one man had rescued another, or some similar historic affair.

Each society, in order of its rank, cantered in single file around the inside of the camp circle. Then they rode out on the opposite side and circled the outside. The Ko-eet-senko were first, followed by the others, with the Rabbits last. At the conclusion of the parade the men unsaddled their horses and went to their lodges, where the women had prepared the evening meal.

The next ten days were given up to singing, dancing, horse racing, buffalo chases, and other entertainment. In the evening the warrior societies met for singing and dancing. Any member who failed to attend or was late was hazed thoroughly the next day. For example, if he were a *T'ai-peko* [a member of one of the six Kiowa warrior societies], he might be accused publicly of being in love with his mother-in-law, a most embarrassing predicament.

The Blackfoot [or Black Leggings] Society had a rule that no member could show jealousy of his wife during the sun dance gathering. Therefore if a man should whip his wife out of jealousy during this time, he would have his sleeves cut off for several days. This was regarded as a crying disgrace.

Each man was assigned a specific part in the work of preparing for the sun dance. For example, one of the war chiefs was responsible for killing and bringing in the sacrificial buffalo. This duty was hereditary. When the time for the dance drew near, he selected several assistants, one of whom might be a woman, especially if she were experienced and skillful in skinning a buffalo.

When they reached the herd, the *to-yop-ke* who was to kill the buffalo sought a two-year-old bull, sound and well fleshed. Having spotted such an animal, he charged alone, cutting it out of the herd and riding alongside for the kill. The buffalo had to be killed with a single arrow driven through the heart. This represented a shot with which the chief had killed an enemy. As he drew near his

62

quarry, he raised an arrow so that the others might see it and shouted that at such and such a time and place he had used an arrow to kill a Ute or other enemy. So that the shot be true, his statement also had to be true. Otherwise he would miss. But for every sun dance the killer always succeeded in driving a single arrow through the heart of the sacrificial buffalo, which was proof, in each case, of the truth of his declaration.

The dying buffalo had to be guided so that he expired on his knees, facing the east. Then the man took a sharp knife and removed most of the hide, starting at the nose. As he worked, he described how he had made his announced coup and scalped his enemy. All the skin on the head and two feet of the hide on either side of the spine had to be removed, including the tail. The horns remained on the skin of the head. While the killer was skinning the buffalo, perhaps with expert help, his assistants built an altar of buffalo chips surmounted by a layer of sage grass. The *to-yop-ke* rolled up the hide and laid it on the altar, first having made four motions as if to do so. Then he brought up his horse and packed the hide across in front of the pommel of his saddle. He mounted his horse, with his party formed in line behind him. The chief cried to the sun a prayer for mercy. He looked to the east, started off, then halted. His followers did the same. This was done four times. After the fourth pause he started off toward the village at a fast trot. The others followed, whooping and singing.

During this entire buffalo hunt the *to-yop-ke* was not supposed to take water or get wet, lest a rainstorm descend to spoil the sun dance.

The party did not enter the village on the day of their arrival. They always halted a little distance outside and bivouacked during the night, so that the village might prepare for their formal entry. Two of the men, representing advance scouts of a war party returning from a successful raid, went in during the night to make ready for the triumphal procession. These plans, formulated by the men in charge of the dance, included a decision as to when and where the party would enter the camp and the route they would follow through the tipis to the inside of the circle. The scouts then returned to their party, taking with them tom-toms to be used the next day.

Before daybreak the buffalo-bringers dressed and decorated themselves. Their black paint of victory and other trappings signified that they were returning from a war expedition, victorious and with scalps. At daybreak, after saddling and mounting their horses, they started, firing their guns in the air, first one shot and then another, and finally a burst of fire. This notified the village of their presence, whereupon a great shout went up from all the people, who had risen early and were waiting to greet them.

The buffalo-killer and his procession always approached on the west side of the camp. They were met at the edge of the village by one of the priests from the medicine tipi, on foot and accompanied by a number of assistants who were lined up behind him. This medicine man was painted over his entire body with white clay, and carried a long-stemmed ceremonial pipe. While his assistants were beating in unison upon a piece of stiff rawhide, he held the pipe in front of him and moved it up and down like a baton. Then he started to walk backward, leading the buffalo-killer into the camp. The procession passed through to the inside of the camp circle, moved around to the south, then approached the medicine tipi from the east. During this parade the drummers kept up a steady thumping, and everyone joined in singing an appropriate song.

Inside the medicine tipi were the ten Grandmother gods, attended by their custodians, singing a buffalo-coming song and whipping a piece of rawhide. On the ground near the center fire was a drawing of a man with a hole in his chest to represent the heart. Into this hole they were pouring hot ashes. In olden times an actual human sacrifice was so used.

As he approached the medicine tipi, the buffalo-slayer made four halts, each time drawing nearer. After the fourth halt he dismounted and unfastened the buffalo hide from his horse. He carried it inside the tent and brought it to an altar of buffalo chips and sage grass that had been prepared. The hide was stretched out on top of this altar with the head facing the sunrise. The *to-yop-ke* then withdrew from the lodge, mounted his horse, and, after making four halts as before, was dismissed and rode away. This concluded his part in the ceremony.

The next part of the program consisted of making offerings to the buffalo. First the family of the *Tai-me* keeper approached and tied their offerings to the hide. A shell was tied to the nose, together with the breast feathers of an eagle. Afterward each family in the village ran to tie its offerings to the hide, these consisting of strips of bright-colored cloth. While tying the pieces of cloth to the buffalo, the adults offered various prayers, generally for good health and good luck. The children were encouraged to rub their hands on the hide, then all over their bodies, to prevent sickness and insure longevity.

After all members of the tribe had been offered an opportunity to bring offerings and make prayers, several famous fighters like Tsen-t'ainte [White Horse] and Quo-to-tai [On Top Of The Eagle] would hurriedly build a sweat house near the medicine tipi. Into this they would carry the buffalo hide with all its offerings attached, where it remained until it was tied to the great forked pole at the center of the sun dance lodge.

On this day, the day the buffalo was brought in, all other entertainment and activities were suspended.

That evening the members of the Old Women's Society dug holes for the poles of the sun dance lodge. The places for these holes were measured and marked by a man who had that special responsibility.

The following morning was devoted to the sham battle and the cutting of the forked pole. First, two groups of men went down into the timber along the stream and built sham adobe forts or walls with leaves and brush. Then every warrior dressed himself in his best finery and carried his weapons for the battle, which was introduced by a short preliminary ceremony. The *Tai-me* keeper, with the old men of the tribe, took position some twenty paces to the west of the postholes which the women had dug the previous evening. Facing eastward, these men began to sing the War News Song, unaccompanied by drums. During the singing the warriors paraded single file through the space between the postholes and the singers.

When a noted chief came through, he was greeted with war whoops by the women spectators, this being their way of showing honor to a brave member of the tribe.

After all who wished to do so had participated in the parade, the

Tai-me keeper gave a signal to start the sham battle. The warriors thereupon ran to attack the imaginary enemy in the "forts" in the timber along the river. There was much showy fighting, advancing, retreating, firing of blanks, and other exhibitions of warlike prowess.

While the sham battle was going on, the older men walked to the spot where the forked tree had been selected. The soldier societies then stopped in the shade of the woods and danced while the forked pole was being cut. The woman who performed this task was a captive member of the tribe. Mooney suggests that captives were designated to perform this and other duties associated with the *Tai-me*, so that if anything went wrong or a taboo was violated, a blood member of the tribe would not suffer as a result.

The actual chopping down of the tree was preceded by another ceremony. Two designated men stood on either side of the tree, shaking *Tai-me* gourd rattles and singing. At the conclusion of the first verse, a woman painted a red ring around the tree trunk. The captive made a motion with her axe, as if to cut. Another verse was sung, a second ring was painted, and the captive made another feint at striking the tree. After this sequence had been performed four times the captive began chopping down the tree, cutting about two feet from the ground. It was necessary that the tree fall to the west. After the captive had trimmed the tree so that it became a long pole forked at the top, the soldiers were notified that the log was ready to be carried to the site where the lodge was to be erected.

One of the warrior societies lined up on either side of the pole and passed rope slings under it so that they could carry it. The *Tai-me* keeper, who could drink no water on this day, stood at the foot of the pole, his body painted yellow, and his rabbit-fur cap on his head. In one hand he had the *Tai-me* whistle, made of eagle bone, in the other, the *Tai-me* medicine fan, made of crow feathers and resembling a fly swatter. While all the spectators stood at attention, the *Tai-me* priest ran down the pole to the fork. If he made it without falling off, everyone yelled for joy. If he lost his balance and stepped off, a great groan went up from the crowd. Perhaps this was why the Mexican captive, Mokeen, was the assistant *Tai-me* priest for a succession of hereditary custodians. Since he never fell from the log, it is to be suspected that he practiced this feat of agility thoroughly before the ceremony.

The soldiers picked up their ropes and carried the pole towards the hole which had been dug for it. At a signal from the priest they halted to permit him to repeat his run down the log, and incidentally to give the men a chance to rest. This ritual was performed four times. The fourth time, the men carrying the log were not permitted to stop until they came to its hole.

Another warrior society was detailed to erect the pole. This was also hard work and required a lot of men. While the older men stood around smoking and offering comments the younger warriors shoved the butt end of the pole into its hole, then raised it erect and tamped it firmly in place. A young medicine man climbed up to the fork where he prayed earnestly to the sun for some ten minutes while the entire assemblage stood at attention.

Meanwhile, two war chiefs were bringing the buffalo hide from the sweat house. Ropes were thrown to the man at the top of the pole, which he then passed to the men who had the robe; they fastened these lines to the front of the buffalo skin, always keeping the head facing to the east. The robe was hoisted to the top of the pole amidst much whooping and yelling, where it was tied over a bundle of willow and cottonwood to resemble a buffalo. This hide-covered bundle was lashed to the fork by the man aloft. Having concluded his part in the preparations for the sun dance, this fellow then slid to the ground.

The succeeding two or three days were devoted to gathering materials for and completing the construction of the medicine lodge. Participated in by practically every member of the tribe, young and old, this was generally regarded as the most enjoyable part of the whole sun dance gathering. It was an informal social event, characterized by much jolly conversation, singing, dancing, laughter, and horseplay. Before breakfast the people marched in groups down to the timber along the stream and under supervision of the men in charge of the sun dance cut designated cottonwood trees and brush.

After breakfast the soldier clubs had the duty of dragging in the heavier poles, beginning with the seventeen wall supports. First the warriors rode around camp, inviting young women to be their partners. Although jealousy was supposed to be banned at this time, a few usually refused the invitation through fear that their husbands might hold a grudge against them if they rode with someone else. But each one who accepted the honor [and this was analogous to being chosen as a partner in a cotillion] took a rope and gleefully mounted up behind the warrior. Having arrived at the place where the poles had been cut, the young women dismounted and, if necessary, helped to fell more trees and trim them. Then they attached their ropes to the poles and to the saddles of the warriors' horses so that the logs could be dragged to the site of the lodge. The seventeen outer poles were cut from straight young cottonwoods about fifteen feet long, each having a fork at the top. They were set in the ground in a circle around the twenty-foot center pole, being nearly evenly spaced. [Had the intervals been exact, there would have been *sixteen* poles.]

Since the completed lodge was to be about sixty feet in diameter, the rafters had to be thirty-five feet long, to allow a little overlap in the center and at the ends. Cottonwood trees of that length were quite large, and it was hard work to cut and drag them to the lodge and still more difficult to lift such heavy, green logs into place overhead. But many people helped, and the whole business was treated as a lark, so it continued to be a happy time. In dragging these timbers, several horses had to be used, the men riding abreast. Each rafter was lashed at one end to the center pole and at the other to one of the seventeen wall supports. The completed frame was like that of a large cylindrical pergola with a somewhat flattened conical roof.

During the early part of each afternoon, while the lodge was being erected, the Old Women's Society entertained themselves and anyone who wished to watch by a musical program and dance which lasted an hour or so. This typical Kiowa dance is difficult to describe, despite its simplicity. The women formed in a line or a circle, hands clasped or arms linked, and alternately advanced or retreated, using a dignified short step somewhat like a two-step, with the first beat accented. The effect was a slight rhythm, the women rising and falling on the balls of their feet in unison. The Kiowas still hold this dance on Armistice Day in the bend of the Washita near Mountain View, Oklahoma.

[Thomas Battey, who witnessed part of a sun dance in 1873, described the dance of the grandmothers as follows: "The music consisted of singing and drumming, done by several old women, who were squatted on the ground in a circle. The dancers—old women sixty to eighty years of age—performed in a circle around them from time to time, finally striking off upon a waddling run, one behind the other; they formed a circle then came back, and, doubling so as to bring two together, threw their arms around each other's neck and trudged around for some time longer; then sat down, while a youngish warrior circulated the pipe, from which each in turn took two or three whiffs, and the ceremony ended."[1]]

When the frame of the lodge was completed, the soldier clubs had a roughhouse in and around it, running, jumping, and leaping. It was a wild frolic, the men wrestling, striking, kicking, and trying to tear the clothes from each other. The small boys particularly enjoyed watching this.

After this free-for-all sport had subsided, the walls and roof were put on the lodge. The wall coverings consisted simply of small cottonwoods with their branches and leaves intact lashed horizontally between the seventeen uprights to form a shade sufficiently open so that the spectators might peer through at the performers. An opening was left for the entrance on the east side, facing the sunrise—always the place for the door of a lodge. Brush was placed as a shade on the outer third of the roof. The central two-thirds was left open to the sky, except for the rafters, so that the priests and dancers might stare up at the sun. Surrounding the lodge, except for the entrance, small cottonwoods were thrust in the ground under which the people might sit in the shade and watch the dance.

Inside the lodge was a screen of cedar trees and small cottonwoods thrust in the ground within three feet of the wall opposite the entrance. Behind this the performers prepared for their acts.

[1] Thomas C. Battey, *The Life and Adventures of a Quaker Among the Indians* (Boston, Lee and Shepard, 1891), 168.

69

[According to Battey, although George Hunt does not mention it, earth had been thrown up around the center lodge pole, making a platform two feet high and five feet in diameter. Battey also says that the central post was "ornamented near the ground with the robes of buffalo calves, their heads up, as if in the act of climbing it; each of the branches above the fork was ornamented in a similar manner, with the addition of shawls, calico, scarfs, etc., and covered at the top with black muslin."[2]]

The final bit of preparation consisted of smoothing the floor of the lodge, removing sticks, stones, and weeds. Then a two-inch layer of clean white sand was spread on the ground. The Old Women's Society and the Rabbits went to the river for the sand, carrying it back in cloths. This work was also done to the accompaniment of music, singing, and dancing.

Four chiefs were appointed to dedicate the completed lodge. They were warriors of renown, being of that honored few entitled to wear scalp shirts and eagle-feather war bonnets. In preparation for this ceremony each chief painted himself in the colors and design peculiar to him and his forebear which always distinguished him in battle. He had on a fine buckskin shirt with long fringes of scalp hair and decorated with beads, porcupine quills, and silver and brass ornaments. Across his chest was a hair-pipe breastplate, and perhaps pendants of the same material hung from his ears and scalp lock. He wore no leggings—only moccasins and a breechclout. On his head was his eagle-feathered war bonnet with its double row of feathers fastened in strips of red flannel hanging down his back to the ground and secured at his waist by an ornamented strap. To the cloth skullcap which formed the upper part of the bonnet might be fastened crow feathers, a crow's head, or a pair of buffalo horns, like the helmet of a viking.

Each chief also carried his war shield, painted with his hereditary design and ornamented with pendants of feathers and scalps. He also carried a lance [and, according to Battey, a medicine pole—perhaps a coup stick] likewise ornamented with feathers. He was armed with a revolver.

[2] *Ibid.*, 170.

These four chiefs went to the sun dance lodge in the afternoon, followed by a great crowd of villagers. Entering the lodge, the chiefs formed in line at the back, facing to the east. Behind them stood the musicians. On either side were many old women, who now began uttering tremolo whoops—hands fluttering over their mouths —to honor the chiefs. The drums began to beat and the four men to dance. They advanced slowly toward the center pole, followed by the musicians, who were beating on a sheet of dried rawhide and shaking rattles while the old women sang and chanted.

The dancers withdrew part way, then advanced again, this time a little farther toward the center. At the fourth advance, they drew their revolvers and fired them through the entrance into the air. Once more the women whooped and then threw their shawls at the feet of the chiefs. The chiefs and the old women returned to their lodges, the shawls remaining on the ground to be picked up by any-one who wanted them.

A steppingstone was now placed in the entrance, in preparation for the arrival of the "buffalo." This was a drama or pageant acted out by about one hundred Indians both large and small, dressed in buffalo robes complete with horns and tails. Each hide was tied over a stick which was held out behind the performer to bring his apparent size more closely to that of a bison. This buffalo herd gathered about a quarter of a mile outside the entrance to the camp, where they lay down together. One poor old buffalo lay apart on the far side of the herd.

One man was detailed to drive the herd into the "corral," which was the sun dance house. Using an enemy coup stick, two noted warriors started a fire on the southern part of the interior of the "corral." They picked up a live coal between two sticks and gave it to the man who was to drive in the buffalo. He walked around the inside of the camp clockwise, carrying the smoking ember, stopped behind the medicine lodge, and peeped out four times at the herd. He ran out the camp entrance, circled the herd, and again stopped. At this the herd began to rise, whereupon he threw away his "incense." At once the herd started to stampede, roaring as they went toward the lodge. They circled the lodge four times, went in, and lay down.

The herd was followed by the feeble old buffalo, who had to stop and rest several times en route, each time falling farther behind. In circling the lodge four times, he tried to run to overtake the herd, but fell down. After a bit he got up and trotted along again.

When the herd was again completed by the arrival of the old buffalo inside the lodge, the thousand or more spectators rushed to the lodge to peer through to the inside. They had been watching the buffalo performance from the open space between the lodge and the inner circle of the encampment.

The buffalo were lying down huddled together around the central lodge pole. The old buffalo with his tattered hide and large shaggy head and wide horns was lying near the entrance, with his head toward it.

At this point the ten medicine priests, dressed in their painted buffalo robes, came out of the *Tai-me* lodge and entered the sun dance lodge. The marks on their robes denoted their war experiences.

The Grandmother god priests began to examine the buffalo, feeling them, punching them, and talking to them. Four of the "fattest" buffalo were selected, each being a famous war chief. As a buffalo was chosen, a short stick was laid along his back, while the priest announced, in a loud voice:

"We have found a great buffalo! If at any time the tribe is in need of service, then we can depend on him. His name is ———!"

At this, all the women uttered their peculiar tremolo whoop to honor the great warrior.

Then the priest found another fat buffalo, a young one this time. The same ritual was enacted.

When the four buffalo had been presented, the head priest closed the ceremony with appropriate remarks and a prayer. A recess until evening was announced.

That evening about sundown, the priests brought the *Tai-me* out of its tipi. Forming a procession, they carried it to the west side of the sun dance lodge, where they stopped and sang four songs. This was repeated on the south, north, and finally the east side. Then they entered the lodge and stood the *Tai-me* against the screen of cedars. To one side of the god was placed a buffalo skull, painted half-red and half-black. In front of each—the idol and the skull—had been dug a small shallow pit in which cedar incense was to be burned. The *Tai-me*, kept concealed in its case during the rest of the year, was now exposed to public view and worship. [It is to be doubted, however, that it could be seen clearly, for it was almost completely covered with a mantle of soft white eagle feathers. This heightened the mystery surrounding the medicine. The *Tai-me* has been described in a previous section.]

Just inside and to the north of the lodge entrance was a group of drummers, squatting in a circle around their drums. Around them were a number of women to aid in the singing and to whoop at appropriate times. There were also several gourd men with their rattles. All these constituted the "orchestra and chorus," or musicians. Using a coup stick, a designated warrior began to kindle the sacred fire in the holes in front of the medicine. Soon he produced thin wisps of smoke which he kept going by adding from time to time a handful of cedar leaves and shavings.

These preparations marked the start of the sun dance proper. When the fire began to smoke, the musicians began a rhythmic pounding on the drums, accompanied by the "Hi-yah-he-yah" of the chanting. The dancers then emerged one at a time from behind the screen and took their places in the center of the lodge facing the *Tai-me*. There were forty or fifty of them, mostly young, vigorous warriors. Their arms and faces, and bodies above the waist, were painted white. They wore soft white buckskin skirts extending from the waist to the ankle. Outside the skirt was a blue loincloth hanging to the ground both fore and aft. Caps of sage grass were on their heads, and wisps of the same material were tied to their wrists. In their mouths were eagle-bone whistles provided by the *Tai-me* keeper. As they jumped about in time with the music, their expelled breath blew toots on the whistles.

During the dance, the performers continued to face the medicine, their eyes fixed on it and their arms outstretched toward it. To maintain this somewhat strenuous exertion for four days and four nights without sleep, food, and water required a high degree of physical fitness and endurance. [As George Hunt remarked in an aside,

73

"Some didn't make it."] There were, however, relieving circumstances. From time to time there were brief interruptions in the dance while some special ceremony was performed. At such times the dancers were allowed to snatch a little refreshment in the form of the tuberous roots of cattails, which their women gathered for them, or, in later years, watermelons or oranges.

The main part of the dance started the following morning. [This session was witnessed by Thomas Battey, who described it as follows: "After some time a middle-aged man painted as the others, but wearing a buffalo robe, issued from behind the screen, facing the entrance, but having his eyes fastened on the sun, upon which he stood gazing, without winking or moving a muscle, for some time, then slowly began to incline his head from side to side, as if to avoid some obstruction in his view of it, swaying his body slightly, then stepping slowly from side to side—forward—backward—increasing his motions, both in rapidity and extent, until, in appearance nearly frantic, his robe fell off, leaving him—except for his blue breech-cloth—entirely naked. In this condition he jumped and ran about the enclosure—head, arms and legs all equally participating in the violence of his gestures—every joint of his body apparently loosened, his eyes only fixed. Thus he continued to exercise without ceasing, or once removing his eyes from the sun, until the sweat ran down in great rolling drops, washing the white paint into streaks no more ornamental than the original painting, and he was at length compelled to retire, from sheer exhaustion, the other dancers still continuing their exercises."[3] This nude performer was Mokeen, the priest's assistant.]

At noon, the high priest came out of the *Tai-me* tipi, entered the sun dance lodge, and disappeared behind the screen. Here he painted and dressed himself for the next ceremony. At length he emerged, painted yellow, wearing his rabbit-fur cap and blue breech-clout, and with a long-haired human scalp tied to his own scalp lock and flowing down his back. He stood facing the entrance and blew loudly on his whistle to summon the people to witness the next important ritual, the pursuit of the dancers.

[3] *Ibid.*, 175–76.

74

The people came running and crowded around the outside wall, at least a thousand being present. First he did a solo dance, a sort of running hop and jump in time with the "music." This brought him around the circle to a position in front of the *Tai-me*. He leaned over the medicine, parted the feathers covering it, and bit off some kind of medicine clay which was adhering to the idol. [Battey thought that he was kissing the god.] After chewing on the medicine clay for a time, he ran around the arena spitting the medicine on the dancers, to impart to them some of the power of the god. Then he went back to the altar, took up the *Tai-me* fan, and fanned first the idol, four times, then the buffalo skull, four times.

The priest now gave the dancers a signal, and at once they started chasing him around the center pole. He looked back over his shoulder and made a motion with his fan, whereupon a number of the pursuers fell over backward, crying for mercy. This was kept up until all the dancers had been fanned out. An intermission followed, during which the dancers seized the opportunity to obtain some refreshments and a bit of rest.

During this pause the fire had apparently gone out, for the man who was tending it started it up again with his coup stick. Then he passed a coal to the Grandmother god priests who used it to light a pipe. After they had smoked reflectively for a time, the dance resumed.

On the following day there was another break in the dance while the *Tai-me* shield custodians were painted. Every soldier club had a number of these shields. Four painters were employed at this time to renew the designs on the shields and to paint the same pattern on their custodians. The artists, who served for four years as such, had to pay a substantial sum for the honor, but they recovered it by charging their successors a like amount. Payment was not in money, but in articles which the Indians valued. Hence to aspire to this office a man had to possess considerable substance and be an honorable and popular member of the tribe. Hunting Horse, who started his adult career as a poor, unrecognized young man, eventually became a *Tai-me* painter. The *Tai-me* painters had certain taboos, one of which was that they dared not see their own image in a looking glass. A tin mirror was, however, quite safe. During their part in the sun dance, these four men had a green moon painted on each side of their breasts, with a red sun in the center. The same design was painted on their backs.

Finally the great medicine dance came to an end. It had started at sunset four days earlier, so just before sundown on the last day there was another short pageant in which everyone was permitted to dance. The closing song was sung, the medicine men took down and packed the medicine and the paraphernalia that went with it, and returned with the sacred objects to the *Tai-me* tipi. The people were then allowed to take as souvenirs or charms the leaves and twigs from the medicine lodge. These were especially to be worn as necklaces by infants, in order to guard them from sickness. Families with small children brought their outworn or outgrown baby clothes to be tied to the great forked post as a sacrifice, with a prayer that sickness and epidemic would not visit them during the ensuing year.

On the following day the tipis were taken down, and the village began to break up into its component bands, each going off in a different direction. The young people were sorry to see the dance come to a close, for to them especially it was a joyful occasion, with much merrymaking and visiting back and forth between families and old friends.

Now the men were allowed to go off on raids or other warlike expeditions.

The medicine lodge was left standing and not thereafter used, even though subsequent assemblies might be held in the same locality. The last Kiowa sun dance, called the Oak Creek Sun Dance, was held in the summer of 1887. ❁

10 ❀ IS THE TAI-ME KEEPER WHITE?

THIS STORY OF A WHITE MAN'S KINDNESS to two captured Kiowas and his eventual reward was told by George Hunt.

❀ Prior to 1840, when the Kiowas and Cheyennes were still bitter enemies, the Cheyennes captured a Kiowa woman and her two daughters. These captives were separated and became the slaves of those who had them in charge; their life was full of misery. The mother, who could not become reconciled to being apart from her children, continually resisted the efforts of her Cheyenne master to tame her. At length, angered by this stubborn attitude, the Cheyenne cut her throat.

Meantime, the elder of the two girls, Pah-gia-goodle, was taken by the chief of the band as his wife, while the younger girl, Tome-gope, was adopted by an elderly couple. These old Cheyennes became so fond of the girl that they treated her as their own daughter. Nevertheless she grieved for her sister.

One day a white trader visited the village. He came from the north with two white-topped wagons, each drawn by several oxen, and had a number of Mexican servants. From this it must be supposed that he was from eastern Colorado, possibly being one of the traders who went out to the upper Arkansas River as a result of a treaty made in 1825. The wagons were loaded with calicoes and other dry goods which the white man had brought to barter for hides and furs. The trader halted his column a little distance from the village and unloaded his articles on the grass. Soon a large crowd of Indians gathered to see what he had and to trade.

The chief, before joining the throng, slashed the bottoms of the feet of the captive Kiowa girl so that she could not run away while he was gone. He left her seated against the front of the tipi, where she could watch from a distance and where he could see her by looking back occasionally. After a time she saw a girl being led forward from the village and being taken to the trader. The latter placed the girl in one of the wagons. The girl with the slashed feet, Pah-gia-goodle, asked a nearby old Cheyenne woman what was happening.

"Your sister has just been sold to the white man," was the reply.

Pah-gia-goodle was heartbroken. She did not see how she could live if her sister was to be taken so far away. Soon she saw the trader packing up to leave. The wagons pulled out, one of them driven by the trader, the other by a Mexican. She saw her sister seated in the second wagon beside the driver. She wanted to run to say good-by. She imagined that her younger sister was looking back toward her, crying.

As soon as the trader had pulled out, the Cheyenne chief departed to hunt buffalo. Pah-gia-goodle determined to join her sister. Her feet pained her dreadfully, so that she could scarcely walk, but she managed to hobble along somehow. The Cheyennes, intent on looking over the goods which they had obtained from the trader, did not see her leave. Soon she disappeared over a rise.

Pah-gia-goodle followed the wagons which were moving slowly ahead of her. The men in the wagons saw her coming. They stopped and waited for her. The white man put Pah-gia-goodle in the wagon with her sister.

They drove on hoping the Cheyennes would not follow. But after two days they saw a smoke signal far to the rear, which meant that the Cheyennes were on the trail. They saw a second, third, and fourth smoke, but they kept on moving. Now they felt safe, for the fourth smoke signal meant that the Cheyennes had lost their trail or had given up the chase. After several more days of travel they came to a trading post, where there was a big store and a number of men working. This was the store of the man who had rescued the girls. From the size of the place and the number of people he employed, the Kiowa women judged that he must be very wealthy.

The trader took both of the Kiowa girls to be his wives. He was a very kind man, and they liked their new home. Two daughters were born to the younger girl and a son to the elder. The boy was named Charley, after his father.

At the main Kiowa camp, in the meantime, the brothers of the two girls had not given up making plans for their recovery. One of them, more active than the others, thought that he was on the point of success several times, but each time he failed. At length, when the Kiowas were raiding in western Kansas, they met a Mexican trader who was well acquainted with the Cheyennes. He knew practically everyone in that tribe. The brothers asked him if he had ever heard anything of their two sisters, describing them. The Mexican knew at once to whom they were referring. He explained that the mother had been killed and that the two girls had been sold to a white trader. He described the country where the trader had his store, telling the Kiowas that the post was at a well-known spring near the Rocky Mountains.

One of the brothers determined to go to this spring and from concealment try to catch sight of his sisters. The Mexican had given such detailed directions that he was sure he could find the place.

After a long journey the young Kiowa came to the spring near the trader's store. Nearby was a deep gully filled with tumble weeds. Here he concealed himself. After a time he heard a woman's voice singing the song of the Blackfoot Society, his own society. He heard the woman saying to herself, aloud, "Oh, if I could just see my brother! What a comfort it is to me to be able to sing his song."

The Kiowa came forth from his hiding place. He looked at the woman. She had been much younger when he had last seen her. He was not sure that it was his sister.

"Is it Pah-gia-goodle?" he asked.

"Yes. Are you my brother?" They embraced and wept for joy. Then he inquired about the other sister.

"She is in the house. I will go and get her."

He asked if there was a chance that the two sisters could run away and go back with him to the tribe.

The woman answered that she would not leave her husband and children. Nevertheless, she said that her husband was a very kind man. Maybe they could persuade him to let her go back to her people and take the children with her. She asked her brother to wait while she went after her sister. Soon there was another happy reunion. The younger sister could hardly believe that the brother had come all this distance to find them.

The Kiowa women returned to the house, where they told their husband that they had met their brother, that they desired to go home, and they asked that he go with them.

"Won't I be killed and scalped by the Kiowas?" he asked.

The women replied that he would not. The Kiowas were friendly to Americans, and besides, he would be a member of the family. So he decided to go with them. He told his servants to tell no one, but to pack two wagons with their baggage and some trade goods which he would take with him. The preparation for the journey took all day, and that night the two wagons departed for the Kiowa country to the south. The brother of the two girls acted as guide and scout. When they reached the raid headquarters from which the Kiowa had come, they found several other warriors there waiting. These men were greatly surprised to see the wagons and the girls. Together they departed for the Kiowa village, many miles to the south.

There was a great reception awaiting them on their arrival, for some of the men had ridden ahead with the news. Shortly after their arrival another daughter was born to the younger sister. This baby was named Addle-da-hodle. A little later a boy, who was named Sau-one-day-tone, was born to the other wife.

The white man had given up his property in the north, left his people, and had come among strangers, all to please his wives. These two ungrateful women repaid him poorly, for both of them soon ran off with other Kiowas. The white man stayed with the Indians and his children for a number of years, but finally went back to his own country, taking with him two of his daughters. Later he made other trading expeditions to the Kiowa villages, but finally they failed to hear from him, and do not know what became of him. ✺

In 1872, James Haworth, the Kiowa-Comanche agent at Fort Sill, tried to trace this trader, whom the Kiowas called Kau-l'ongoodle (Red Wrinkled Neck) or, more familiarly, Tsali (Charley), but died before he could solve the mystery. James Mooney, who studied the Kiowa tribe in 1892, speaks of a trader named Charles Whitacre or Whittaker, whom the Kiowas called Tsali. Perhaps this man was the hero of this true story.

However, the history of Tsali's descendants is no mystery. The son, Charley, was named Kau-au-k'odle. His daughter, Hone-a-bone, furnished this story to George Hunt. In 1935, Hone-a-bone was about sixty-eight years old. She died in 1950. Her father, Charley, died many years before, but his descendants have estimated that the events related herein must have occurred about 1844 or 1845.

The trader's other descendants are the Bo-tone family, who live on the Fort Cobb–Mountain View highway, about four miles east of Mountain View, Oklahoma. The present *Tai-me* keeper, the great high priest of the tribal medicine, is a Bo-tone. Thus we have the curious fact that a white man founded the present dynasty of *Tai-me* keepers.

II ❋ WITHOUT MEDICINE

ZEPKO-ETTE, OR BIG BOW, inherited his powerful physique, warlike spirit, and good looks from his father, a war chief who was also called Big Bow. The grandfather, likewise known as Big Bow, had led at least two expeditions into Tamaulipas, on the east coast of Mexico. On the second of these raids, Grandfather Big Bow had been killed by the Mexicans, whereupon his son led a revenge raid to the same region. The third Big Bow, who is the hero of this story, was born in 1833, the Year the Stars Fell, on Elk Creek, a tributary of the North Fork of Red River.

Through the influence and training of his father, Big Bow learned to be a warrior at an unusually early age. By the time he was eighteen, he had already been on two raids, and that year, 1851, he was made a *to-yop-ke*. With this auspicious start he should have become a prominent chief, but two things militated against it. First, in the winter of the year in which he won his title of *to-yop-ke*, he ran off with the pretty wife of another warrior who was absent on the warpath. He took her to his home camp and left her standing outside in the deep snow while he went to his family tipi to get some food. His father, who knew what had happened, held him in the lodge all night. The woman, who waited patiently in the timber, had her feet frozen. This unsavory incident subjected the young Big Bow to so much criticism that he tended to draw off to himself and thus forfeited much of his earlier popularity. Second, he offended many of the Kiowas by his skeptical attitude toward religion. They were especially repelled and even frightened by the way he treated the medicine man while they were the warpath. A medicine man usually accompanied an expedition of any magnitude, for the purpose of interpreting the omens and predicting success. A favorite medicine man was the Owl Prophet, a fakir who carried the feathered skin of a screech owl which he would inflate and hold in his hand, and then by ventriloquism he would produce the quavering, muted call of the bird. This owl talk was then interpreted, for a price, to each warrior in turn.

Big Bow laughed and scoffed at all this, boasting that he did not require the aid of a bird to give him success in battle. He said that it was cowardly and the work of a weakling to solicit the aid of a medicine man; he himself won his fights through his own courage and strength. Naturally this sort of talk was resented by the other Kiowas. Repeated publicly at the victory (scalp) dance, it brought so much criticism that thereafter Big Bow went on raids by himself, or accompanied by only one or two others. He associated a good deal with the Quahadi Comanches, who roamed in the Staked Plains and along the Cap Rocks. He became more familiar than most of his tribesmen with the arid country between the Pecos and the Río Grande, knowing the location of the crossings and the water holes. He went far down into Chihuahua.

On one of these trips, Big Bow was gone for three years. On his return, the tribe had very nearly forgotten about him. When he rode into camp late one night in the year 1855, lustily singing the song of his society, the Wild Sheep, they were greatly surprised, and assembled to hear where he had been and what he had done. One of his experiences, which he related at this time, dealt with a raid against the Navahos. This story, which is a favorite in the tribe, has been preserved in considerable detail, and I have heard it from several old Kiowas. The following version closely approximates the account of the raid which George Hunt wrote down at my request in 1941.

☼ As usual, when he decided to go to the Navaho country, Big Bow took with him only two companions. One was a Mexican captive member of the tribe who remembered enough of his mother tongue to be able to act as an interpreter in case any Mexicans were encountered. The other was a Kiowa on whom Big Bow felt that he could rely in an emergency.

They rode in a northwesterly direction for several days, crossing the upper Pecos River and ascending the long, arid plain that rose gradually toward the Rocky Mountains. Passing through a region dotted with stunted cedars, they came to an adobe house, the home of a *comanchero*, or Mexican who traded with the Comanches and Kiowas. An old friend of Big Bow, he received the Indians cordially. Big Bow explained that they were on their way to capture some horses from the Navahos. He inquired as to the best route. The Mexican replied that this was difficult to describe and that he doubted whether they could find their way through the rough, mountainous country which lay ahead or locate the Navahos. Big Bow asked if a guide were available. The Mexican said that he did not think that anyone living in the area would be willing to guide them against the Navahos, with whom the Mexicans had to live at peace. Big Bow then stated that he could guide himself and that he was sure he could find some of the enemy.

"Wait a few days," protested his Mexican friend. "My son, who is now on a trip to Santa Fe, will return. He will act as your guide."

Big Bow thanked the Mexican, and said they would wait.

Before they departed, the Kiowas established their headquarters at the home of their Mexican friend. They changed to fresh horses and left their spare mounts, together with their saddles and blankets, to be picked up on their way out of the country. Big Bow asked the Mexican to keep their horses saddled day and night. He had a feeling that when they returned, it would be on the run and in need of making a quick getaway. This proved to be a wise precaution.

After riding west for two days, they came to a range of mountains. Their young Mexican guide led them to the summit of one of the highest peaks. Here they rested under some tall pines while he described the country that lay beyond. He pointed out a trader's store, possibly Maxwell's, in the valley below, with a trail leading west from it into a wooded plateau which sloped up to the foothills of another mountain range. Sunlight glistened on a distant stream that emerged from a canyon and tumbled along beside the path. The Mexican told them that this was the route followed by the Navahos in going between their village and the trading post.

Big Bow thought that if he followed this trail, he would come to a clearing where the enemy pastured their horses. He told his men that they would follow the trail and thus could probably locate the horse herd.

The Kiowas descended the mountain, detoured wide around the trader's store, and moved through the timber until they came to the mountains on the far side of the valley. Here they tied their horses and proceeded on foot. Soon they heard a bell, which Big Bow was certain came from the bell mare of the Navaho herd. Following the sound, they came to an upland meadow where thirty or more animals were grazing. They easily caught the bell mare, which was hobbled, and by leading it away, moved off with most of the horses. They picked up their own mounts, then took their captured stock across the valley to the mountains which they previously had climbed and concealed the herd in a side canyon. They staked out the bell mare so that the other animals would not wander away.

Then they turned back to the west. Big Bow wanted to complete their success by taking at least one enemy scalp. By lending their Mexican guide some of their clothing, they disguised him so that the Navahos would not recognize him as a local inhabitant.

Beyond the meadow where they had found the enemy horses was a marsh beside the trail. Big Bow saw that anyone passing this way would have to stay on the path in order to avoid bogging down in the swampy ground. An ideal place for an ambush, he thought. He had his men tie their mounts in the timber east of the marsh, then they all concealed themselves at the narrowest part of the defile. About noon they heard a gunshot on the other side of the mountain spur to the west. Soon they saw a Navaho riding toward them, the carcass of a deer tied behind his saddle. Big Bow whispered to his men to stay under cover until the enemy was within bowshot range.

A moment later he gave a whoop, whereupon they sprang up and ran toward the Navaho, shooting arrows. The Navaho wheeled his mount around in an attempt to escape. But the animal lunged off into the marsh and sank in the boggy ground up to his knees. In a flash Big Bow was upon his victim. He dragged the man to the ground, stabbed him, and expertly tore off the scalp. He seized the horse, pulled it out of the mud, then they all ran back to get their horses. He knew that other Navahos would soon come along the trail, and he wanted to get a good head-start on them.

Big Bow was right about this. As the Navahos told the Kiowas many years later when the tribes had made peace, a group of them did discover the body of the deer hunter soon after Big Bow and his men had departed. The man was still alive. Eventually, through the aid of a white doctor at their agency, he recovered.

The six Navahos hastened eastward on the trail of the retreating Kiowas, overtaking them a mile or two short of where Big Bow had hidden the captured horses. It was in a place surrounded on three sides by high mountains, heavily timbered. The Mexican guide, armed with an old musket, held the Navahos out of bowshot range for a time, for none of the other Indians on either side had firearms. But he wasn't enough of a marksman to hit any of the fast-moving Navahos, and soon he was out of ammunition. From then on it was a fight at long range with bows and arrows.

This type of skirmishing, which began shortly after noon, lasted until the shadows were lengthening in the canyon before any really dangerous attack was made. The Navahos didn't seem to be in any hurry to close with Big Bow and his men. Perhaps they were sure of themselves, or, even more likely, they recognized Big Bow as a formidable opponent. The Kiowa-Mexican had been hit with an arrow in the back part of the leg, but the others had no opportunity to offer him first aid. The enemy were circling closer and closer.

Now Big Bow ordered his men to shoot at the horses of the Navahos. That method had often helped him in previous fights. At once this brought success. One of the enemy made a charge—individually, in the custom of the Indians. Big Bow and his two unwounded companions sent a shower of arrows at him, aiming at the horse. Hit in several places, the horse reared and threw his rider to the ground. Big Bow ran forward and pinned the man to the ground with his lance, then scalped him and added the trophy to the other fresh scalp hanging at his belt.

Meanwhile the Navaho chief was parading up and down in front of his men, gesticulating and haranguing them in a loud voice. Big Bow, who by now had an arrow in the upper part of his thigh, could virtually tell what his enemy was saying. He felt sure that the enemy leader was going to charge Big Bow himself, as he was the only one who was really dangerous to them. If he were slain, the others in his party would quickly be massacred by the Navahos. He told his companions to get ready to cover him by shooting at the other Navahos when the chief charged.

There was a short lull while the Navaho chief was making his medicine and preparing to charge. Big Bow fitted an arrow to his bowstring and waited.

Suddenly the loud talking among the Navahos stopped. The chief wheeled his horse and dashed straight at Big Bow, his lance leveled.

Instead of dodging or running, Big Bow leaped straight at the charging horseman. This brought the enemy's mount up short for

an instant, throwing the Navaho off balance. As the enemy's lance wavered, Big Bow stepped in close and drove an arrow upward into the man's heart, through his body, and on into the air. The Navaho slumped and fell off on the other side of the horse.

Now Big Bow had to dodge a flight of arrows. He wanted to run in and get the scalp, but several Navahos galloped up, reached down, and dragged their leader away. It was now almost dark. The leaderless Navahos withdrew rapidly, taking the body of the chief with them. Big Bow and his men were left to jerk out the arrows protruding from their legs. Then, without further delay, they hastened back into the canyon where they had left the stolen stock. They knew that the enemy had gone for reinforcements and would soon be on their trail again. They took with them a few of the stolen horses, but left most of them because they didn't want to be burdened by driving the herd during their flight. It was a painful journey because of their wounds and the need for traveling rapidly over unfamiliar ground in the darkness. Big Bow kept urging them to make more speed. He felt sure that the unwounded Navahos, despite their late start, would gain rapidly on the fugitives.

When they reached the home of the Mexican trader, Big Bow declined to spend the night there, or even to stop for a meal. The Indians merely accepted some hot *atole* (a thin corn-meal gruel), which they drank as they went on. So they continued to ride on through the following night. As Big Bow learned later, the Navahos arrived at the Mexican's house within a few minutes after the Kiowas had disappeared. The Mexican, replying to their question as to whether the Kiowas had come that way, said that they had. But he added that they had been gone for a considerable time, that they now had fresh horses, and that they had picked up some help from another party of Kiowas who were in the vicinity. They had all gone eastward, discussing among themselves where they would lie in ambush for their pursuers.

This was too much for the Navahos, who returned to their village.

On his arrival at the Kiowa camp, Big Bow displayed one of the scalps he had taken. He had given the other to the kind Mexican's son, who had been so much help to them. At the victory dance the next night, Big Bow was asked by the chiefs and warriors to give the details of his fight with the Navahos. At the conclusion of his story they asked him very pointedly why, if he had killed three enemies as he had claimed, did he return with only one scalp?

Big Bow explained that he had been unable to scalp the Navaho leader because the body had been carried away before he could get to it, and he had given to the Mexicans one of his two scalps.

The chiefs did not believe this story.

Big Bow indignantly informed them that if they didn't believe him, he would be glad to take any number of them to the scene of the fight and also let them question the Mexican.

Stumbling Bear, alone of the war chiefs, appeared to accept Big Bow's story. When the other Kiowa leaders said that they thought Big Bow was too young to have performed these deeds, he said that he would go with Big Bow to obtain verification. The winter season was now upon them, so the expedition was postponed until the following spring, in 1856. Then Big Bow, accompanied by Stumbling Bear and several other chiefs, started out toward the Navaho country.

The journey was a long and tiresome one. Some of the Kiowas dropped out and returned to their home camps. Ah-lay-te, one of Big Bow's friends, overheard some of the other chiefs say that Big Bow was dragging out the trip so that others would be discouraged and refuse to go any farther. Some of them also dropped out and turned back. Now only Stumbling Bear and a few of Big Bow's firm friends continued on into New Mexico.

On their arrival at the home of the Mexican trader, the latter embraced Big Bow and hugged him joyfully. Later, when they had eaten and rested, he verified what he knew from his son of the whole adventure. He displayed the Navaho scalp which Big Bow had given them. The Kiowas spent several days at the home of the Mexican friend. Then they rode west to view the scene of the fighting in the canyon. On their arrival they easily identified the spot, because some of the arrows were still sticking in the ground, and the place was exactly as Big Bow had described it. He told his companions to take the Navaho arrows back to the village to show to the people as evidence of the truth of Big Bow's story. They then went to the marshy place where Big Bow had shot the first Navaho. There was evidence there, too, of what had occurred, signs that only an Indian could read, but unmistakable nevertheless. The members of the party were satisfied that Big Bow had actually done what he had described.

Before they turned back, the Kiowas stole some more Navaho horses, so the home-coming was a happy one. When the announcement was made that Big Bow's story was true, the whoops of the women doing him honor could be heard all through the village. All criticism was now stilled, and the reputation of Big Bow continued to grow. Despite this, the Kiowas were never entirely happy over the fact that he was able to win his victories without the aid of medicine. ✺

12 ✾ HOW TO CATCH AN EAGLE

Iseeo tells of the customs surrounding the catching of eagles and the uses of eagle feathers.

✾ We Kiowas didn't wear feathers as hair ornaments until we learned it from the Sioux. Many years ago, after we had finished our annual sun dance on the Washita near the site of Cloud Chief, a big party of Sioux came down from the north to visit us. They all wore eagle feathers in their hair, and they taught us a feather dance in which they used dance wands decorated with eagle feathers. We have called this dance the Sioux dance ever since.

But we have always used eagle feathers for other purposes. We used the wing feathers to decorate our lances and shields and to feather our arrows. In battle we sometimes wore little caps on which we fastened a special medicine such as a buffalo horn or hair, or the head of a crow, or the fluffy feathers taken from the breast or under the tail of an eagle. But certain warriors, only the *to-yop-kes*, were allowed to wear in battle an eagle-feather war bonnet. Such a bonnet was strong medicine. It was almost as powerful as that of the shield. Furthermore, each feather represented some honor won by the owner or previous owner. Many war bonnets were made a long time ago and were handed down from father to son, or from uncle to nephew.

Sometimes a man made his own war bonnet, or it was made by some-one else, like old man Black Horse, who made several famous bon-nets a long time ago.

Only the tail feathers of a war eagle [golden eagle] are used to make a war bonnet. We never use the white-headed eagle for any-thing. Since there are not many feathers in the tail of a single eagle, it takes six or seven birds for one war bonnet. A man who has need of eagle feathers must catch the bird alive. It would be very bad luck, and spoil the medicine entirely, to wear a war bonnet made of feathers of an eagle that had been shot.

You know very well that the eagle is the wisest of birds. He can-not be caught in an ordinary snare. Here is the way you must do it:

A man who wants to catch an eagle goes out on the prairie, away from his lodge, and digs a large hole at the point of a ridge. This hole must be deep enough to be two feet over my head as I sit here on this log and at least as wide as a man is long. As he digs the hole, the man throws all the dirt on a hide or blanket, then carries it a good distance from the hole to hide it in the brush. Then he cuts a number of saplings as thick as my wrist and lays them flat over the hole. Again, he goes out quite a ways from the hole and cuts some slabs of grassy sod which he lays on the poles to cover the pit. He leaves a hole so that he can get down into the pit himself.

Next he kills a coyote. He opens it and thrusts through it a sharp-ened stake. He lays the coyote on the sod over the hole and pegs it down by driving the lower end of the stake into the bottom of the pit. A fork or notch in the stake at the upper end holds the coyote fast. He uses a coyote as bait because its strong odor attracts the eagle.

He goes out before daylight the next morning, gets down into the pit, smooths everything over outside, and places some sod to cover the place where he entered. He can see up between the poles and can shove his hands up beside the bait.

The eagle has a custom of soaring over the prairie at daybreak. He is hungry and looking for something to eat. When he sees the dead coyote lying in the grass, he dives down and strikes it with both feet, sinking his talons deeply into it. He is not long about it, but strikes swiftly.

92

The Indian, who has seen him through the poles, sits very still. The eagle stands quietly on the coyote, looking all around, until he is satisfied there is no danger. Then he begins pecking at the meat. After the bird has eaten for awhile, and is getting heavy and slow moving, the man puts his hands up softly between the saplings and grabs the eagle by both legs. He shoves aside the stakes and jerks the bird down into the pit and breaks its neck.

The eagle must be jerked down suddenly, not pulled, and its neck broken at once. In that way it dies all over, just as if it had been scared to death. But if you make only a weak pull, or catch him by one leg only, he will be dangerous.

I know a Kiowa man who sat for two days in an eagle pit. On the third day he saw an eagle light on his coyote. He reached up but caught the bird by one leg only and pulled him down. The bird was quiet at first, but quickly got over his fright. He struck his talons through the man's wrist, cutting an artery. The blood gushed out as they fought and struggled like two men in the pit. Finally the Indian, though weak from loss of blood, managed to choke the bird to death. He tied up his wrist and took the eagle back to camp. When he got there, his arm was badly swollen, as big as the calf of his leg. It was very slow healing.

It takes some time to catch enough eagles to make a war bonnet. But a man keeps at it, day after day, until he gets as many as he needs. One of the best places to catch eagles is at the head of the Arkansas River, where there are very high mountains.

The only men who may wear war bonnets in the medicine dance [sun dance] parade are the *to-yop-kes*, and only then if they have worn their war bonnets in battle.

Eagle feathers are good medicine. But a man who is poor in spirit does not have an eagle-feather war bonnet. They are worn only by men with strong hearts—chiefs! That has always been the custom, from earliest times. ☀

13 ❋ THE LOST SHIELD

To an Indian warrior, his war shield was just about his most important medicine. Its power to protect him was mystic as well as material. He guarded it carefully at all times, kept it covered when not in use, and in camp hung it from a special tripod outside his tipi where it would be aloof from any possible contamination. There were definite rules concerning the war shield, and taboos as well. A man who violated any of these was facing certain disgrace. This is the story of how a brave who abandoned his war shield redeemed himself.

It was related to me by Andrew Stumbling Bear, an old Kiowa who was the son of Chief Stumbling Bear.

The latter, a cousin and close companion of Chief Kicking Bird, was in nearly every battle fought by the Kiowas from about 1850 to 1872. At that time he became identified with the peaceable portion of the tribe, and thereafter fought no more. Andrew was still a boy when the Indian wars ended, and so had no personal experiences to describe. But he well remembered the many tales often told by his father, one of which follows.

Iseeo, the central figure of this story, was an uncle of the Kiowa scout of the same name who furnished a number of other stories.

94

✿ In the late fall of 1853, the Kiowas were camped in what is now northern Oklahoma near where Camp Supply was later built. Iseeo and Tsain-hay-te [Big Horse], father of Kicking Bird, recruited a war party for an expedition deep into Chihuahua. This semiarid and partly mountainous region south of the Rio Grande was a favorite raiding ground because of the weak resistance offered by the Mexicans and the fact that they owned numerous horses, mules, and cattle. The usual method of operation was to establish a raid headquarters in the lofty Sierra Madre Mountains, from which forays would be made against the settlements in the lowlands.

Iseeo was a chief and an *on-de*. A man attained this highest caste by individual prowess in war rather than by birth. But this entailed responsibilities, one of the most important being that in battle an *on-de* never deserted or abandoned that special personal medicine, his war shield. The Kiowas had a well-developed system of heraldry, in which a man's horse, his body, and his shield were painted, for battle, in a specific design of symbols and colors. Iseeo painted himself and his shield sky blue with large red dots. No one could fail to mark him in a fracas.

Iseeo took his wife with him to Mexico in 1853. It was unusual for women to accompany so extended a raid, but was not forbidden. It was their duty to care for the extra horses, cook the food, and remain in charge of the raid headquarters while the warriors were on the prowl. Iseeo's wife was proud to have this honor. She was an unusually good-looking young woman, and Iseeo was quite jealous of her. After the expedition was well under way, he whipped her soundly several times to let her know that he would tolerate no foolishness while his back was turned.

The girl's uncle, old Bait-sopte, resented this. "Here we are on a raid," he complained. "Iseeo had no business bringing this girl along. And now he is making trouble with her. He is only a poor, slim boy. I don't think he has any right to be called an *on-de* or a chief."

Iseeo made no reply. But he was irked by the criticism.

After many days of travel the Kiowas came to the no-water country. Here hundreds of cattle grazed through the sparse shrub of the plains. But at a few of the larger towns were garrisons of Mexican lancers. The Indians held these militia in low esteem, but it was well to be careful. They had just slaughtered several beeves for a meal when they saw a party of lancers following their trail.

Now there would be some fun! Not many soldiers were in the troop, whereas the Indian war party was a powerful one containing Comanches and Cheyennes as well as the hard core of Kiowas. The Indians leisurely took positions behind rocks at the foot of a timbered hill and waited until the Mexicans were within bowshot range. Few of the warriors possessed firearms in those days.

Suddenly the lancers deployed. They looked much more numerous now than when they were in a compact column. Many of the Indians lost their lust for battle and retired hastily up the hill.

Only Chief Stumbling Bear and two lesser warriors remained on the firing line. Stumbling Bear never ran from battle unless forced to do so. The Mexicans did not notice that he was almost alone, or perhaps they suspected a trap, for they advanced cautiously on foot, leading their horses. Soon they were closing in, firing their pistols.

Stumbling Bear, hearing other Indians calling to him from the crags, realized that he was unsupported. He and his two companions began to scramble back up the slope, closely followed by the enemy. A few Mexicans mounted up, but their horses were slowed by the rocks. Stumbling Bear and his two companions stopped now and then to fire at them, which further slowed the pursuit. One of the three Indians paused too long. His old muzzle-loader misfired, and the lancers closed in and pierced him with their spears.

Soon Stumbling Bear and the other survivor were winded. They slowed to a straggling walk. Just as they were about to be overtaken, Iseeo dashed down the hill to rescue them. Racing past, he charged the enemy singlehanded. The Mexicans, thinking that Iseeo was leading the expected counterattack, turned back down the hill. Now and then one of them would stop and shoot at Iseeo. One of the bullets hit him in the pit of the stomach, knocking him to the ground.

By now, several other braves were following Iseeo in his headlong attack. They picked him up and unwound the folded sheet

96

which was wrapped about his waist. A bullet fell out. It had pene-
trated several folds, but the chief was only bruised. Presently he sat
up and saw the Mexicans disappearing far down the valley. Then
his gaze fell on Bait-sopte, who was sitting on a rock combing his hair.

"Hah!" cried Iseeo. "So I'm not a chief! I guess you saw what
kind of a man I am!" He grasped Bait-sopte by the hair, twisted him
to his knees, and knuckled the old man's eyes severely.

"You're a woman yourself," he snorted, flinging Bait-sopte
sprawling.

After resting for half an hour, the Indians continued southward.
Toward sunset they came to a pueblo on the outskirts of which were
grazing many horses, tended by two peons. Iseeo and Big Horse
rode down and shot the horseherders while the other Indians drove
the animals into a nearby corral. After stripping the clothing from
their victims, but not otherwise disturbing their bodies, Iseeo and
Big Horse discussed what they would do next. Big Horse favored
heading north with the captured stock before the nearby garrison
should become aware of their presence. But Iseeo, emboldened by
his recent success, wanted to enter the town to stir up some devil-
ment. He had little fear of the Mexicans. He was accustomed to
seeing them flee from him. Therefore he told Big Horse to bring
up the rest of the band to where they had killed the beeves and wait
there for him. Hone-zeptai and Au-an-todal volunteered to accompany him into the village.

It was almost dark. Near the corral Iseeo and his companions
could see the naked bodies of the two fallen Mexicans gleaming
faintly through the dusk. Iseeo rode over and idly stuck his lance
into one of them. The miserable fellow was not dead, only "playing
possum." His anguished scream startled Iseeo's horse, tossing the
young chief to the ground. As he landed on his head, he emitted a
yelp. The main party of Indians rode away laughing heartily at
his mishap.

Iseeo and the other two rode toward the town. Not far away they
could hear the village band giving its nightly concert in the plaza.
The customary evening promenade was in progress.

The Indians came to the high adobe wall enclosing the village.

They tied their horses to a post and climbed over to the inside. Here they sat down to rest, with their backs against the wall. Iseeo unslung his shield and began to rub his aching head. Soon all three were dozing in the quiet evening air.

Presently a sentry approached, walking his beat around the top of the wall. He stopped to peer at the three recumbent Indians. As he was about to challenge them, an officer of the guard came up the street with a patrol. The sentry pointed out what he saw. The Mexicans conferred in low tones, but this still aroused the Indians. They sprang to their feet. There was a blinding flash as the sentry fired his piece. The Kiowas went back over the wall like monkeys and fled into the fields, not stopping to untie and mount their horses. Though they ran headlong into a cactus fence, they did not feel the spines. On through a plowed field they floundered, falling into an irrigation ditch. They scrambled up the far bank and stopped to listen to the sounds of pursuit.

A hundred paces from them could be heard the horses' hoofs pounding along the road. Shrill orders were being shouted in excited Spanish. There was much dashing to and fro.

Suddenly Iseeo gave an awful cry. "I've left my shield," he moaned. "I'm going back after it!"

"No you don't," replied the others, seizing him. "If you try it, we'll all be wiped out! Come—let's get out of here!"

Now the soldiers were in front of them, running back and forth across the field like beagles on a scent. The Kiowas had to drag Iseeo away. He dug his heels in the ground, still insisting that he must go back after his shield.

"Be quiet!" hissed Hone-zeptai. "You can't do it. We will make up a story when we get back, saying that you lost your shield when you were thrown from your horse at the corral. You didn't notice that it was missing from your back; the carrying strap must have broken."

They jumped into a rocky arroyo and crawled under an overhanging rock in front of which was a screen of weeds. They had to keep a restraining hold on Iseeo, despite the voices of soldiers all about them in the darkness. The Mexicans scattered out and began

98

to comb the ravine. Several of them rode within a few feet of the fugitives. Finally, when the tumult had died away, the Indians slipped out of their hiding place and started to run north. They travelled through the night, coming to the rendezvous at daylight weary and forlorn. The other Indians were eating breakfast.

"What is this?" asked Stumbling Bear in astonishment. "You went after more horses, yet you return without even your own!"

The other Indians gathered to hear the explanation. Their faces were expressionless, but they did not fail to notice the absence of Iseeo's shield.

"We got a large bunch of horses," lied Hone-zeptai, "but we got tired, and as you see, poor Iseeo lost his shield in the darkness when his horse threw him."

But Iseeo's hang-dog look gave him away. "A fine story!" snorted the other Kiowas.

Iseeo sat apart, silent and troubled. The outcome of the raid, which had started out so well, worried him intolerably. He wished he had told the truth, but now it was too late.

The band traveled north for several nights. On the fourth morning, Iseeo walked alone to the top of a nearby knoll. He stood for a time looking down at the camp. Suddenly a great cry of anguish was wrenched from his heart.

"I've disgraced myself! I left my shield! I ran from the enemy! Ai-ee! Ai-ee!"

Old Bait-sopte heard the wail. His eyes narrowed. "Everyone come here," he called. "Listen to Iseeo!"

The other Indians came running to listen coldly while the young chief walked up to them and poured out the whole miserable story.

"I have no sympathy for you," snarled Bait-sopte when he heard the story. "I always knew you were that kind of a man. You are no chief. You are no *on-de*. You are lower than a dog."

The others nodded in solemn agreement. Then and there they voted to withdraw Iseeo's title of war chief and to reduce him to the lowest caste of the tribe.

Nevertheless, Iseeo felt better for having confessed.

When the expedition returned to the tribal camps, the Kiowas were all informed of Iseeo's disgrace. For a year no one except his father would even talk to him. Old friends failed to recognize him when they met him face to face. Iseeo wilted under this treatment. There came a time when he would not venture outside his tipi during daylight hours.

His father attempted to cheer him. "I will see the medicine man," he said. "He will help us."

He returned from his visit to the shaman bringing a rabbitskin cap topped with a pure white eagle feather. "This is like the cap worn by the *Tai-me* priest at the sun dance," he explained. "The next time the Kiowas are in a fight, you must wear it. It will bring you so much bravery that the chiefs will reinstate you."

Iseeo promised to do his best.

It was not long before he was given his chance. They were again in Mexico. A troop of soldiers, accompanied by a brass cannon drawn by mules, was following them. The Kiowas took position beside a little creek, with a rough, rocky slope to their rear. The enemy approached on the other side of the stream and deployed in full view. The Indians saw the Mexicans tie their horses together in a sheltered hollow and come forward to lie behind an irregularly spaced line of rocks bordering the creek.

The firing became general. A number of Indians mounted their ponies to make individual charges. It was their way of displaying their courage.

But who was this? It was that disgraced Iseeo on a white horse! He was wearing his white-feathered medicine cap, which made him invulnerable and strengthened his heart. His red blanket was hooked over his shoulders like a military cape, and his body was painted in his traditional colors. His only weapon was a long, polished spear. He galloped full speed toward the enemy. The firing had slackened, but now picked up again as Iseeo came out into the open. Iseeo circled out across the front of the enemy and returned unhurt to the shelter of a gully. Immediately he repeated the performance, this time at a canter. A third time he rode across the enemy front at a slow trot and much closer to the firing line.

This was too much for the Kiowa chiefs. No low-down, unrecognized dog could best them in a show of bravery. The mighty Do-hauson came forth and circled even closer to the enemy than Iseeo. But before he had regained the shelter of the gulch, he saw Iseeo following him, riding even closer to the Mexicans.

Iseeo was not hit. He rested himself and his mount for a few minutes, looking around to see if anyone dared better his feat. No one seemed anxious to try. Iseeo gazed scornfully at the hesitant braves, then gathered his reins and dashed straight toward the Mexican firing line. They saw his horse rearing and plunging in the very midst of the stabbing gun flashes and billowing smoke.

But he came back untouched.

Now Stumbling Bear was getting ready to make a charge. Iseeo dismounted near him. "I have no shield," he shouted. "I am not allowed to carry a bow and arrow. Only a lance. I will even leave my special war pony behind. But I'm going forward again. This time on foot!" He and Stumbling Bear rushed forward simultaneously.

"Someone catch my son!" shrilled Iseeo's father. "Save him!"

Several Kiowas snatched at Iseeo as he ran past, but were only able to tear loose the empty quiver on his back. Iseeo ran on alone. The other warriors, fired by his example, followed.

Iseeo did not know they were coming. He thought he was alone except for Stumbling Bear. To the front boomed the cannon. Dust spurted up between the Indians from the musketry fire. Then the Indians reached the firing line, Iseeo still in the lead. The Mexicans stood up from behind the rocks to receive the assault. In the middle of their line was a bald-headed man, their commander. He and Iseeo thrust at each other at the same moment. The officer tumbled over backward, his back broken by Iseeo's lance thrust. Iseeo was struck in the knee. As he went down, several Mexicans fired practically in his face.

The redcoats could not stand the shock. The air was filled with pursuing arrows. The Mexicans were knocking each other down in their efforts to escape. Those who were not cut down from behind reached a second creek, much wider. They jumped into a deep pool, which the Kiowas immediately surrounded. Hundreds of arrows flashed into the struggling mass of bodies in the water. Soon there was only a tangle of dead men. Widening swirls of scarlet spread through the pool.

The shooting died down. Not an enemy remained alive. The Indians lay panting on the ground.

Stumbling Bear tried to cut the mules loose from the cannon. He saw a group of Kiowas behind the breastwork swabbing off one of the wounded braves. It was Iseeo. His face was black from powder burns, and the Indians were licking and sucking the grains from his face and eyes. The buffalo medicine men were howling and shaking gourd rattles. But this didn't help Iseeo. He had been blinded by the gunflash in his face.

The Kiowas stripped the red uniforms from the fallen Mexicans and dressed themselves in this finery. They untied the captured horses and led them to their own herd. When they arrived at their own position, they found one man shot through the temples by a spent bullet. His eyes were hanging out on his cheeks. It was Bait-sopte. He was dead.

For the first hours of their return journey the Kiowas rode in a column of fours to imitate the enemy. As they crossed some flats, they saw two Mexicans on a hill signaling to them. They waved back, whereupon the Mexicans rode to join them. The Kiowas took considerable satisfaction in killing and scalping them. Soon they encountered another peon whom they fooled in the same manner and with the same fatal conclusion to the episode. The whole expedition was regarded as being a thoroughgoing success despite the death of Bait-sopte.

When they returned to the base camps on the Arkansas River, Iseeo was still blind. The wound in his knee failed to heal, and infection eventually brought death. Nevertheless, at the time of the triumphal return, he was happy. Once more he was a recognized chief. Once again he was an *on-de*.

Although Iseeo had no further use for a war shield, his friends made a new one and presented it to him in a public ceremony witnessed by the entire tribe. ❁

14 ❧ SATANTA'S SHIELD

TAY-BODAL, an old Kiowa alive in the 1890's, told Captain H. L. Scott this story of a famous war shield once owned by Satanta. When Set-tain-te (Satanta, White Bear), as he is known in Kiowa, was taken to prison in 1875 to serve out a life sentence for murder, he gave his shield to his son Tsal'-au-te. The latter, before his death in 1894, willed it to Captain Scott who in turn presented it to the museum of the University of California.

❧ Black Horse made that shield long before I was born. He made six, but that one is the only one left now. It had strips of red cloth fastened on one side and yellow on the other. In the center of the shield was painted a sun, with two rings around it just like the rings you see sometimes around the moon. There was a crane's head fastened to it, and when Black Horse went to war, carrying the shield, he had in his hair the longest wing feathers of a crane. He wore a buckskin shirt painted red on one side and yellow on the other. In camp he kept the shield on a tripod about two hundred paces from his lodge. Above it, tied to a pole, was a crane's wing.

When I became old enough to know things, I saw that shield. Black Horse was an old man when he was killed in the fight with the Sah-kee-bo. But before he went into that battle, he gave his shield to

Satanta, who was then a young war chief. That shield has been in fights with every kind of red man, and has been many times on long raids deep into Old Mexico. Satanta carried it to Durango the time the Mexicans came out to fight us with ropes. Satanta was lassoed by a Mexican who tied the rope to the horn of his saddle and jerked Satanta off his horse. Then the Mexican galloped off, dragging Satanta behind him. The Indian was jerked and dragged, first on one side and then on the other. Frizzlehead, whom you know very well, came up and charged the Mexican with his spear. Frightened, the Mexican dropped the rope and dashed away.

Thus Satanta was saved. But both of his legs and his sides were badly skinned, and he was sore and very stiff for a long time. The famous shield was with him when that fight took place, and it probably helped save him.

I was along on a raid myself when Satanta, carrying his red and yellow shield, killed a Mexican with a spear near Chihuahua. Again I was there when he killed a Sah-kee-bo on the other side of the Arkansas and a Pawnee near Bent's Fort on the Arkansas. I know that Stumbling Bear and another man now dead saw him kill a Ute with a spear, one night in New Mexico. He had that shield in every one of those fights. It has had a strong road. It has been in more than one hundred battles. It had the honor of being hung in the medicine lodge during the sun dance. ☼

15 ❁ TAY-BODAL THE SURGEON

GEORGE HUNT RECALLED FOR ME the accomplishments of this talented Kiowa.

❁ Old Tay-bodal was not a medicine man. Nevertheless he was a clever healer and a very wise fellow. He lived to be over a hundred years old.

In the summer of 1854, during the fight with the Sah-kee-bo, one of the wounded was a Kiowa named Maunte-pah-hodal, or Kills-It-With-A-Gun. He had a bullet deeply embedded in his rump, not an honorable spot in which to be shot by the enemy. For several days and nights he was in such pain that he couldn't ride a horse. The wound was festering. Things looked mighty gloomy for Maunte-pah-hodal.

The Buffalo Society tried their medicine, but Maunte grew steadily worse. At length Tay-bodal was brought in for consultation. He hadn't volunteered because he was not a recognized medicine man. Professional ethics were strong in those days. If he were not successful, things would go hard with him. But as Maunte-pah-hodal was in a desperate condition, Tay-bodal agreed to take the case.

He honed his long-bladed knife on a stone until it was like a stiletto. He took a brass arm band from one of the spectators, cut and straightened it, then fashioned it into a probe, with a short hook at one end. He passed the knife and the hook through a flame several times to purify them, then wiped the tools thoroughly with a dirty rag.

When all was ready, he had some of the men spread-eagle the patient buttocks-up over a pile of blankets, to raise the man to a height convenient for operating and to force open the wound.

He stuffed a rag wad into Maunte's mouth and told him to bite it hard.

"Are you ready?" he asked the four assistants.

"Yes. Go ahead."

"Are you ready to risk his life?"

"We are willing."

"All right," said Tay-bodal. "Hold him tightly by both arms and legs."

He peered at his victim, who was showing the whites of his eyes. "Bite down hard on that rag," he cautioned.

He rolled up his sleeves, seized the knife, and thrust the eight-inch blade straight down into the wound until he touched the slug. As he probed around, the blood spurted up through his fingers.

"Hold him down good!" he repeated to the assistant technicians. "Bite down hard!" He withdrew the knife, twisting it to further open the wound. He wiped his hands, took the brass hook, and rammed it down the gaping hole. Carefully he fished around and withdrew the bullet, which was followed by much evil-looking matter. It was an ugly slug, mashed at one end. Blood streamed from the wound.

Tay-bodal flushed the hole out thoroughly with water from a gourd. He had the men melt some buffalo tallow, which he poured hot into the hole. At this Maunte gave a great cry, spitting out his gag.

"You're going too far," he complained.

"Silence," was Tay-bodal's reply. "Get down there again. I am not through."

He whittled a shallow cup about four inches wide from a piece of soft cottonwood. He twisted this over the wound, tying it in place.

The cup was to hold the edges together and to keep out the flies. Within an hour Maunte was sleeping quietly, for the first time since he had been injured. His fever went down. The next day they took up their journey, carrying Maunte in an improvised travois. It would be some time before he could ride a horse in the normal manner.

Each night Tay-bodal removed the cup and let the wound drain. He renewed the tallow dressing. Soon the wound began to heal from the inside out. It had stopped festering. By the time they had reached their home camp, Maunte was able to walk. He was feeling fine. In grateful appreciation he offered his two sisters to Tay-bodal as wives.

"Fine," said Tay-bodal. "I certainly thank you. But one of them is already married."

Maunte brushed that aside. "No matter. You can have her anyway."

But Tay-bodal, who was not looking for unnecessary trouble, accepted only the unmarried sister. Her name was Bodal-tay-dal. That certainly sounds like Tay-bodal backwards.

Zay-baidal, or Big Arrow, was another of Tay-bodal's beneficiaries. He was ambitious and thrifty, not easily tempted. Unlike nearly all Indians of those days, he did not gamble. Once when nearly two hundred men were gathered to watch some horse races, Big Arrow alone placed no bets. This aroused the scorn of some of the Kogui band who were present.

Gotebo, a prominent member of that order, remarked loudly to those nearby, "I wonder if Zay-baidal is likely to die in battle? He is so afraid to take a risk at a horse race, I don't suppose he would ever place himself in danger."

Big Arrow brooded over this for two years. Then many of the Kiowas went on a raid to Texas. During a fight with some Texans, the Indians were chasing a lone man, who seemed to be gaining on them. Big Arrow was in the dust to the rear of the pack.

Suddenly they heard him shout, "Now my time has come! The Koguis said I was afraid to die. Today is my die-day!" Whipping his horse vigorously, Big Arrow passed the other Indians and drew near the Texan. The white man turned in his saddle and shot the Indian with his pistol at point-blank range. The bullet struck Big Arrow in the eye, ranged down through his throat, and lodged under his shoulder blade. Half his teeth were shot out, too.

Big Arrow didn't fall, but he had to abandon the fight. In a moment the other Indians surrounded him, chattering over his awful appearance. The Buffalo Society began to minister to him. They made their buffalo-hoof rattles hum. They waved their buffalo-tail medicine switches back and forth, singing and chanting. Some of them bawled and bellowed, in imitation of a bull in distress over a sick cow.

The wounded man stayed in the saddle. Though they led him slowly to a safe place, it was obvious that the activities of the buffalo men were not effective. The victim was growing gray and swaying in the saddle.

An appeal was made to Tay-bodal, who had been quietly observing the efforts of the medicine men. He looked at them to see if they objected to his taking over. They gave him the go-ahead signal.

First, Tay-bodal got some water from a nearby tank and washed Big Arrow thoroughly. He gave the poor fellow a drink, but the water came out the hole in his throat. Tay-bodal held one hand over this gaping wound and poured some more water into Big Arrow. Up came his breakfast, together with much blood.

"That's fine," said Tay-bodal encouragingly. "Just what I want. Let's flush him out again." Which they did.

Now Tay-bodal removed the bark from a dead cottonwood tree. Underneath was a soft, silky fiber, from which he fashioned a little vacuum cup the size of a silver dollar. He had the patient lie down, after which he reamed out the wound with a piece of soft wood, cleaning out the foreign matter which had been shot into it. Then he drew the edges together with his suction cup and tied this plug in place.

After Big Arrow had rested for an hour or so, Tay-bodal had him drink a little warm broth made of buffalo jerky pounded up and boiled. He probed for the bullet and cut it out with his knife. When this was finished, he washed and greased the incision and tied it together as before.

The patient fell asleep. They kept him alive for several days with soup, moving him out of the enemy territory in a travois. Within two days, Tay-bodal was able to remove the plug. The wound was growing together. He applied buffalo tallow, and installed a larger suction cup. Two days later he again dressed the wound. Big Arrow had to continue for some time on a liquid diet, on account of his missing teeth. His eye socket healed nicely, however, and in spite of considerable suffering he was recovering. Within a week, Tay-bodal was able to take the suction cup off altogether.

Big Arrow had terrible scars and wore a black patch over one eye, which gave him somewhat the look of a pirate. He lived to be about ninety. He was a nephew of Satank and a cousin of Kicking Bird, but never attained their fame in battle.

The wars were long over, but the medicine men were still plying their trade. Old White Horse, the famous raider, developed a swelling under the skin of his abdomen. He thought it might be the result of some old war injury. It continued to get larger, and eventually he had a high fever. Never having had much faith in the medicine man, the old chief called in Tay-bodal, who was by then a genuine ancient, close to one hundred years old. Tay-bodal said that an abdominal operation would be very dangerous, probably beyond his capabilities. But White Horse insisted that he try.

By that time, many years of inactivity had piled considerable fat around White Horse's midsection. In addition, his skin was unusually thick. Tay-bodal probed the lump thoroughly with his fingers. He found one place that stayed depressed when he pushed in. Here he decided to explore with a knife.

When everything was ready, and White Horse had prepared himself mentally, Tay-bodal gathered up a bundle of flesh in his fist and plunged his sharp, narrow-pointed knife into it. Pus spurted out. It was allowed to drain, then Tay-bodal squeezed more out with his fingers. He dressed the wound as in previous cases, renewing the dressing every two or three days. White Horse recovered fully, to die in bed some years later still unrepentant for the many atrocities he had committed in his young days.

In the year of the Peninsular sun dance, which was held in a bend of the Washita, a boy was run over by a horse and his leg broken. This boy, whose name was Tap-to, was not helped by the medicine men. His parents finally took him to Tay-bodal. After studying the case for some time, Tay-bodal went to the creek, cut dogwood branches, and fastened them together in the form of a cradle splint. He manipulated the fracture until he had reduced it fairly well, then he fitted his wicker contraption around the leg like a cast and tied it in place securely. He required the boy to wear it for a long time. The leg bone knit well, and the boy recovered entirely without any lameness. It had been a compound fracture.

Tay-bodal was also something of a horse doctor. Once a valuable horse was bitten by a rattlesnake just above the pastern. The whole leg swelled, all the way to the shoulder. Tay-bodal had the horse thrown on its side and hog-tied. He got a pan of warm water and soap and washed the leg thoroughly. He scrubbed it with a brush made of broomstraw. After whetting his knife, he thrust it through a piece of wood to mark the depth to which he would cut. Leaving this piece of wood on the blade, he gashed the horse's leg in numerous places wherever there was swelling. Yellow poison came out. He took a three-foot stick and scraped down the leg as with a draw knife, forcing out more of the poison. He kept up this treatment until he had reduced the swelling. Then he applied salt to the cuts.

The next day the swelling was almost gone. Tay-bodal soaked the leg with water to keep the gashes soft and open, so they could continue to ooze poison. In a few days the hair came off around the cuts, but the horse recovered, and the hair grew back.

He also doctored a horse which had distemper. The treatment consisted of burning rags in a skillet of coals under the horse's nostrils. On this fire he sprinkled damp cedar leaves. This primitive vaporizer loosened up the congestion in the animal's nasal passages.

He kept up this treatment for some time, continually dampening the cedar with water so that it would smoke instead of burn. After two daily applications, the horse recovered. The Indians often used this method thereafter. It always cured the horse.

His treatment for curing a horse that was wind broken was to cut some veins on the nose and tip of the ears and under the elbows. He let them bleed for a time, then required the animal be rested for several months before being used again. Sometimes this therapy worked, sometimes not.

Once, a white man showed up at the Rainy Mountain mission who had been bitten by a rattlesnake. Tay-bodal, who happened to be in the vicinity, was called in to help. Instead of applying any of the secret herbs which the Indians are commonly reputed to use, he cut open the place of the bite and sucked out the poison. Then he poured into the cut a pinch of gunpowder which he touched off with a match. Under the circumstances, who could have done better?

Definitely, Tay-bodal was good medicine. ☼

16 ✦ A REMARKABLE CURE

OLD SATANK, the chief who was shot to death while trying to escape from a guard wagon near Fort Sill in the summer of 1871, was more of a warrior than a medicine man. But he had at least one psychiatric cure to his credit, not less outstanding than any of Tay-bodal's achievements. His oldest son, An-pay-kau-te, tells the story.

✦ I was born tongue-tied, and reached my seventh birthday without having said a word. One day my cousin, a grown man, sent for me. He had a pint of whiskey. "Now, boy," he said, "Make your heart strong! I'm going to tell you something. I have here a little pinto pony which you have been wanting very hard. I am going to give it to you if you will take a big drink of this crazy water. Maybe-so you'll be able to talk."

I took a big drink. Then I took another. It burned all the way down. But I kept on taking swallows until I became drunk. All at once I began to say a few words. The first thing I said was, "Now give me the pony!" A crowd of young boys were standing around watching me act the fool. But I didn't care. I had found my tongue. And I had a horse.

"Here," my cousin said to my mother, "take this bottle. Give him a drink every once in a while."

112

Next morning I could still say a few words. Just then my father came in from a raid. "What's this all about?" he asked. They told him. "Let me see that bottle," he demanded. There was just one drink left in it. My father tested that. "Good," he said. "I'll get some more." So he bought a bottle from some Osage. When that was gone he bought another. And another. Each time I got a dose of this medicine he took one too. Had to test it, he said. It seemed to do him good.

As for myself, the firewater completed my cure. I became a great talker. ☙

This seems to be the first recorded instance in America of successful speech therapy. One often wonders, however, just what this medicine would do to the sign talker. Surely the signals would get a bit mixed at times!

17 ✿ TAPE-DAY-AH BECOMES A MAN

UPON THE OUTBREAK of the Civil War, the United States withdrew the bulk of its army units from New Mexico, because they were required elsewhere in the prosecution of the war. Unrestrained by the presence of troops in their country, the Kiowas and Comanches began to raid more frequently against the border settlements and down into Old Mexico.

A map of eastern New Mexico published in 1862 as a part of a Senate document shows that the Comanches at that time were generally in the Staked Plains south of Beaver Creek, as the Canadian River was then called. The Mescalero Apaches, by that time friendly with the Comanches, were west of the Pecos. The Kiowas were not shown. General Carleton reported that the Comanches had a large pool of stolen stock somewhere west of the Pecos, which they were selling or trading in New Mexico. These animals had been captured in Mexico and Texas. The Indians sold them in New Mexico, whence they were sold back to their original owners, from whom the wild Indians stole them again. Thus an interesting cycle was established, which kept the Plains Indians entertained.

Sometimes young Indian boys went on raids with the older men. They were used to guard the spare horses, saddles, and other equipment which the Indians would cache at a "raid headquarters" prior to descending on the settlements. Boys who were less than sixteen or seventeen years of age had to secure the permission of their fathers to go on such expeditions, for the older men did not care to be responsible for the safety of such inexperienced youths. It was under these conditions that in 1861 a warrior named Hone-zep-tai took two boys, Set-koi-k'e and Tape-day-ah, with him on a long raid into Old Mexico. Tape-day-ah was then about thirteen, and Set-koi-k'e was perhaps a year older. Hone-zep-tai was an experienced raider who had been to Mexico several times. He planned to join the Comanches on one of their expeditions and stay with them until he had built up a considerable herd of stolen animals.

The story of their adventures was later told by Tape-day-ah to Iseeo, his younger brother, who in turn told it to his nephew George Hunt. The following version was furnished to me by the latter, whom I have substantially followed.

✿ The three Kiowas left their tribal camps on the banks of the Arkansas River and drifted south along the edge of the Staked Plains. After many days of travel, they crossed the Pau-aidle-san or Little Río Grande [the Pecos]; not finding the Comanches, they continued across the desert into Mexico. It was a long, dangerous trip, but Hone-zep-tai had been there before, was acquainted with every landmark, and knew the location of every waterhole along the route usually followed by war parties. He and his companions rode towards the purple heights of the Sierra Madre Mountains, where they expected to make their headquarters.

They were grateful to leave the heat of the lowlands and climb up among the cool pines where there were sparkling springs of water and where a refreshing breeze blew constantly. Far below them was the grassy plain of Chihuahua, spotted with occasional clumps of mesquite. They also observed extensive ranchos with oases of fruit trees surrounded by high adobe walls. In the distance was a village consisting of a few flat-topped adobe huts, and here and there a more pretentious *casa* with a plastered facade tinted sky blue or pink—all clustered around a lofty church.

Hone-zep-tai was sure that some of the Comanches had established their base of operations in these mountains. He made a brief search, and presently he located them. The Comanches proved to be so hospitable that the three Kiowas remained with them for two years. During this time they made it a practice to descend stealthily on the Mexican settlements, steal a few head of stock, then drive the animals swiftly back to the mountain hideout before the Mexicans could organize a pursuit. When the captured herd became unwieldy on account of its size, the Indians would return with it to Texas, where they turned the booty over to the Indians who had been left in charge of the "pool." Then the raiders returned to Mexico for more stock.

By spring of 1863, Hone-zep-tai and the two boys had obtained so many horses and mules that they decided to return to their own people. They realized that if they remained away from home much longer their relatives would give them up for dead. Hone-zep-tai wanted to travel to the Arkansas River by a new route. He was an unusually restless nomad, a true explorer. It was his theory that they could follow the Rocky Mountains north to near the source of the Arkansas. They would then follow the stream east until they came to the Kiowa camps. This route would avoid the desert and the arid Staked Plains. Possibly it would be less dangerous, because it would avoid Texas, where rangers were apt to make an inconvenient appearance, and Kansas, where there were United States troops. Anyway, it was something novel, and he wanted to try it.

Probably no small part of his motive lay in a desire to have experiences which no other Kiowa had been through, to have tall tales to tell when he returned to the tribal campfires. It was not difficult for him to persuade the two boys to agree to this plan. They were too inexperienced to appreciate properly the probable hardships which lay ahead of them. Trusting implicitly in their leader, they anticipated only a pleasant and interesting series of adventures.

They told the Comanches to hold their share of the stock, that they would either come to the Pecos for it later in the year, or that some of their kinfolk would do so. Then they made preparations for the long journey north. They killed a few stolen beeves, jerked the meat, tanned the hides, and made extra pairs of moccasins. They selected several of the hardiest horses, to ride and to be used as pack animals. But they did not care to be burdened with a large herd of extra horses.

At first the explorers traveled slowly, and by easy stages, to harden themselves and their horses for the rough trip which they anticipated. As the summer wore on, and the mountain ridges still stretched far away to the north, they knew that they would have to push faster if they were to finish the trip before winter set in. But the country was becoming more and more rugged, and their ponies were developing tender feet from the continual contact with sharp rock and rough lava instead of the prairie sod to which they were accustomed.

Finally, one after another, the animals began to give evidence of complete exhaustion. The Indians were forced to shoot and butcher them for food. Eventually they were reduced to one mount apiece, and these were failing rapidly owing to the scarcity of food and the hard going. The Indians had been moving constantly north, keeping along the eastern edge of the mountains in order to avoid the fierce Utes and Navahos who lived farther west. By the time that all their horses, except those they were riding, had been killed, they were far north—probably somewhere in the vicinity of Raton Pass.

One day they looked far down in the canyon below them and saw a wagon train toiling along a narrow road. A body of men who appeared to be soldiers were riding as escorts. [This may have been one of the gold or silver convoys from the mines in New Mexico, destined for the United States mints in the east. Large shipments of bullion were passing over the Santa Fe Trail during the Civil War to assist the Federal Government in meeting heavy expenses of the war.] At once Hone-zep-tai began making plans to raid this train at night in order to secure fresh horses. He had no idea what the wagons carried, and he was not interested in finding out, for he realized full well that three tired Indians could accomplish little against so strong a party.

Toward evening the Kiowas saw the white men halt the wagons and form them into a circle for the night camp. Here was the chance they had been waiting for. Before it became too dark to see the trail, they began to pick their way down the mountainside. As they got deeper into the pass, they noticed that some of the streams flowed east from this point, others west. They were on the divide between the headwaters of the Río Grande and the Arkansas. At the foot of the peak they found a beautiful little creek lined with timber. There they tied their weary animals, then on foot they began to sneak down the creek bed to where they thought the white men had pastured their horse herd.

It was entirely dark by the time they arrived opposite the camp, but they were able to make their way because of the dim light of the dying camp fires reflected from the surrounding pine trees. While the Indians were crouching below the bank of the stream, a man approached from the direction of the camp carrying a musket on his shoulder. Just as they decided he must have seen or heard them, he turned and walked slowly back in the direction from which he had come. They realized he was a sentry pacing a regular beat. They conferred in low tones and determined to kill him when he approached on his next round. They strung their bows and waited, tense with excitement. Suddenly Hone-zep-tai whispered, "Here he comes!"

The Kiowas ran silently towards the soldier, loosing a shower of arrows as they ran. The man gave a great cry and discharged his gun. Almost instantly the little valley was lighted by the flashing of fifty guns. The canyon reverberated with the sound, which was practically continuous. Later, in discussing the affair, the Indians decided that the white men must have seen them on the mountainside, during the afternoon, possibly through field glasses, and were on the alert for an attack.

The Indians fled in confusion. But when they reached the timber, the two younger Indians paused, having discovered that their leader was not with them. They looked back hastily. He was not in sight. They stared at each other in dismay. Hone-zep-tai must have been struck down by the first volley! But the bullets were still flying overhead, so they resumed their flight, fearful that they too would be hit. Presently they came to a safer place, sheltered by a low spur of the mountain. They stopped again and called to Hone-zep-tai. The only answer was an angry increase in gunfire. They were sure then that their leader was dead. They began to weep.

Soon they reached the place where they had tethered their horses. There stood Hone-zep-tai's pony, saddled and bridled just as he had left it a short time ago. The boys' lamentations broke out with renewed vigor. They untied their mounts, including Hone-zep-tai's, and began to climb the mountainside. As they made their way slowly in darkness through brush and rocks, they could hear the shooting still going on in the valley, growing fainter now. The jumpy white men continued to "repel" the supposed Indian attack. By midnight the Kiowa boys reached the top of the mountain, where they sat down among some boulders and waited for daylight to come.

In the morning they could see the white men preparing to break camp. Thin blue smoke from their campfires rose straight in the quiet morning air. The Kiowas knew that their enemies were eating breakfast. They gnawed reflectively on the few remaining bits of dried beef which they carried in their saddle bags and watched dismally while the wagon train formed in column and marched slowly east. Toward sunset the Indians felt it was safe to go down and search for Hone-zep-tai's body.

Far below they saw a flock of crows circling and knew that he must be lying somewhere near the deserted campsite. However the darkness of the canyon brought back their fears. They imagined that the enemy was waiting for them in ambush, or that other and more evil things lurked in the darkness. They turned and retreated hastily up the mountainside. Here they remained for three days, trying unsuccessfully to gather their courage sufficiently to descend into the pass.

"What shall we do?" they asked. "Shall we go on or shall we turn back?" They doubted their ability to find the headwaters of the Arkansas, or to distinguish it from any other streams which rose in the mountains. They feared lest they perish in this hostile region, so far from their tribe. Reluctantly, they decided to return to Mexico; from there they felt that they could find their way home even though it involved crossing the no-water country without a guide. It was a hard decision to make, to travel by such a roundabout route, but they chose it as the lesser of the two evils, preferring the known to the unknown.

Sadly, they killed Hone-zep-tai's horse, butchered it, and dried the meat in preparation for the long journey. Then they turned their faces south once more. Their hearts were full of foreboding. Winter was close at hand, it would be fatal to stay in the north until the snows overtook them. They were uncertain of the route and worried lest they be unable to find sufficient water along the way.

After a week or so, their horses, already in a pitiable condition, gave out entirely and had to be shot. They cured some of the meat, but were unable to pack much of it. They realized that they must reduce themselves to short rations to conserve their supplies as long as possible. They were able to kill some game, but not much. There were no buffalo in the mountain ranges, and little game of any kind.

The youths did not dare go down into the lowlands, even though they sometimes saw settlements and ranches with grazing cattle. Like the wild wolves, they knew that the hand of every man was set against them and that they would be killed on sight.

Soon their clothing was rotting and falling from them. Their moccasins had worn through and they were forced to walk barefoot through the sharp rocks. Mounted or "horse" Indians that they were, this form of locomotion was not merely unpleasant, it was actual hardship. Before long their feet were cut and bruised, and their flesh torn by briars and cactus spines.

Eventually, they came to an exceptionally rugged part of the mountains, a region which was bleak and dry. They had been without water all day. Toward mid-afternoon, Set-koi-k'e, the older boy, went eastward to look for water. Tape-day-ah waited for him until the evening shadows blackened in the canyons; then he became fearful that something had happened to his companion. He felt that he ought to go in search of him, but hesitated to do so lest they miss each other in the darkness. The chill of night descended on the mountaintop.

At length, Tape-day-ah arose and began to grope his way forward along the ridge running to the east. Now and then he stopped to call. There was no reply except weird echoes thrown back from the sides of the mountains. The Kiowa youth stopped, afraid to go farther because of the danger of falling over a cliff. In the meantime, Set-koi-k'e was searching for him. Both were lost. During their searches they passed each other in the darkness, on opposite sides of the ridge.

In some way the horrible night was endured. But when daylight came, they were little better off. They kept up the search, but were only able to straggle along, weakened by thirst, hunger, and panic. Finally on the third day, when he had almost given up hope, Tape-day-ah saw Set-koi-k'e at a distance. He called hoarsely, but the other did not look his way. Tape-day-ah tried to run in that direction, but his legs failed him, and the other boy had turned away. Then Set-koi-k'e turned around again and saw the younger boy. They limped painfully toward each other. It was a joyous reunion, with much weeping and embracing. The boys felt that having overcome such hardships during the last few days, nothing worse could be in store for them, provided they stayed together. And so with a better spirit they resumed their journey southward. Early in the winter they arrived back at their old headquarters in the Sierra Madre Mountains.

Looking around, they found the deserted campfires of the Comanches. There was no sign that the Indians had been there recently. In a clearing in the woods they saw an old broken-down burro, feeding peacefully. They shot the animal and butchered him for food. While they were cooking the meat, they saw something moving in the timber on the opposite side of the meadow. At once they concealed themselves in the high grass. A group of strange Indians had been attracted by the smoke of their fire. The leader of this band rode forward to investigate. The Kiowas recognized him as a Comanche, but they did not know him. However, they knew he was a member of a friendly tribe, so they came out of their hiding place and gestured to him.

The Comanche was shocked by the appearance of the two young men. They looked like animals with their naked, lacerated bodies, their hair unkempt and matted with dirt and briars, and their eyes bloodshot from lack of sleep and from hardship. Plains Indians were accustomed to keeping themselves well clothed and neatly groomed, especially the hair. They considered it shameful to be seen in a disreputable condition.

"Who are you?" the Comanche called.

"Kiowas," they answered.

The Comanche chief embraced them and cried over them. "Stay here until I can collect some clothing for you," he said. Then he returned to his party, borrowed several garments, a comb, and a small looking glass. No self-respecting Comanche ever set forth on a trip without these necessary toilet articles. When the Kiowas had made themselves presentable, he took them to join his companions. They would have lost great face had they appeared in their original destitute condition.

A great welcome was prepared, and a fine feast was held at the Comanche camp fire that night. The Kiowas related the entire story of their misfortunes, while the Comanches listened sympathetically. The Comanche chief then told them he was going on a final raid of the season and that he would be glad to have them accompany him, after which they would all go home together. The Kiowas were glad to accept. The Comanche chief was kindhearted and, although the Kiowas were not very successful in the raid, he gave them some horses and took them north with him.

Weeks later, they reached their camp on the Arkansas River. It was a sad duty to have to report the death of Hone-zep-tai, but the survivors were proud to be able to tell what hardships they had overcome in making their way back. Iseeo said that when his brother had left home, he was a boy, but that when he returned, he was a man. Already his medicine power was good. ✸

18 ❁ GOD'S GIFT

ACCORDING TO GEORGE HUNT, the Kiowas believed that the buffalo were God's gift to the Indians. From these animals the Plains Indians obtained nearly everything needed to sustain life. In addition, the buffalo became a religious symbol, featured in the medicine dance or sun dance. The Indian loved the buffalo, and had no part in its extermination. It was an integral part of his daily life, and when it had vanished, he felt that life was not worth living. He could not comprehend how and why the buffalo disappeared, apparently within such a short space of time. For several decades thereafter he hoped against hope that some miracle would bring back the great herds.

George Hunt was able to recall about seventy-five uses which the Indians made of the buffalo, but even then he wasn't sure that he had not overlooked a few. The following is a composite of what he had to say on this subject.

❁ Of course, the most important thing which the buffalo gave the Indians was food. They consumed nearly every part of it except the hide, hair, bones, and horns. In emergencies even the hide was eaten —pieces of rawhide shaved up and boiled to make them soft. Marrow from the bones was always eaten, sometimes being preserved

123

like sausage by stuffing it into the buffalo windpipe or stomach lining. The stomach lining was also used as a water bag, and the stomach contents of a freshly killed animal were eaten.

Special dishes were made from the blood, nose, ears, vital organs, and brains. The tongue, liver, and udders were delicacies. The liver was eaten raw while the carcass was being cut up, generally dipped in or sprinkled with gall. Gall was also used to clear the throat during a prolonged song session.

[Old-time Indians claimed that buffalo meat tasted better and was more healthful than beef from cattle. I have eaten buffalo meat obtained from the Wild Life Preserve and was unable to detect any difference in the taste, but I am not a connoisseur.]

The meat was commonly prepared by throwing a good-sized chunk on an open fire and barbecuing it until the outside was charred and the inside rare. [This is in accordance with the best cook-out practices of today.] The Indian women also boiled it in their camp kettles. They had no facilities for baking or frying. In order to preserve meat, it was cut into sheets about half an inch thick and hung in the sun. The dry air soon converted the meat into jerky, which could be kept indefinitely. It could then be chewed up raw or soaked in water and boiled. Dried meat was also pounded up with suet to form a pemmican, which was made more tasty by the addition of dried wild plums when available.

The next most useful part of the buffalo was the hide. It was staked out on the grass to dry, after which it was divested of all hair, flesh, and fat by scraping it with a tool made of elk horn or the rib of a buffalo. This backbreaking job, performed by the women, was a source of pride when properly done. The hide was then tanned by rubbing into it a mixture of brains and liver.

Tanned hides were sewed together to form coverings for the tipis, lodges requiring from ten to thirty hides each, depending on the size of the structure. Although all women were trained to do this work, the making of a tipi cover was usually a group enterprise supervised by an expert, and the occasion was a sort of sewing bee. The thread used was sinew, which lies along the spine of the buffalo next to the loin.

124

Hides tanned with the wool on them were used for bedding, and in lieu of overcoats. In the winter some lodge covers were also made of hides with the hair on the inside. When the wool was removed from a hide, some of it was saved to stuff pillows, or pad cradles, saddles, and the like.

Leather made of tanned buffalo hide had many other uses. From it was fashioned all the various articles of horse gear, such as saddles, bridles, halters, hobbles, and lariats. The saddle frame was made of elm wood, which was covered first with green rawhide shrunk on, then with tanned leather. Saddle blankets were pieces of hide.

Leggings and moccasins were made of buffalo hide, but other articles of clothing were made of buckskin or cloth.

Rawhide was used extensively. The thick, tough skin on the neck was used in covering war shields. Ordinary rawhide was fashioned into cases or envelopes called parfleches, in which were packed food, clothing, and equipment. Moccasin soles were rawhide, as were many of the plaited ropes used for tying together the lodge poles, tying packs on the animals, erecting the sun dance lodge, and the like. Sweat lodges were covered with rawhide. Rawhide thongs were used to tie stones to wooden handles to make war clubs. Knife cases and scabbards were made of rawhide and, rarely, quivers were also made of it. Panther skin was the approved material for this latter purpose.

A sheet of rawhide was tied to the center pole of the medicine lodge, and a buffalo skull was placed on the altar.

Medicine men, especially the buffalo medicine men, used the buffalo tail as a ceremonial or medicine switch. All Indians carried buffalo-hide quirts. The hoofs were made into rattles, used in songfests and by medicine men. The sinew, in addition to its use as ordinary thread, was used to fasten spear points to their shafts, as well as arrow heads and feathers. These were made more secure by using a glue made by boiling the lips, gums, and forehead of the buffalo.

Buffalo horns were fastened to a leather skull cap to make a warrior's helmet, something like those worn by the vikings. Few Kiowas and Comanches wore feathered headdresses in battle—few were entitled to do so. The horn was also made into spoons, dippers, and match cases, and often served as a powder horn in the days when muzzle-loaders were common.

Finally, even the dung of the buffalo was useful. On the prairie, when distant from timber, the Indians used dried buffalo chips for fuel. They also piled it up in the form of a little altar on certain ceremonial occasions. ☼

19 ✦ HOLDING THE BUFFALO

L̲ike all the prairie tribes the Kiowas had a pseudomilitary organization, which they called the *Yä'-pähe* and which consisted of six warrior orders. These societies, called "dog soldiers" by the whites, were responsible for the security of the village and for maintaining order. They were in charge of tribal ceremonies, were the leaders in battle, and when a controlled hunt was necessary, they "held the buffalo." Old Iseeo explained what this meant and gave an interesting example.

✦ Small camps did not hold the buffalo. But when the Kiowas were all in a large village, as at the time of the sun dance, it was necessary for the herd to be held. If this was not done, individual hunters would go out in different directions before daylight and thus drive the buffalo away from the village. This might mean that others in need of meat would be unable to find any buffalo, or that the whole village would have to pack up and move again to follow the herd. The soldier society which was holding the buffalo would keep a close watch over the camp to prevent anyone from going out to hunt deer or anything else. They would whip any man whom they caught trying to do so.

When the chiefs decided it was time to make a run on the buffalo,

127

all the hunters would go out mounted until they got within charging distance of the herd. Then they would form a line, with the soldiers scattered along the front to hold back any impatient young men who wanted to start before the signal was given. When everyone had arrived on the line, the chief would give the signal, and the whole crowd would ride straight at the buffalo and start shooting them with bows and arrows. The old men always advised against using guns or revolvers on a buffalo hunt of this kind because the firing frightened the herd so badly that it ran too far from the village. But the buffalo were not usually stampeded by men on horseback killing them with silent weapons.

A bear will run over mountain after mountain before he gets so tired that he must stop. But the buffalo only runs for about three miles before he slows down to a walk. He continues walking for another three miles until his heart quiets down, when he begins to eat grass. Therefore, during the controlled hunt, the men cut out enough meat to last ten or twelve days. During that period the buffalo have again returned to graze not far from the camp, and it is time to make another run.

One summer the Kiowas were holding the buffalo in an area west

of the Wichita Mountains near the North Fork of Red River. They were in the midst of moving camp. Men of the Rattle band, of which Satanta was the head, were acting as soldiers. There were over fifty of us out in front, sitting on our horses on a hill and watching the great buffalo herd that covered the country far out to the front. Behind us, the village was just going into camp.

"Our horses are panting," said Satanta. "We will dismount here and let them rest."

Just then we saw three men far off to the right moving up to run some buffalo. Every one of us saw them.

"Five of you come with me," said Satanta, pointing out several of us. And we rode down the slope to where the three men were getting ready to run the buffalo.

"Hold up!" shouted Satanta. "We are holding the buffalo."

Two of the men were scowling. They would not answer. Satanta asked them, "What is the matter? Are you mad? I am going to tell you something wise. You pick it up and hold it fast. You go back to the village!"

One of the men, who was Kicking Bird's brother-in-law, then replied, "My sister, who is Kicking Bird's wife, is very sick. Coming along the trail today she was all played out. So I am mad."

Satanta told him, "You poor, weak little man! You go back! We are holding the buffalo."

At that, the man struck Satanta's horse across the nose with his quirt, and with the other angry man he bolted forward toward the buffalo. The third man, whose heart had been wiped out [he was subdued], remained behind.

Satanta pulled up his horse, which had begun to run. He told me to bring up our whole group of soldiers. I galloped to where they were resting on the hill. Then, when we had rejoined Satanta, we all started after the two men who were chasing the buffalo. When we got to the top of the ridge, we saw them charge a herd of buffalo, firing their revolvers in the air to scare the animals. After they had scattered the herd, they did the same to another. They weren't getting meat. They were just acting smart.

We all charged after these men, Satanta coming along behind

because his horse was played out. As we got near the two men, one of them stopped, whereupon a soldier shot his horse through the head. It dropped in its tracks without rolling over, and the man stepped off. The soldiers took all his weapons and other things. In a few minutes the other man rode up. Each soldier shot an arrow into his horse and killed it. Satanta took all their arrows and broke them. He broke their bows and cut their robes to pieces.

"You are mad, are you?" he said. "You talk mad to me, and I'll cut you the same way."

Both men stood silent, while Satanta continued to give them good advice. After the soldiers had slashed their saddles and bridles and other belongings, Satanta said, "Every soldier whip them!"

Each soldier rode up to the men and struck them across the face and shoulders with his quirt.

Satanta then said to the two men, "Now I leave you here afoot. No one is allowed to take you up and give you a ride."

It was a very hot day and a long way to water. One man complained, "I didn't do it of my own accord. Kicking Bird told me to do it." The other man, who was Kicking Bird's brother, also said, "Kicking Bird told us to do it."

Satanta replied, "I will go and see Kicking Bird about this." And he went back to where the camp movers were putting up the lodges.

Satanta asked for Kicking Bird. Presently someone answered, "Kicking Bird has not come into camp. His wife is sick. He stopped somewhere back on the trail and will come in later."

We watched for a long time, but Kicking Bird did not come.

Finally we saw two men coming towards the village on foot. Some of us went out to meet them. They were the two whipped men, their faces swollen and bloody. We lent them robes to cover their faces, and they came into camp with their faces covered.

After a while a man came into camp and said, "Kicking Bird has heard about what happened. He is mad. He is going to whip Satanta because Satanta whipped his brother and brother-in-law."

Satanta said, "All right! He started the trouble. Now let him go ahead and whip."

But several days went by and Kicking Bird did not come into

camp. Finally Satanta couldn't stand it any longer. He called all the soldiers to a council and said, "Tomorrow we will go and make peace with Kicking Bird. Everybody saddle up! Bring something that you have that is valuable."

Next day we brought the valuable things—four horses, a white mule, two saddles and bridles, a gun, and some blankets. We made a big pile of these things, then packed them on pack horses. We rode to make peace with Kicking Bird.

He was sitting under his shade when we rode up.

"What have you come here for?" he asked. "To fight?"

Satanta answered, "We have come to give you presents. We want to make peace."

After we had given the presents to Kicking Bird, he said, "All right. I began the trouble. But I do not now feel my heart stabbed anywhere [he was not resentful]. I shake hands with everyone."

Later he explained that he had sent out his two men to drive away the buffalo herd because the village had moved in disobedience to his orders. He had directed that the village stay in place while the buffalo were being held.

Satanta was a big man, and he was older than Kicking Bird. But he was not as wise. Furthermore, I think that Kicking Bird had the stronger medicine. ⚙

20 ❀ A SMALL BOY PROVES HIS COURAGE

J IMMY G UI-TONE RELATED the following story of his boyhood.

❀ I have never taken a scalp. I was too young to go on the raids. The wars were over, and the soldiers had driven us onto the reservation while I was still a boy. But I used to like to sit around the fire and listen to the men tell of the great days on the warpath on the Arkansas, the Cimarron, and south of Red River. Two of the best storytellers were my grandfather, An-zah-te, and his friend Tsen-goodle-cap-tan.

One night these two were arguing and boasting about themselves. An-zah-te said, "You claim to be a warrior, but I see no scars."

"I have some, look!" bragged Tsen-goodle. He had been wounded during the fight when our Kiowas captured a war bonnet from the Cheyennes. My grandfather had never been wounded, but he was a brave man. "I walked from the northern Arkansas River far down into Mexico. Wore out twenty pairs of moccasins. You never did that!"

I couldn't keep quiet. "I wish I had a chance to prove how brave a warrior I am," I said.

The old men laughed. I was only eight years old.

On the following day our village moved out toward the Cap

Rocks, about where the town of Gotebo is now. Tsen-goodle rode up on his pony and asked us boys to come and get some coyote pups out of a den. Several of us went, including Son-to, Do-ya-te, White Arrow, my brother, and myself. My grandfather, his wife, and Son-to's mother were also there.

The old man said, "Everybody get ready now. Dismount. I'm going to test these prospective warriors."

It was my chance. I ran forward to go into the den. The other boys weren't in such a hurry. They gave me a strip of rawhide to tie the legs of the pups. The den was awful deep. And dark. It stunk like a skunk. I could hear something whimpering in there. I lay still a moment. Then I reached out and caught something hairy. It was a tail. I fastened the rawhide to it and began to scramble out backwards, dragging the animal after me. When I was almost clear of the cave there was a terrible snarling. The thing ran out past me, slashing at me with its teeth. It was a big gray wolf, not a coyote. I lost my rawhide. All the people were roaring with laughter. I was trembling all over and wouldn't go in again.

We rode on a ways and found another den.

"Come on boys! who is going to get me a coyote pup?" An-zah-te tried to encourage us. I said nothing. I thought it was some other boy's turn to be a warrior.

My older brother went slowly into the hole. He wasn't laughing now. But he only went in up to his feet. Out he came.

"Can't make it," he said. "Hole is too small."

Then they tried to get Son-to to go. He objected. Said there might be snakes. White Arrow also backed out. So it was up to me.

I was sweating with fear. But I wanted to be a big chief.

It was very dark. Maybe there was another wolf in there. Or some kind of evil god. I crawled slowly on. The rocks and dirt crumbled over my head. Maybe it might cave in on me. A black hairy tarantula ran across my wrist. I wanted to quit. To back out. Then I was again surrounded by that terrible stink. Ahead in the darkness I could see glowing pairs of eyes staring at me. I was quivering all over. But I reached out a bare hand, expecting something to bite it off. I felt something soft and furry. I caught hold of it and squirmed out backwards as fast as I could crawl. I was drag-ging by its tail a coyote pup.

The old women were singing victory songs: "Hi-yah! he-yah! Hi-yah!" honoring the new warrior. The old men were smiling. The other boys' eyes were big and staring. I was very proud. My grandfather was hugely pleased. I handed him the pup.

Then he said, "Who's next? Come on now, let's have some more big warriors!"

My brother must have grown smaller. The hole wasn't too small for him now. He went in and brought out a pup. The other boys forgot about snakes. They went in. I took another turn. Altogether we got eight pups.

Did my grandfather want them for pets? Of course not. He knocked each one on the head and put it in a sack. The old women made a fire and brought up a kettle. My grandmother singed the hair from the carcasses. Then she cut one open, took out the liver and the yellow leaf fat and roasted these delicacies for us. I ate some, as a warrior should. It was fine. Then she dumped the pups in the boiling water and cooked them until they were tender. We peeled the skin off, salted, and ate the meat. It was tender and juicy, much like a suckling pig. My grandfather was extremely fond of it.

That was my medicine. They named me Gui-tone, which means Wolf Tail. ✦

21 ❀ WHAT HAPPENED TO MARY HAMLETON?

Sarina Myres, a white girl, said that her half sister, Mary Hamleton, was murdered. It happened in April, 1867, when the Indians made a raid into the northwestern part of Tarrant County, Texas. But Mary Hamleton lived until 1924, and never knew her own name. She was a captive member of the Kiowa tribe for fifty-seven years.

In the autumn of 1860, James Myres, with his wife and six children, came from Missouri and homesteaded on Walnut Creek in the northern end of Tarrant County. His wife Sally was the daughter of Nathan Allman, who had settled in that area in 1850 and on whose farm a country church had been built.

Myres died a few months after his arrival in Texas. A year later his widow married William Hamleton, by whom she had two children. In the spring of 1867, when tragedy came to this family, the Myres children were William, sixteen, Mahala Emiline, fifteen, Eliza, thirteen, Sarina, eleven, Samuel, nine, and John, seven; the two Hamleton children were Mary L., about five years old, and Gus, an infant of eighteen months.

On the day of the Indian attack, Hamleton had gone some distance to a mill to have his corn ground. The elder son was also away from home herding the cattle. Mahala, Eliza, Samuel, and

John were working in a cotton field; Sarina, Mary, and little Gus were in the house with their mother, who was weaving cloth on a hand loom.

Suddenly, a large band of painted Indians burst from the timber which bordered the nearby stream and rushed toward the cabin, shooting arrows at the children in the field. The latter fled and the Indians, who were intent on attacking the house, did not pursue them.

The raiders were after plunder, and they had learned from past experience that it was a good idea to ransack the farm buildings before attempting to kill any persons who might be outside in the fields. The settlers had a dangerous habit of barricading themselves in their buildings and shooting down any warriors who failed to get inside during the first rush.

In the case of the Hamleton family, no men were present to defend the house. Furthermore, the Indians gained the inside almost before Mrs. Hamleton knew that an attack had occurred. She was killed immediately, the place plundered of everything portable, and the three children seized and carried off.

The next few hours were a nightmare for the terrified children. Sarina, who later told what had happened, remembered a rough, hard ride. She said she was held in front of a brawny savage on his horse, then thrown roughly to the ground when they stopped to camp for the night. Young as the child was, she had enough presence of mind to endure her hardships without a murmur. Little Mary was sick with fever and chills and too young to maintain a stoic attitude like that of Sarina. She cried now and then, which greatly annoyed her captors. The next morning when they broke camp, they abandoned her. Sarina thought that shortly afterward Mary was killed, for none of the family ever saw her again.

Six months later, word was received in Texas that the commanding officer at Fort Arbuckle had ransomed, through the assistance of a friendly Comanche chief named Asa-Havey, two white captives. One of these gave her name as Sarina Myres. Hamleton went to Fort Arbuckle and brought home Sarina and Gus. The Indians said that Mary was dead.

Sarina, on her return to Texas, said the Indians who had captured her were led by Chiefs "Santag" and "Santana." She was referring to Satank and Satanta. The Indian account of the raid, as told by An-pay-kau-te, Satank's oldest son, is as follows:

⚙ In the spring of the year in which the Medicine Lodge Treaty was held [1867], a party of about sixty of us went on a raid into northern Texas. The *to-yop-kes* were Satanta and my father, Satank. We left our camp on the North Fork of Red River, rode south across Red River, about where Doan's store now is, and presently came near a fort where the soldiers kept some Tonkawa Indians as scouts.[1] From there we rode down along the Brazos River for half a day. I think we were somewhere in the timbered country southeast of where Graham, Texas, is now. We found a single white man, killed him, and rode on. Finally we came to a log house. There were some people in the field. I think we killed two; anyway, we had a fight there. Some of them got away.

Some of our men went up to the house and kicked in the door. There was a great big fat woman inside and some children. The woman tried to defend herself, so we killed her. I don't remember how many children there were in the house. We grabbed them and came out on the run. Sait-aim-pay-toy had one girl captive, Ho-to-yeah had another. We rode back toward our own country. That night we stopped to camp in a grove of trees. The next morning when we were breaking camp, one of our men became excited.

"Look at that dust rising in the air behind us on our trail!" he cried. "The Texans are chasing us!" At once we left in a hurry. Sait-aim-pay-toy had wrapped his captive in a blanket. But he thought she would be in the way if we were chased, so he dropped her beside an oak tree. After a few minutes of hard riding, we found that the dust cloud which we had seen was coming from a herd of stampeding cattle. We slowed down.

Sait-aim-pay-toy said, "I left a child behind!"

[1] Fort Griffin, Fort Belknap, and Fort Richardson were in the area in question, about twenty miles apart. I believe that Fort Richardson, near Jacksboro, is referred to here.

"Where did you drop it?" asked Hah-bay-te. "Did you stab it?"

"No. It's back there where we camped last night."

"Then I'm going back after it," said Hah-bay-te. "I want to give it to my daughter. She has no children of her own."

Hah-bay-te took another man with him and went back to pick up the child. I saw it later when he brought it into our village. When he let it down off the horse, it ran around camp in a very lively way. It had fair hair and light blue eyes. We sold our other captives at some army post, but Hah-bay-te's little captive girl never was given up. We all told the army officers that she was dead, but she was brought up in a good Kiowa family, being raised as an Indian girl. Her foster mother's name was Tope-kau-da [Oak Tree or Acorn], and the foster father was a warrior named Tan-goodle, who died a few years later and left his famous medicine lance to Satanta. Tope-kau-da, lonely after the death of her husband, was glad to have the captive white girl as a companion and never would be separated from her.

In the autumn of that year in which we made the raid, we received word that all the tribes were supposed to assemble at Medicine Lodge, in southern Kansas, where the people from Washington were going to give us some annuity goods. They were going to make a treaty with us, but we would not have assembled just for that. The reason that we went there was that we were told the soldiers were going to give us some free food.

It was a big gathering, and we had a fine time. A lot of speeches were made, which we did not understand. The interpreter [Philip McCusker] kept mumbling something, but he spoke only Comanche, and all of us did not know that language. Afterward we learned that they were going to put us on a reservation near the Wichita Mountains; we heard also that all white captives had to be given up. Tan-goodle and Tope-kau-da went off south on the prairie and hid their little white girl.

Some years later, when we were finally driven into Fort Sill and disarmed in the old stone corral, Tope-kau-da painted her foster daughter's hair green, her face red, and kept her covered with a shawl. She taught the girl to keep her eyes down when she was around the white people. In that manner the Kiowas were able to prevent the agent from learning that we had this captive. We had to give up most of our captives, but this little girl and the one you call Millie Durgan remained among us all their lives.

Of course we had lots of Mexican captives too. They preferred to stay with us; they all liked the Indian life. Many captives liked the Indian road because in the old days there were no rules or regulations. We went to bed when we felt like it, got up when we pleased, didn't go to school or office, never had to rush, and we were friendly among ourselves, not quarreling and killing each other. We liked our own food better than yours. Even today we would eat meat three times a day if we could get it.

At first we called the little white girl Tay-han [meaning Tejan or Texan], which we usually named captives from Texas. Later this was changed to To-goam-gat-ty, which means "the woman who holds the medicine, standing in rear of the tipi." This was shortened to To-goam. ✸

George Hunt gave me the story of Mary Hamleton's subsequent life, substantially as follows:

✸ The little captive soon learned to play happily with the other Indian girls. Some of these in later years said that she was generally good natured, but that she had a temper and when angry would "whip them all." She quickly learned to speak perfect Kiowa, and after a few years was unable to remember even one word of English. Like other Indian girls she was taught to ride a horse, and became expert in the use of the lasso. She even enjoyed riding a mustang. No matter how many times she was thrown, she merely laughed and mounted again. As it was the duty of the Indian women to care for the livestock, To-goam soon became expert in raising, training, and doctoring animals.

To-goam grew into a tall, strong woman with a heavy frame and deeply tanned skin. Her hair stayed light brown. In manner, she was an old-time "Indian," but her face still showed that she was white.

When To-goam was about seventeen, the young Kiowa men began to loiter around her foster mother's lodge, watching for an opportunity to "steal" the girl. It was the custom that a young man who threw a sheet or blanket over an unmarried girl and ran away with her was considered to have married her—that is, to have eloped with her. In such a case the man did not have to make presents to the girl's parents. The best families tried to keep their girls from doing this.

Tope-kau-da cut a long elm club which she kept for use on any young man who tried to make off with To-goam. It was desirable that the girl be married properly by Indian custom. Gotebo, brother-in-law of Big Tree and leading male member of Tope-kau-da's family, made plans to marry the girl to a Mexican captive named Ko-do-seet, or Calisay. This fellow was about thirty-two and a widower with several children by a former wife. But he had, or Gotebo had for him, the number of ponies needed to buy a wife. Tope-kau-da hated to give up her foster daughter, but it was the custom.

To-goam, herself, had to do what she was told. After her marriage she used to lie in her tipi and cry for her foster mother. At the same time Tope-kau-da in her lodge was weeping because she missed the girl.

All young Kiowas learned to swim, even the girls, but To-goam was a better swimmer than most. I remember when she showed how strong she was in the water. The old cattle trail which in the eighties and nineties ran north from Texas to Kansas, crossing Red River at Doan's store, had a branch which ran down the valley of Rainy Mountain Creek. This trail crossed Rainy Mountain Creek about five miles south of the present town of Mountain View, Oklahoma, near where Chief Big Tree lived. It was called Big Tree crossing. South of the crossing a smaller creek ran into the main stream, forming a **Y**.

Once a valuable pony tied to a tree in the center of this **Y** was marooned by a flood caused by a cloudburst in the mountains. The animal was about to drown. A number of young Indian men were there, staring at the horse, but none of them were willing to risk swimming the stream to save it.

140

To-goam came up and offered to cut the animal loose. They asked her not to try it, but she took a butcher knife between her teeth, and went into the swiftly running flood. Swimming strongly, she reached the terrified horse, cut him loose, then turned about through a great whirlpool and made her way safely back to the bank. The Kiowa men stood ashamed that they had been outdared by a white captive girl.

To-goam was shy in the presence of white people. This may have been caused by her childhood training, when she was taught always to keep her eyes down when they were around. She seemed ashamed of being a member of the white race. When she had to go to town at Mountain View to buy supplies, she usually painted her face and wore a shawl over her head so as to be taken for an Indian woman. Once she was noticed by a strange white woman who asked the store-keeper if she was part white.

"No," he replied, "she is *pure* white, but cannot speak English."

To-goam apparently realized that they were talking about her, for she quickly swung to her shoulder a sack of flour, as easily as if it had been a sack of feathers, walked out of the store, threw the flour into her wagon, and drove away. She was as strong as a man.

To-goam was brought up in the religion of the Indians, but she became a Christian when the Baptist missionaries came to Rainy Mountain and was baptized by J. J. Clous.

The agency officials realized in later years that she was a white woman, but they made no attempt to return her to Texas. By that time it was too late. She was an "Indian" with a husband and children. They recalled that Cynthia Ann Parker, a white captive from childhood, had died of homesickness when torn away from the Comanches. So To-goam lived and died among the Kiowas. She never knew her white name, never knew whether she had living relatives, nor from what part of Texas she came.

On July 22, 1924, To-goam had a heart attack and died. She is buried in the Rainy Mountain Baptist Mission cemetery, where Big Tree and many other famous warriors now lie. She was survived by two sons, five daughters, and many grandchildren, one of whom attended the University of Kansas. These children consider themselves to be Kiowa, although their mother was a white woman and their father a Mexican.

We Kiowas wonder whether any of Mary Hamleton's white kinfolk are still living in Texas and whether they have heard what happened to her. She led a happy life with her foster people. Her medicine was good. ✲

22 ☼ WHITE HORSE CATCHES
A NAVAHO

AY-TAH, at one time the wife of Set-maunte, furnished the details of this story.

☼ White Horse had a reputation in the Kiowa tribe as being an active, tough, and reckless fellow. It was the practice for Indian boys to become proficient in horsemanship by constant training from childhood. They learned how to pick up objects from the ground while at a full gallop and how to rescue comrades who were wounded, or even how to pick up and carry off the bodies of men who had been killed. Of course, it required two or more men acting as a team to pick up a man without dismounting, and usually the man who was being rescued had to be able to assist by hobbling along and lifting his arms. Another trick which the boys learned to perform was to pick up a lariat by flipping it into the air with the end of a bow.

White Horse was adept in all these things, and because of his unusual strength, he could even pick up a child while at a gallop. He demonstrated this ability in a spectacular fashion on a raid against the Navahos.

In the summer of 1867, the Kiowas and Comanches went on a revenge raid against the Navahos in New Mexico. The Navahos had killed a Comanche, and one of his closest relatives had circulated the pipe among both the Kiowa and Comanche tribes. A large number of warriors accepted the pipe. Furthermore, special preparations were made before the raid started. The Navahos, whose tribe numbered ten thousand, were able to muster more fighters than the Kiowas and Comanches combined. Consequently, extra pains and time were taken to insure that the expedition was well equipped and heavily armed.

When the war party neared the Navaho country, scouts were sent out far ahead of the main body to locate small parties of the enemy or some isolated village. The Kiowas and Comanches had no intention of attacking any substantial number of Navahos. Iseeo, who was on this raid, said that they all were constantly on the alert and kept their attention fixed on the distant scouts, who would signal to them when the enemy was sighted.

Late one evening, they saw three scouts on a far ridge making individual circles with their horses. This was the customary signal that the enemy had been discovered. The number of circles had a specific meaning as to the strength and activity of the enemy.

At once the warriors started to build altars of buffalo chips, all a part of the ritual of preparing for battle. Behind the altars stood the older men, singing the Scout-Coming-Song, "Ko'k-eah-day-dau-gia." At the same time the other warriors began to parade by galloping across between the altars and the approaching scouts. The excitement increased.

On arrival within easy shouting distance, the scouts halted on line while their leader rode out to the front to give the news which they were bringing. One of the song leaders, usually the *to-yop-ke* of the raid, took a long straw in his hand and walked up to the leader of the scouts. The scout leaned down and the leader thrust the straw in his hair. That was the cue for him to tell his story. He withdrew the straw and gave a full report of everything the scout detachment had seen and done. The scouts had to be accurate and truthful, but not wordy. The time might be short, and the enemy approaching.

In the case of this raid, the scout leader stated that they had discovered a Navaho mud village about a half a night's journey to the west.

At once the war party started in that direction. During the night they stopped once to take food. At this halt the Comanche who had gotten up the raid began crying again for his slain relative. Probably this was for effect and to stimulate all the warriors to great effort to wipe out the sorrow. It was the custom.

He offered the horse that he was riding as a prize to anyone who would make a real effort to kill a Navaho and thus insure that the revenge was accomplished. The animal was a valuable one, being brown with black ears, especially prized by the Indians. For a time there was no response. Acceptance of the horse meant that a man had to incur a very real risk and make every effort to kill one of the enemy. He couldn't back out of the bargain once it had been made. A Kiowa named Kaun-pah-te had recently been refused admittance into the Ko-eet-senko because the degree of his bravery was still questioned. This was preying on his mind. He was in a reckless mood, but he was not reckless enough to accept the offer of the Comanche.

Finally Lone Wolf sent for the horse, and was duly thanked by the Comanche for accepting the hazardous mission.

As the advance continued, it began to get light in the east. They halted to await the dawn. As the shadows began to lift, they could see the smoke rising from the Navaho village, now dimly visible straight ahead. With its cluster of low mud hogans, it looked in the distance, except for the smoke, like a prairie-dog town.

The war party slipped closer for the final assault. Just as they were nearing the outskirts of the village, they saw a few children running to the nearest hogans. White Horse dashed after them. He seized a half-grown Navaho boy by the hair and yanked the youth up behind him. It was like an eagle snatching a rabbit.

By this time the attack was well under way. There was much whooping and shouting from the men and screaming from the women and children. A few guns were fired, and the air was filled with arrows.

More and more Navahos poured from their hogans. None of the allies had been able to get a scalp. But it was seen that White Horse had a captive. They could scalp him, so they began to withdraw.

The enemy was stronger than they had bargained for. They were pressing the pursuit relentlessly. The Kiowas and Comanches began to ride faster. Then they made a short stand, but in a moment they were fleeing again. Some of the men were wounded. Two or three horses fell, but the riders were instantly taken up by others.

The loss of the horses worked in their favor, for the Navahos, who evidently had been short of food for some time, stopped to butcher the wounded animals. The Kiowas, who should have used this opportunity to gain distance on their pursuers, stopped, turned about, and some of them made a charge on the Navahos. Most of the latter were still mounted, but in some cases they were riding two to a horse. The Kiowas noticed that one of the enemy who was riding tandem had dropped off and was shooting at the Kiowas and Comanches. About this time Kaun-pah-te's horse stopped and shuddered. It was dying from exhaustion. A Navaho ran up and drew his bow on Kaun-pah-te. The latter swung his shield around to the front, but held it too high. The Navaho drove an arrow up under it and into Kaun-pah-te. The Kiowa fell to the ground. No one was able to rescue his body.

The distance between the opposing sides had now lengthened to about three hundred yards. The Kiowas and Comanches were chattering about the Navaho marksman who had knocked off Kaun-pah-te. He seemed to be a dead shot. They decided to make an attempt to get him. When the Navahos made their next charge, they watched for a chance.

The Comanche chief Black Horse, wearing a long war bonnet, and Lone Wolf made a dash after the enemy bowman. Black Horse was in the lead. At this point the Navahos abandoned their marksman and withdrew. The latter, seeing he was alone, turned to flee, but it was too late. Black Horse lanced him at full speed, and the victim rolled over and over. When Black Horse and Lone Wolf dismounted to collect the scalp, they could see and hear the Navahos in a heated argument among themselves over having abandoned their sharpshooting hero to his fate.

The Kiowas and Comanches resumed their withdrawal. It was a terrible experience, for the pursuit lasted for twenty-five to thirty miles. The enemy hung on to their flank and rear grimly, trying to pick some of them off. Two more men were lost, a Kiowa and a Comanche. Finally, when they were nearly exhausted, the enemy gave up the chase.

White Horse brought his captive boy back to the home camp. He soon became tame and adjusted to living with the Kiowas. White Horse adopted him as his son, and the boy grew up to be a Kiowa warrior. Later he married Gia-gi-hodle, and had two sons. One of these, Au-sau-hay, lived to old age and has stepchildren living today. ☼

23 ✸ STUMBLING BEAR
SCALPS A UTE

ONE OF THE MOST TRAGIC EPISODES in Kiowa history occurred in the summer of 1868, when Chief Heap-of-Bears and six of his men were killed by the Utes. The latter also captured two of the *Tai-me* idols, which were never recovered. Andrew Stumbling Bear told me the story of the revenge raid which inevitably followed.

✸ After the Medicine Lodge Treaty, we Kiowas moved down to Fort Cobb, where our new agent had promised to issue rations. He wasn't there when we arrived. Therefore, since it was late in the fall, Kicking Bird took all of us who were in his band up the Washita on a buffalo chase to get our winter meat supply. Stumbling Bear then brought the pipe around to get men to go with him to recover the bodies of Heap-of-Bears and his party and to try to get revenge on the Utes. Several men joined him—he wanted only a few.

Since Stumbling Bear had been in the fight, he knew where to go. He led the group beyond the head of the Washita, then northwest to Beaver Creek [the South Canadian]. They followed its north bank for several days until they came to Red River Spring.[1] Here they found the dead, all of them skeletons. But Stumbling Bear could tell who each was by the scattered clothing and other belong-

[1] Near where the South Canadian crosses the New Mexico border.

148

ings. The Utes had made a beaten circle around Heap-of-Bears, evidently in a victory dance. He had been carrying two of the *Tai-mes* in a bag on his back, but they were gone, and we have never seen them again.

After Stumbling Bear and his friends had buried the bones in a safe place, they rode westward again, hoping to kill one or two Utes so that our hearts would feel better. They didn't plan to attack a large party of Utes, but only hoped to catch one off by himself. The Utes had a custom that when they saw men of a strange tribe, they would charge instantly. Therefore Stumbling Bear's party would be in great danger as soon as they entered the Ute country.

Two scouts were sent out ahead. On the second day they were just at the top of a long hill when they signalled that they had sighted the enemy on the other side of the crest. Stumbling Bear, riding a little ahead of the main body, hurried to overtake the scouts. They motioned to him that there was only one Ute, evidently out hunting. All three men immediately galloped over the hill and down the far slope to catch him.

Years later, when we had made peace with the Utes, we learned their side of this story. Their chief had forbidden anyone to go out alone, because a Kiowa revenge raid was expected. Two Utes had gone deer hunting before daylight and had become separated. The man seen by our scouts was following the trail of a wounded deer and had his eyes on the ground. Thus, he didn't see the Kiowas until they were bearing down on him at full speed.

The Ute started to ride down the hill, loading his gun as he went. Then he turned to fire. As he did so, his horse jumped a deep-worn buffalo trail, throwing him to the ground. At once the Kiowas were upon him, thrusting at him ineffectually with their spears as he dodged about. The scouts then jumped from their horses, seized the Ute, and threw him flat. They held him down while Stumbling Bear scalped him. All three at once mounted and rode quickly back to rejoin their group. The whole party began a rapid withdrawal from the Ute country, having accomplished all they had come for.

After the Kiowas vanished, the scalped Ute walked toward his village. On the way he stopped at the house of a white man, apparently a doctor, who treated his wound, bandaged his head, and took him in a wagon to his tipi.

By the following summer the Ute had practically recovered from his injury when his tipi was entered suddenly early one foggy morning by Big Bow. The lone Kiowa raider killed the Ute silently with a knife. No one else was in the tipi, and no one had seen him enter. When Big Bow started to take the scalp, he found to his astonishment that the man had already been scalped. So he took the war bonnet instead, as a trophy.

For this reason the Kiowas named the medicine dance in the summer of 1869 "the Sun Dance When He Brought the War Bonnet."

When Big Bow visited the Utes in 1893, they told him that the man he killed was the same one that Stumbling Bear had scalped. ✣

24 ❀ HAU-VAH-TE AND THE OWL

HOODLE-TAU-GOODLE, daughter of the famous Maman-ti, supplied this story about one of her father's apprentices.

❀ The Kiowas were very superstitious about owl prophecies. They dared not make fun of this medicine in any way, lest misfortune, even death, overtake them. When they went off to war or on raids, they always tried to take with them a medicine man who was an owl prophet. It was his duty to prophesy the outcome of the raid, especially telling what booty each man would capture and whether any of them would be hurt or killed. If the omens happened to be unfavorable in some cases, the man or men affected might turn back, or even the whole expedition might be abandoned.

Maman-ti was the great owl prophet, and so experienced and wise was he that his presence on a raid almost guaranteed success. Often he was the real leader, even though one or more chiefs might be a member of the party. In his medicine pouch he carried the cured skin of an owl, which was a triumph of the taxidermist's art. It was perfectly lifelike when slipped on over the magician's hand, even to its eyes, which were made of yellow buttons with pupils painted on them. When Maman-ti exhibited this little creature apparently perched on his wrist, turned its head around to gaze at the crowd and, without moving his lips, made a twittering soft call of the screech owl, few Kiowas doubted that he had a real bird. Few wished to doubt. They came eagerly with gifts, which the medicine man graciously accepted in the name of the owl.

As each man came forward and offered a prayer, the prophet responded with a short forecast which was sufficiently ambiguous to be susceptible of later interpretation in the light of what actually happened. And so Maman-ti's reputation increased greatly with each successful raid. It became increasingly difficult to get up a raid unless he was a member.

On one occasion, however, a crowd of some seventy to eighty men assembled for a horse-stealing expedition down into Texas. It was hoped, too, that some of the buffalo soldiers [Negroes of the Tenth Cavalry] might sally from Fort Concho or one of the other frontier posts and give chase. In this case additional fun might be anticipated. But at the last minute Maman-ti was unable to go. Perhaps he had an infected foot or other ailment. This was pretty serious. For a time it was thought that the raid would be called off. But all arrangements had been made, the dance had been held, and there were quite a few young men for whom this was to be a first experience on the warpath. They didn't want to be disappointed.

So Maman-ti proposed that one of his three apprentice medicine men go in his stead. He selected Tape-day-ah, who was something of a hero anyway because of his grueling experience on the raid in the mountains when Hone-zep-tai was lost. He had been studying under Maman-ti faithfully for a long time, and the great owl prophet felt that the young shaman could stage a creditable performance. Maman-ti would not, however, trust the imitation owl out of his possession. Privately he instructed Tape-day-ah to try to capture a live owl, and suggested places where he would be most apt to find one. Most Indians would have nothing to do with owls and knew little about their roosting or nesting places.

The great raiding party crossed Red River at their favorite ford near the present location of Quanah, Texas, and moved southward for two nights. They traveled only after dark and rested and slept in groves of trees during daylight. On the third morning they bivouacked in some woods along a little creek. Toward evening Tape-day-ah went alone to the edge of the stream and searched through the hollow trees for an owl. Presently he caught one, probably a fledgling which, though fully feathered, had not yet left the nest. As he brought it back to the bivouac, one of the men spied him holding the bird in his hand. At once there was a commotion.

"Everyone come here," the man called. "Tape-day-ah has a live owl! Something very important about our journey is about to be told, I think."

Each Indian was awakened as the word was passed softly along. Every man began going through his possessions to select some present to make to the owl.

All except Hau-vah-te. He asked his partner, Set-maunte, "I don't have anything. What are they giving?"

Set-maunte replied, "Anything you have is quite all right. Surely you have something that you can give! It is very important that we have a good forecast."

Already the men were getting into line to take turns making gifts to the owl, such as colored handkerchiefs, rings, pieces of hair-pipe, or other ornaments. But Hau-vah-te had stripped himself of all such things before he started on the raid.

"I wonder if it would be satisfactory if I gave him an arrow?" he asked his partner.

Set-maunte laughed. "Don't be foolish," he said. "No one gives away his weapons when on the warpath."

Quite an argument ensued between the two friends, following which the annoyed Hau-vah-te slipped off into the brush and cut a small club, which he concealed next to his chest under his blanket. By the time he returned to where the medicine show was in progress, his place was at the end of the line. The line moved slowly; as each man approached the sacred bird and made his offering, which he placed at the feet of the prophet, he laid his hand gently on the owl's head, spoke an earnest prayer, and received his prophecy. Finally it was Hau-vah-te's turn. All the rest of the crowd were standing around to hear what would be said in his case.

"I have nothing to give but *this*!" cried Hau-vah-te, stepping

153

forward. He pulled out his concealed club and struck the owl on the head, killing it.

The apprentice prophet, Tape-day-ah, stood looking at the owl with its lifeless head hanging over on one side. A sheepish grin spread slowly over his face, for he was under no illusion about the nature of the whole business. Seeing this, a number of Indians, led by Big Bow, laughed heartily. But not the majority. A gasp of dismay and a groan swept over the crowd. This was the worst omen they could imagine. A few of the more timorous and apprehensive even wept. Things looked hopeless. Then an angry muttering spread through the assembly. Some of them wanted to give Hau-vah-te a severe beating. One man continued to pray to the owl. "Oh Grandmother," he moaned, "make Hau-vah-te's face be all twisted. And don't fix him up afterwards!"

This was in reference to the fact that the Kiowas frequently suffered from Bell's palsy, a temporary paralysis of the side of the face, thought by them to be caused by having offended a god or violated a taboo. But Tape-day-ah intervened. He persuaded the Indians to go ahead with the raid. He had secret medicine, he said, very powerful, which would overcome the effect of Hau-vah-te's horrid deed.

And so it turned out. Nothing untoward occurred during the raid, which was in fact a mild success. Not a thing happened to Hau-vah-te. He had killed the owl to prove that he didn't suffer from that superstition. Since he didn't believe in it, it couldn't hurt him! ❖

25 ✿ THE MEDICINE HORSE

VIOLENT STORMS STRUCK THE PLAINS at times. Bolts of lightning often started holocausts when the grass was dry. Not too uncommon were the freak hailstroms in which chunks of ice as big as hen's eggs were hurled upon the prairie. But most of all, the Indian dreaded the tornado. In much of its wide expanse the land offered no place of refuge. The Indians believed that the cataclysmic whirlwind had a demoniac origin. An old Kiowa once told me of a day when he saw a great black cloud rushing toward him. In its midst, a hundred feet or more above the earth, was a group of struggling black objects. Suddenly the whirlwind veered and roared past him. In the cloud he saw that the tumbling objects were buffalo. They had been sucked up in the vortex and were being carried along through the air.

Here, Iseeo describes a tornado which he saw at close range.

✿ One time a Kiowa war party was returning from the Ute country. Plenty Stars was the leader, though among the ordinary members were several famous chiefs including old Lone Wolf, principal chief of the Kiowas. I was with them also.

We came to the big bend in the upper Washita where the year before Custer wiped out Black Kettle's village. The skeletons of the Cheyenne still lay where they had fallen. As we sat on our horses looking at the dead Cheyennes, we saw a great black cloud coming from the southwest.

Plenty Stars shouted, "Dismount! It is going to rain hard!"

We all dismounted and started to make shelters. Soon we heard an approaching roar that sounded like buffalo in the rutting season. We all looked to see what it was. Gradually the black cloud dipped a leg down to the earth. The center was red. Bolts of lightning shot down through the center, setting the grass on fire. The leg began tearing through the timber along the Washita, uprooting trees and flinging them in the air.

It was coming straight toward us. We were terribly afraid. As it got near, it made our hair stand straight up.

We wanted to try and get away by running. But the old men said, "No! Try hard! Try hard now! Brace up! We understand about this. It is the horse that Sindi[1] and the Boys made that is causing the big whirlwind. Get out all the pipes and light them!"

Then the chiefs got out seven or eight pipes, lighted them, and pointed the stems to the cloud, calling out to it, "Smoke it! Smoke it!" They begged the storm to go around and pass us by without hurting us.

"Don't come here!" they cried. "Pass on around us!"

They prayed hard to the cloud, and it heard them. It understood Kiowa. They prayed to it, and it passed around us and went away. We were saved, but it was very close.

Then we went and looked at its trail. It had twisted off several big trees in the middle. It had torn out others by the roots, trees so big that a man could hardly reach his arms around their trunks. It carried these great trees through the air like birds. It cut a wide path through the timber. It even sucked up the grass and weeds, leaving the ground bare. In one place a rock had been shattered, and was in pieces.

That storm was the great medicine horse whom we called "Monka-yee." *Monka* means "sleeve." I don't know what *yee* means.[2] ⚙

[1] Sindi was a mythical hero.
[2] John P. Harrington's *Vocabulary of the Kiowa Language* (Washington, Government Printing Office, 1928) states that *man-ka-ih* means "cyclone." Probably this is because of the resemblance of the tornado funnel to a giant sleeve.

26 ✦ THE TENDER-SKIN RAID

OLD AN-ZAH-TE HAD A FRIEND whom the Kiowas called Red-Clay Paint Man because he went around naked all the time, his nudity concealed only by a coat of red paint. The Indians regarded this behavior as highly eccentric and even comical, which brings out the little known fact that these people were sometimes embarrassed if they were seen in the "raw" by strangers. At least they felt that way as early as 1870, having by that time had sufficient contact with white men to realize that it was then considered extremely unstylish to go around unclad.

In preparing for almost any desperate enterprise, however, an Indian warrior generally stripped off his clothing and divested himself of any equipment that would impede his movements. When the occasion for this was over, he hurried to dress himself, and if he was unable to do so, he was not at all comfortable, as is illustrated by several stories I have heard. The one which follows is a good example, and a later one involving Big Bow is another. The tale given below also indicates that the Indians, like fighters of other races, were not always bold and courageous, but experienced moments of panic.

George Hunt tells the story; he heard it from Komalty, one of the participants.

☀ In the spring of the year in which the Warren Wagon Train Massacre occurred [1871], A-to-tain, brother of Pago-to-goodle and Sun Boy, led a small raid into Texas. The group included another experienced warrior named Komalty [Friendship Tree], a sixteen-year-old apprentice, A-man-te, and a Kiowa-Mexican named Podo-say for whom this was the first warpath experience. They headed south across Red River toward the timbered country below where Graham [Texas] is now. Before reaching the settlements, the raid-ers established a headquarters where they cached their extra cloth-ing and equipment, their saddles, and their horses. The mounts of A-to-tain, Komalty, and A-man-te were left hobbled, but they took with them Podosay's scrawny pony as a pack horse. To it they tied their bridles and lariats and a bag of dried meat. They carried only their weapons and war shields, and traveled on foot—all except Podosay, who was allowed to ride the pack animal.

They started out from the raid headquarters early in the evening and traveled through the night. Toward dawn they bivouacked in a mesquite thicket. The pack horse was thrown on his side and hog-tied, for he might disclose their presence if allowed to graze. He lay there all day, moaning and sighing while they slept. At dusk they untied him, let him drink and graze for a while. Then they resumed the journey.

The Indians traveled by night in this fashion for two days, by the end of which they had consumed most of their food and still had not seen any horses which A-to-tain considered safe to steal. They prowled around the ranches and farms after dark, hoping to see some unguarded stock in the moonlight and to hear a cowbell which would lead them to an animal they could kill for food. At length they saw a pair of yoked oxen in an open shed. Two of the men wanted to kill one of these, but A-to-tain would not permit it.

"We can't stay here long enough to butcher the meat, and besides, if we kill one of the oxen, the other will take fright and drag away the carcass," he said.

As they were leaving the farmyard, they heard a wagon coming up the road. As they prepared to attack it, they heard two men in the vehicle singing lustily. For some unexplained reason this caused the Indians to abandon the attack. As they stole away, one of them said, "Listen to those fellows singing as they drive to their home!"

Later, A-to-tain said, "We'll get a good night's rest, then travel for a longer stretch until we come to a settlement near a timbered mountain, where I feel sure we will find some horses, and something to eat, as well."

While they were lying on the ground in a thicket, unable to sleep on account of their gnawing hunger, the men heard Podosay chewing on something. "He must have hidden some food," whispered Komalty. "Let's search him." But when they grabbed Podosay, they found that he was chewing on a piece of sinew. "If we don't get something to eat pretty soon," he complained, "we'll be eating our bowstrings."

By daylight the Indians were well on their way once more. They came to a timbered hill, beyond which was a settlement of painted houses. As they neared the crest of the hill, they heard some loud talking on the other side. Peering cautiously over the top, they saw a crowd of soldiers unsaddling their horses and turning them loose to graze. It appeared that they had just completed an all-night march and were making camp.

A-to-tain and Komalty got some ropes from the pack horse and stole through the woods to where the horses were grazing. While the soldiers were occupied with making camp, the two Kiowas lassoed a couple of the horses. Just as they were tying lariats to the halters to lead them away, they were spied by a soldier who began shouting to his companions. Though the Indians wanted to drive away the herd, they feared that there was not time enough to do so before the whole group of soldiers came up, so they decided to withdraw at once. They called to A-man-te and Podosay to jump on the pack horse and ride away as fast as they could go. They mounted the two animals they had captured and started to follow.

Most of the soldiers were unable to catch horses quickly enough to follow them because the herd had started to stampede at the commotion set up by the discovery of the raiders. But several of them, armed only with pistols, jumped on their mounts and, guiding them only by the halters, went in pursuit.

Podosay's old nag, a slow horse at best, and now burdened with two riders, wasn't making much speed. A-to-tain dashed up and began applying the quirt, but without marked success. He saw that the soldiers would be sure to overtake them unless some desperate measure was undertaken. He saw also that the other three men were in a state of panic. They were forgetting to use their bows and arrows to slow down the pursuers. Indeed, they didn't seem to remember that they had weapons with them, but were intent only on escape.

A-to-tain yelled to Komalty, "I'm going ahead into the timber, where I will stop and start shooting at them while the rest of you try to get away." As he gained the timber, the soldiers had come within range, but they were slowing down, suspicious that more Indians might be waiting in ambush. This pause gave A-to-tain time to dismount, tie his horse to a tree, and start using his repeating rifle on the enemy. The soldiers began firing their pistols back into the trees, making the dust fly on all sides of A-to-tain. But their shooting was wild because they were having a hard time controlling their mounts, using only the halters.

A-to-tain saw that his companions had not deserted him. They had dismounted, secured their horses, and were dodging back and forth behind the tree trunks. Just then a group of the enemy came close enough to shoot the bark from the trees in front of their very noses. This threw A-man-te and Podosay into another state of shock. A-man-te threw himself to the ground and started to pray in a loud voice. "O listen to me, great god of the Grandmother medicine," he howled, "if our lives are spared by your protection, I will offer a sweat lodge to you!"

Podosay was lying on his face, absolutely frozen with fright. On his back was a full quiver of arrows, but he had not used a single one.

When Komalty and A-to-tain saw this, they began to laugh, in spite of the sharp peril facing them all. Stripping off their clothes, the two warriors called to the two younger men to do the same. "And get busy with your bows and arrows!" yelled the leader. This brought the two apprentices out of their befuddled state. This episode, especially Podosay's discreditable part in it, has been a standing joke in the tribe ever since.

In a few moments all four Indians were completely naked and were stringing their bows. A-to-tain called to Komalty, "Now we are up against it. I have a cartridge jammed in my gun!"

"I have a ramrod tied to my back," answered Komalty. "Take it and clear your rifle." A-to-tain was soon able to resume firing.

He was just in time, for at that moment a sergeant rode up and fired his pistol at A-to-tain. The latter shot the man's horse, throwing the sergeant to the ground. He got up and started to run, but fell again. He had been hit. A-to-tain wanted to make coup, but the other soldiers were trying to rescue their comrade. The Indians pulled back deeper into the woods. The enemy did not follow, and for a few minutes the firing died out.

A-to-tain took advantage of the lull to order his men to get on their horses and clear out. He said that he would follow them.

"My horse has been hit," called Komalty.

"Take mine, I'll follow on foot. Hurry!" shouted A-to-tain. He continued to fire until he saw that the soldiers had pulled back to the edge of the woods. He could see that what had saved his party was the fact that the enemy were riding bareback with only halters for bridles and that they could not guide their mounts well enough to follow the Indians closely and fire their pistols accurately at the same time. Komalty said later that if the soldiers had had saddles, bridles, and rifles, they would have wiped out the small party of Kiowas.

While the soldiers were carrying their wounded leader back to a safe place, A-to-tain ran to the rear. His men had not gone far, but were waiting for him. Komalty picked him up, and they all dashed away. As they rode, they heard the firing break out again to the rear.

After riding several miles down a country road, the Kiowas passed a house, in front of which were tied several saddled horses. In a nearby field was a herd of loose horses and two or three that were hobbled. The men didn't dare go up to the house to take the saddled horses, but they turned into the pasture, where they readily caught two of the hobbled animals, thus providing mounts for all four of them. They started to drive away the loose herd.

About this time several white men came out of the house, saw the Indians, mounted their horses, and started in pursuit. Since they quickly began to overtake the Indians, Komalty and A-to-tain pulled up and fired back at them. The white men stopped and began to discuss this among themselves. They seemed uncertain about what to do next.

"They must have seen how awful we looked without our clothes," said Komalty later. "We felt very uncomfortable about it. We started out again to follow the other two. We thought for a minute that the whites had given up the chase, but here they came again. On their fast horses they drew near enough to fire their pistols at us. They made it so hot for us that we had to give up trying to drive away the loose horses and pay attention to getting away safely.

"After the enemy had fallen behind and were no longer to be seen, we calmed down enough to realize that we were still naked. We also noticed that we were blistering our legs by riding bareback without pants or leggings. Finally we got so sore that we dismounted and grabbed some grass with which to make pads in place of saddles or blankets. But grass wouldn't stay in place, and was soon gone.

"At last we arrived back at our headquarters. We were in bad shape. Remembering that we were hungry, we killed one of our ponies, roasted, and ate some of the meat. Then we felt better. All

of us had left saddles and spare clothing at the headquarters except Podosay. He had lost his saddle during the raid. So he had to ride all the way home without clothing or saddle. It was a tough ride for all of us, with the skin gone from the inside of our legs, but it was especially hard for Podosay.

"When we got back to the village, A-man-te made the sweat lodge he had promised to the Grandmother medicine. Since his prayers for safety had been answered, he had thereafter a strong faith in the medicine to which he had cried for help.

"Podosay started bragging about his bravery as a warrior, and what big things he had done on the warpath. He kept this up so much that no one in the tribe could stand him. He married a Comanche woman and went to live with Parra-o-coom's band. When Mackenzie attacked that camp the next year, Podosay ran away, leaving his wife to be killed or captured. We laugh about Podosay's big scare every time we get together for a session of storytelling." ✿

27 ✿ QUITAN'S MEDICINE FAILS

GEORGE HUNT TOLD ME THIS STORY of a Kiowa-Mexican's bad luck.

✿ Quitan, a captive Mexican member of the Kiowa tribe, was the grandfather of Parker Mackenzie, a prominent Kiowa of modern times. He was born about 1852 of Spanish parents in the city of Chihuahua, Mexico. His father, a member of the Mexican army, was traveling with his wife and children from one military post to another when the party was attacked by Comanche Indians. All were killed except the boy, then named Esteban. A year later the Comanches traded him to the Kiowas for a spotted pony.

The captive grew up as a member of the tribe, becoming popular because of his good humor, his willing, active spirit, and later for his enterprise and courage on the warpath. He often accompanied Big Bow on the latter's solitary raids. Big Bow grew so fond of Quitan that he gave him one of his sisters as a wife.

In spite of his unfailing good cheer and normally generous nature, Quitan kept a few things to himself. One was his medicine, which he didn't discuss with anyone. Another item was his supply of pipe tobacco. Though he was willing to share his tobacco to a certain extent, he always reserved a little private supply for himself while on a long raid.

164

All the Kiowas relished a good smoke when they were on the warpath—or at any time—but when they were gone from the home camps for a long time, their supplies usually ran out. They were not thrifty like Quitan.

Quitan knew that if he carried his mixture of tobacco and dried sumac leaves in the ordinary way in the usual beaded pouch, he would either have to share it freely, or the others would take it from him. If generosity was not forthcoming, force would be applied. Therefore, he devised a secret hiding place. In those days all Indians wore their hair long, usually in braids around which they wrapped red flannel or otter fur for decoration. Some aging men suffered from baldness, so that their locks were too thin and scraggly to make an attractive long and fat braid. In such cases they usually made a "rat" out of buffalo wool or hair with which they stuffed their braids to make them more full. Quitan did not need to augment his braids, but he carefully thinned them out, then devised a rat from a long hollow tube. In this he stuffed his smoking mixture, plugged up the open end, and wrapped his braid around it. He carried, in this manner, a generous supply in each braid. Since Quitan's hair was obviously thick, no one remarked on the rather full appearance of his braids.

The Indians had been out on a raid for a long time. Their tobacco had been exhausted for a week or more, and already they were starved for a smoke. Even Quitan's supply seemed to have been used up. But presently several members of the party noticed that the Mexican occasionally reeked of tobacco smoke. No one ever saw him using his pipe, yet they suspected that he had a supply concealed somewhere in his equipment or on his person. They searched him thoroughly several times but found nothing. Yet the odor of tobacco smoke was still on him, especially in the evening or early morning.

What was happening was that Quitan would sneak off into the darkness for a quiet, private smoke. The other Indians, still suspicious, took to watching him carefully but not ostentatiously. Quitan realized what was going on, so he refrained from smoking for several nights. But the urge was too powerful. So one evening, instead of going off into the brush for a smoke, he rolled up in his blanket somewhat apart from the rest of the group, but still in sight of them.

He pulled his blanket over his head, took out his bone pipe, stuffed it with tobacco, and lit up. Knowing that he had only a few moments of privacy, he smoked furiously. In his eagerness and greed he puffed so hard that he almost asphyxiated himself. He passed out. The pipe fell from his hands and set his blankets to smoldering.

The Kiowas, seeing this, rushed toward him and rolled him out of the blanket. The open air revived Quitan, who opened his eyes, saw the commotion, and thought, pitifully, that his friends had come to pour water on him and put out the fire. Not at all. They simply snatched his pipe, appropriated his tobacco supply, and proceeded to use up the entire hoard. To the hapless Quitan they paid not the slightest attention. If he had burned up, no one would have been concerned.

Quitan feared that something was wrong with his medicine.

A few days later they were straggling along on foot through the no-water country, having left their horses far behind in a raid headquarters near Sun Spring. The water holes where they stopped had mostly dried up as a result of a drouth. Heat waves were shimmering across the alkali flats. The sky was lemon yellow. Even the jack rabbits stayed in the shade of the cacti, and the prairie dogs were in their burrows. The Indians' eyes were bloodshot, their mouths dry and cotton-like.

All of a sudden the leading man saw a little pool in the trail ahead. At once they raced, each man for himself, striving to be the first to reach the muddy water. There didn't appear to be enough to go around.

In the lead was Quitan, fleet of foot and a noted runner in the tribe. He reached the pool at headlong speed, slipped in the mud at its edge, and fell flat and outspread in the middle of the puddle. All the water splashed out and was lost in the sand. No one got a drink.

Truly, Quitan's medicine had grown weak. ✸

28 ✹ TOO YOUNG TO DIE

GEORGE HUNT HEARD THE FOLLOWING STORY from his Uncle Iseeo, who was an eyewitness to some of the events described. They occurred in 1869 and 1872.

✹ In the summer of the War Bonnet Sun Dance, forty Kiowas went on a raid into southwest Texas. White Horse's younger brother, Kom-pai-te, a boy of fourteen, wanted to go with them. Though he was told that he was too young, he tagged along anyway, accompanied by a friend of the same age. The older Indians, though annoyed, did not send the boys back.

After crossing Red River, the party came to the place where they were to make their raid headquarters. Two men were left there to guard the extra equipment. The *to-yop-ke* wanted to leave the boys there also, but the youngsters insisted on continuing with the group. Finally an area was reached where the boys would be a serious handicap. Iseeo was deputized to tell them that they would simply *have* to turn back to the headquarters.

So Iseeo said, "Now boys, you are too young to go any farther. You can't stand this day-and-night travel. I want you to turn back." But they obstinately refused.

At midday the Indians were resting, with their horses unsaddled.

Finally Kom-pai-te told Iseeo that they would go back if he would give them a plug of tobacco. They happened to know that Iseeo had found five plugs which had been cached by some Mexican traders.

Iseeo gave them the tobacco, whereupon the boys saddled a horse and a mule and mounted up. Before they left, Kom-pai-te went to where the men were resting and smoking and said, "When we came on this journey we thought we were going to get some help from you men. You can go on now; we are returning to the headquarters. But don't bring too many horses. They would be hard to drive. We'll wait for you at the headquarters."

The boys disappeared over a hill, while the raiders continued southward, much relieved to be rid of the two.

That evening, ten Comanches came by the raid headquarters, also on their way into southern Texas. Kom-pai-te asked if he and his friend might go with them.

The Comanche leader replied, "Yes, if you think you are men enough to keep up with us."

After a continuous ride of two nights and a day, the Comanches came to a thickly settled farming area. The leader said he knew where there was a lot of good stock, and he pointed out barns and corrals where many horses and mules were kept. It was a bright moonlit night. The raiding party was too small to make a daylight raid. Instead they would approach stealthily in pairs to take the animals without arousing the ranchers.

"Now everyone scatter out," said the leader. "We'll meet here before sunup."

The two boys went eastward to a pasture beyond a little peak. Here a number of horses were grazing in the moonlight. They easily caught two hobbled mares. When they led these two away, the other animals followed. In the bunch were a number of good saddle horses.

At the assembly point the other Comanches began to come in, bringing several horses apiece. Soon they all had a good-sized herd. The leader was surprised when he saw what the boys had. He told them to remember which horses were theirs. He detailed two of the older men to help the boys drive the herd, while the other warriors followed in rear.

After traveling for a night and a day the Comanches rested for a time, then set out again at midnight, expecting to reach the Kiowa raid headquarters by noon of the following day.

The Kiowas had arrived back at the headquarters after an unsuccessful raid. They had captured a few horses, but were attacked on their way back, losing all the captured animals and some of their own as well. They had arrived at the headquarters tired, hungry, and dispirited. They asked the two guards who had remained there what had happened to Kom-pai-te and the other boy.

"They went off with some Comanches," was the answer.

The Kiowas hung around waiting for the Comanches to return, becoming more worried as the hours passed.

Finally they saw the Comanches approaching, with the two boys in the lead, driving the captured stock. The youngsters had fifteen horses as their share. The Comanche leader increased their pride by complimenting them and praising them to the Kiowas, who looked even more glum. Kom-pai-te turned to the Kiowa *to-yop-ke* and asked, "How many did you get?" He knew very well that they had returned empty handed.

The chief did not answer.

"Well, we are going to give the Comanche leader one of our horses and one to Iseeo, who was good to us, but none to any of the rest of you," said Kom-pai-te.

After that the boys would not go on raids with the Kiowas. They hung out with the Comanches and went on further raids with them. At the end of three years, though still very young, they had become experienced warriors. In the summer of 1872, they were on a raid with Long Horn and a few Comanches. On May 19, when they were seven miles east of Round Timbers, twenty-five miles below Fort Belknap, they got into a fight with a well-armed party of surveyors. At this time Long Horn, who was leader of the party and felt responsible for the two young warriors, was temporarily separated from them.

When the fight started, the white men fired so accurately and rapidly that the Indians took cover in a little ditch at the head of a wooded ravine. There were three Comanches in addition to the two Kiowas. First one of the Comanches was hit, then Kom-pai-te, then the other Kiowa boy. Pohocsucut, brother of Tabananica, was wounded. The third Comanche escaped after dark to take the bad news to Long Horn.

Long Horn couldn't sleep that night. The next morning he again questioned the survivor of the fight, who insisted that the two Kiowa boys were dead, but that he wasn't sure about the others. When the sun was about an hour high, Long Horn rode back to find the bodies. As he approached the ravine, he noticed crows circling overhead. Then he saw the sun shining on their bodies. The two young Kiowas were lying close together.

The tears ran down Long Horn's face. He saw that the crows had pecked open the boys' abdomens and dragged out their entrails. He moved them gently side by side, covered them with a blanket, and piled rocks over them.

He followed some drops of blood to the edge of the timber, where he found a blood-stained rag. Soon he came upon the two Comanches, Pohocscut and the other, both wounded. He gave them food and water, helped then to bandage their wounds, then went back to get the unhurt Comanche and their horses.

At that time Long Horn, a Yaqui captured in Mexico when a child, was considered to be a Comanche, though later he lived with the Kiowas.

When he and his men returned to the Comanche camp with the report of the disaster, there was much wailing for Kom-pai-te and his friend. Some of the Comanches went to tell the Kiowas about it.

White Horse organized a strong revenge raid for his brother. He said he was not going to come back until he had killed someone in Texas or had been killed himself. Vengeance had to be obtained in the same country where Kom-pai-te had died.

They came to a house with the two rooms connected by a long, roofed porch. A man in a white shirt was sitting in a rocking chair on the porch, reading a newspaper. The Indians sneaked up a gulch. White Horse took aim and shot the man. Then they rushed the house, took several children and perhaps a woman. ☼

This revenge raid took place on Sunday, June 9, at the home of Abel Lee, sixteen miles down the Clear Fork of the Brazos from

Fort Griffin. Mr. and Mrs. Lee and one daughter were slain and three other children taken captive. They remained slaves in the Kiowa camps for several months before being ransomed.

29 ❀ "I SCALPED A MAN ONCE"

AN-PAY-KAU-TE, the oldest son of Satank, whose speech defect was cured by the liberal use of firewater, participated in a number of raids while still in his teens. After his father was killed at Fort Sill in 1871, he inherited one of the Grandmother gods, which he kept in a buffalo hide pouch together with his father's "Washington Medal." Once he took out and wore the medal while I was taking his photograph, but of course he never showed me the medicine. Presumably he had never seen it himself. He furnished me with much valuable information about the period 1868–74, having been a participant in or eyewitness of many of the important events. He lived until the late 1930's, one of the last of the old-time warriors. The following personal experience story illustrates how the raiding parties wandered, apparently aimlessly, in the arid wastes of southwest Texas, looking for adventure and enjoying the scenery. It was one way of escaping boredom.

❀ I scalped a man once. It was in the summer of the year that Mackenzie captured the Comanche women and children [1872]. Ten of us went on a raid way down below where Quanah, Texas, is now. Pago-to-goodle was the leader, Set-maunte his assistant, and the others whose names I remember were A-to-tainte, Hau-vah-te, and Mamay-day-te.

172

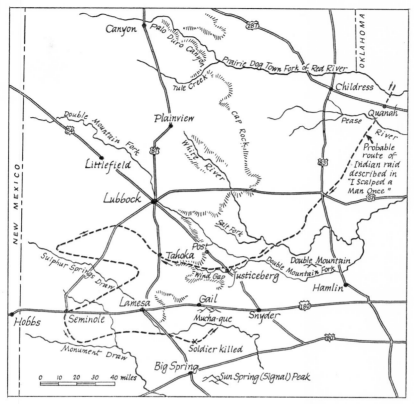

The Staked Plains Region (showing modern cities and highways)

We crossed Red River between the sites of Vernon and Quanah and rode southwest toward Double Mountain, a customary landmark for our raiding parties. When we reached Sun Spring, a little above Double Mountain, we turned west. We crossed Trading River and went up through Wind Gap [west of the present Justiceburg]. After leaving the gap, we came to a place we called Cloudy-Dirt Creek, where the ground was shale. From there our route took us to Timber Spring, where we camped on the side of a hill. Our next campsite was at another "Sun Spring," a well-known water hole on the old war trail leading down into Mexico. Then we went to Sulphur Springs, probably near the head of Sulphur Springs Creek [it is marked on Mackenzie's campaign map], also well known to Indians. The leader now took us eastward to Great Stinking Lake. Many years before, wagons had bogged down here in the mud. We could still see some of the pieces of wagon wheels.

Next we turned north and met some Apaches who told us that their tribe, the Mescaleros, were camped at Chinaberry Tree Springs and that traders were coming there from New Mexico. So we all went there, but the Apaches had gone. We turned back southward to where Eagle Creek heads up into the Cap Rocks, and followed the creek to where it flows into a lake named Tone-gui-ah, which has many cattails growing in it. From there we moved to a place where many wagon trails crossed Pecan Creek. This part of the country was traveled by freighters and others going through in wagons. We hoped to intercept a small group, but we saw no one.

We now came to a big pile of stones near a mountain [a monument for surveyors, perhaps]. Turning south from here we found a saucer-like depression in the rock which was filled with water. We drank some water and watered our horses. Then we continued on to the point where the war trail forked, and from there went to Muddy Wells, a place I had often heard mentioned by the older men. Near the wells we caught a white soldier who was staggering along, apparently lost and starving for water. We killed and scalped him.

This victory meant that we had accomplished the main purpose of the raid. Now there was no need of risking the lives of any of our men further, and we could go home. We turned eastward, and had crossed Pecan Creek again when we were overtaken by a few Apaches. We told them about killing the soldier and invited them to join us in the victory dance that we were planning to hold.

While we were traveling along together, the Apaches got a signal from two of their advance scouts who were on a hill. These men were facing each other and touching the tips of their bows together to form a rainbow. This meant that they saw dead bodies or a place where Indians had been killed. Knowing that their people had been camped on the other side of the hill, the Apache leader began to cry.

As we approached the campsite, the Apaches pointed out the tracks where men on shod horses had scouted the village. Then we

saw where these troops had made their charge. But when we got to
the campsite we found that the people had fled, escaping before the
troops had ridden in. They had abandoned some of their property;
the sight of these bundles lying on the ground here and there had
led the scouts to think that they saw bodies.

The Apache leader made a signal smoke and presently had gathered more men who were hiding in the area. Now we all followed
the trail of the troops, who seemed to be weak from lack of water,
not knowing the location of the water holes in that country. Finally
we sighted them on the edge of some timber, just at dusk. But they
escaped from us during the night. They had only a small party,
probably less than a troop.

The Apaches wanted us to stay with them and visit their village,
but Pago-to-goodle declined, saying that we had been out long
enough and were on our way home.

Heading eastward again, we passed White-Clay Springs, a favorite camping ground of the Apaches and went over a long ridge
that lies south of Muts-a-que[1] and north of Sun Spring Peak, which
the Comanches call Tabby-paritsope-que. Our leader said that the
soldiers would never follow us to this place, so we camped there and
rested for ten days.

We resumed the journey before sunrise on the eleventh day. Soon
after daybreak we stopped at a water hole to wash our faces, drink
some water, and eat some of the hard cakes made of mesquite berry
meal that we were carrying. Just as I was dipping up some water to
drink, a shot was fired not far away. Our two rear scouts came up
and asked us if we had heard someone shooting.

"You fellows get back up on that hill," said Pago-to-goodle,
angrily. "Probably soldiers are following us, and you should be up
there where you can see them and signal to us."

The scouts climbed up the hill to the right rear of us. Soon they
signaled that they saw enemy approaching. Then instead of staying
there in observation, they hid themselves among the rocks.

"Every man tie up his sheet and get ready to fight," said Pago-to-

[1] Also called Mucha-que. It is a Comanche word meaning "bearded peak," and
on today's map shows as Muchakooago, a few miles south of Gail, Texas.

goodle. "We'll fight on foot, all except Set-maunte, who will stay mounted." He led us to a deep gully where we hobbled our horses, then made an ambush under an overhanging bank just below where the horse trail passed above us. As we were moving into this position, we saw the soldiers about a quarter of a mile away, riding slowly along the creek and coming toward us. Evidently they had found our campsite of the past ten days and were following our trail. There were about twenty of them, with one man on a black horse well out to the front. Seeing the fresh manure of our horses, he started his horse trotting.

"We had better get out of here," said Pago-to-goodle. "There are too many of them. Let's ride over the ridge and keep on going."

Hau-vah-te objected. He had a breech-loading repeater and two revolvers and wanted to show them off. "First let me shoot at them," he said. Pago-to-goodle agreed.

We had no sooner gotten under the bank than the leading soldier appeared right in front of us. He saw us at the same instant that we saw him. Drawing his pistol, and holding it up, he took off his hat, turned in the saddle, and waved to the others to hurry forward to join him. As he turned his back on us, Hau-vah-te and another man fired at him. One of the guns only snapped, but Hau-vah-te shot the man in the back. He fell to the ground. Seeing this, the other soldiers wheeled and galloped in the opposite direction, firing their pistols to the rear.

We all raced to make coup. I was making my holler the same as the others. Set-maunte, being mounted, got there first. But his horse, having a sore back, started to buck violently just as he got to the body, so Set-maunte didn't get to make coup. Hau-vah-te made first coup, and A-to-tainte second coup. Then we all mounted up and followed Set-maunte, who was charging after the other soldiers. As we got nearer to them, they stopped and began firing at us through some mesquite trees. On beyond them, in the distance, we could see more soldiers coming. So we turned back and started to clear out. Just after we passed the fallen soldier, Mamay-day said to me, "Let's go back and get the scalp."

176

There he lay on his face, not moving. I got down off my mule, at Mamay-day's order. "You scalp him," he said.

I jerked the man over and cut off the scalp. I saw that he was middle aged, with brown hair. He had blue pants with a broad yellow stripe, and a duck coat. Since it was raining, he was wearing a raincoat. In front he had tied to his waist a gold chain with a watch. I didn't know, at that time, what a watch was, but I cut the chain with my knife and carried off the watch as a trophy. Mamay-day got the scalp, Hau-vah-te the carbine, and A-to-tainte the revolver.

When we stopped for lunch, I examined my trophy. It was still alive! I could hear its heart ticking! So I smashed it between two rocks to kill it. Then I threw away the pieces; they were of no use to me.

The following summer we visited this place again. The soldiers must have camped there for some time, because they had dug a nice grave for the dead man and put up a cross and a flag over it. Around the grave they had built a picket fence. This place was about a day's journey south of Muts-a-que. ☼

30 ✿ QUANAH AT ADOBE WALLS

In July of 1874, a group of twenty-seven professional buffalo hunters had established a base camp at Bent's long-abandoned adobe trading post on the Canadian River in the Texas panhandle. Their slaughter of the buffalo enraged the Plains Indians, who determined to wipe out the hunters. The expedition was led by Isatai, a Quahadi Comanche medicine man, and Quanah, a young Nokoni war chief. These leaders had recruited a few Kiowas and a substantial contingent of Cheyennes and Arapahoes, as well as many Comanches. But they attacked on Sunday, when all the hunters were assembled at Adobe Walls rather than scattered out in hunting parties. This fact, plus the superior marksmanship of the whites, who had high-powered rifles with telescopic sights, resulted in the repulse of the Indians. The story has been told many times by white survivors (only three of the twenty-seven were killed) and has become an epic of plains warfare.

Not much has been said from the Indian viewpoint. Here is one account by Iseeo, a Kiowa, and another by Quanah.

✿ Quanah [said Iseeo] had a nephew killed in Texas. He was a good-looking young man, and Quanah was going about giving the pipe. Our Kiowa village was on Elk Creek. We heard that Quanah

178

was coming to see us. One day we saw somebody coming across the prairie, crying. We said, "There he is—Quanah!" He was bringing the pipe, and it was the custom in such cases to cry for a dead man who was unavenged. He had already gathered many Comanches to smoke the pipe.

Quanah came into the village and asked, "Where is the chief's lodge?"

I pointed out my uncle's lodge to him. He went by the left of the door and clear around the outside of the lodge as was the custom, then entered and sat down at the back. Soon my uncle came and called all his young men to assemble in the lodge. I went in, too, and sat down with them.

Quanah said, "My nephew was killed by the white people. His body is lying on the ground in Texas. I want to get even. I am coming looking for you. I give you the pipe to smoke."

Everybody heard him. All the young men watched to see if the chief would smoke the pipe. If he was afraid of that pipe, they would not smoke it. If he was not afraid, everybody that wanted to would smoke it with him.

The chief said, "I am not afraid of that pipe. But hold up. Wait until all the old men hear about it. If they say 'Good,' I will smoke it."

Quanah said, "All right. I will go talk to the old men."

But the old men were afraid of that pipe.

Quanah then went to a big Cheyenne village which was farther up the creek. Many Cheyennes smoked the pipe. Six or seven foolish young Kiowas also smoked it. With the Comanches, they all went over to the Canadian to attack some white men's adobe houses on the Canadian above Antelope Hills. This place is now [1897] the headquarters of the Hansford Land and Cattle Company, J. M. Coburn, manager—the turkey-track brand.

Isatai, the leader, had a strong medicine. He told the Indians, "Go ahead. Those white men can't shoot you. With my medicine I will stop up their guns. When you charge, you will wipe them all out."

The Indians went up close early in the morning before sunrise.

They charged and killed two white men outside the fort and one inside. But quite a few Indians were killed. Isatai's medicine was no good. The Indians lost the fight. Later, after the hunters had gone, the Indians came and gathered up the bones of their dead, wrapped them in robes and blankets, and put them in the hills on the south side of the Canadian upstream from Adobe Walls. Nine Indians were killed. ✻

✻ A long time ago [said Quanah][1] I had a friend killed by the Tonkawas on Double Mountain Fork of the Brazos. That make me feel bad. We had grown up together, gone to war together. We were all very sorry that man was killed. The Tonkawa killed him— it make my heart hot. I want to make it even.

At that time I was a pretty big young man and knew how to fight pretty good. I work for one month trying to get Comanches to go to war with me. I go to the Nokoni camp first, on head of Cache Creek. I call in everybody. I tell them my friend he killed in Texas. I fill pipe, I say to man, "You want to smoke?" He take pipe and smoke. I give pipe to other men. One man say, "I not want to smoke. If I smoke pipe, I go to war." I say, "You not excused. God kill you if you be afraid."

I go see Kiowas on Elk Creek, then Quahadis, then I go see Cheyennes. Lots of them smoke pipe. Cheyenne camp on Washita near where Fort Elliott later built, where Washita forks around hill. Lots of Comanches there—Otter Belt, He Bear [Parra-o-coom], Tabananica, Old Man Esa Rosa [White Wolf]. Camps in different places.

They say, "When you go to war, Quanah?"

I say, "Maybe tomorrow, maybe next day. Have big dance tonight. Big Horse Society dance here; Little Horse Society dance there; Fox Quirts on this side."

Then I hear somebody call, "Quanah, the old men want to see you over here!" I see Old Man Otter Belt, White Wolf, and lots of other old men.

[1] By 1890, Quanah was able to talk in broken English. His story concerning the Adobe Walls fight was communicated to General Scott in that language, and is set down here in the words used in Scott's notes.

They say, "You pretty good fighter, Quanah, but you not know everything. We think better you take pipe first against white buffalo-killers. You kill them first and make your heart feel good. After that you come back, take all the young men, go to war, Texas!"

I say, "Otter Belt and He Bear, you take pipe yourself, after I take young men to go to Texas."

They say, "All right."

Isatai make big talk at that time. He says, "God tell me we going to kill lots of white men. I stop bullets in their guns. Bullets not pierce our shirts. We kill all, just like old women. God told me the truth."

Before that Isatai was pretty good medicine man, make pretty good medicine. He had sat down far away and listen. God tell him, "Maybeso on little creek, fifty miles away, is white soldiers. We must go kill them." This time he listen to what God tell him.

Soon we move to Fort Elliott—no got fort there at this time. I pick seven scouts to go look for white men's adobe houses on Canadian. Old Man White Wolf go with them. They gone all night. Next day our watchers on a little hill call out, "Here they come!" We see our scouts circle four times to the right and know they find the houses. Our whole village, the women and children and everybody, make a long line in front of the camp, Old Man Black Beard

in the middle. Then the seven scouts come in single file in front of Black Beard.

He ask, "Tell the truth, what did you see?"

First scout say, "I see four log houses. I see horses moving about." All the scouts say the same thing.

Black Beard say, "All right. Pretty soon we kill some white men."

Everybody saddled up, took their war bonnets and shields. We started when sun there [about eleven], we stopped when sun there [about four]. We took off the saddles and blankets from our horses, hobbled the extra horses, make medicine, paint faces, put on war bonnets, then move in fours across the Canadian at sundown. We kept along the river to pretty near Red Hill near Adobe Creek, where houses were. We all walk our horses, because enemy could hear horses trotting a long way off.

At dark some men want to go to sleep. He Bear[2] say, "Dismount. Hold lariats in your hands. When I call, you mount again."

While we wait, some sleep, some smoke and talk. Finally He Bear and Tabananica call them, "Everybody mount." All mount again and travel until there is just a little daylight. Pretty soon we make a line. All the chiefs try to hold the young men back: "You go too fast. No good to go so fast."

Pretty soon the chiefs call, "All right. Go ahead!" We charge pretty fast on our horses, throwing up dust high. Many prairie dog holes. I see men and horses roll over and over. Some men who were ahead drove off the white men's horses.

I was in the middle of the line. I got up into the adobe houses with another Comanche. We poked holes through roof to shoot. Two white men killed in wagon. I not see any other killed. Four Cheyenne, some Arapahoes and Comanches killed. My first wife's father got leg broken by bullet. I got shot in side.

That pretty big fight. Lasted from sunrise to midday. Then we go back. All Cheyennes heap mad at Isatai, tell him, "What's the matter your medicine? You got polecat medicine!"

[2] Quanah must have been mistaken about this. He Bear's son states that the great chief was ill with pneumonia at that time and died in his camp on Elk Creek or North Fork at about the time the battle was fought or shortly thereafter.

One Comanche killed was a yellow nigger painted like Comanche. He had left nigger soldiers' company, everybody know that [deserter from the Tenth Cavalry].

Pretty soon we all go back, get saddles, go to village. I take all young men, go war Texas. ☼

It was said that the Cheyennes came to kill Isatai to avenge themselves, but found that he had run away at night and could not be found. On his return he was asked about his medicine, whereupon he excused himself by saying, "Somebody killed skunk. This broke my medicine."

Be that as it may, at Adobe Walls, Isatai's medicine, and Quanah's as well, was no good.

31 ❀ HE WOULDN'T LISTEN

In the fall of 1874, about half of the Kiowa tribe participated in an outbreak which was triggered by a skirmish at the agency near Anadarko with four troops of the Tenth Cavalry. Few casualties were suffered by either side, but after looting Shirley's store the dis-affected Kiowas and Comanches fled to the Staked Plains. Most of them were rounded up during the winter and brought back to Fort Sill. They were disarmed and the guilty leaders confined. This ended the Indian "wars" in the southwest plains.

Botalye, who in 1874 was about seventeen years old, describes in the following narrative his adventures during this, his first and only experience on the warpath.

❀ I was in Poor Buffalo's band, which in August of 1874 was camped just east of Mount Scott. Early in September we moved to Cobb Creek, where we remained peaceably until a Kiowa rode into the village with a report of some fighting at the Anadarko agency on issue day. He said that a Negro had been killed near the store, as well as four white men who were working in a hayfield several miles from the agency. Indians from several tribes had taken part in robbing Shirley's store, but there was still a lot of good stuff re-maining, if any of us were interested.

184

Our two *to-yop-kes*, Co-yan-te and Ay-an-te, said that we ought to go down there. The Kiowas might need us. Consequently, during the night all the young men in our camp rode down the Washita toward Anadarko. I went with them.

We arrived on the high ground north of the agency before daybreak and waited for the first light before going down to the river valley. The sun's early rays shone on some bright-colored cloth scattered on the grass around the trader's store, part way down the slope. The usual places where the Indians camped at ration-issue time were deserted, but as the shadows in the river valley disappeared, we could see Indians riding around in the big bend of the river. Some scattering gunfire broke out. The Indians were skirmishing with the Negro soldiers who were in a trench across the river. We started down the hill to join in the fun. I was pretty excited, never having been in battle before.

But when we reached the flat ground, the other Indians crowded around us, all talking at once, telling us what had happened the day before. They pointed to where the Negro had been killed. Others told us how they had ridden down to the hayfields in the afternoon and had gotten four scalps.

We wanted to go to the trader's store to get a share of the loot. They advised us to be careful, because there were some soldiers just around the hill, near the store. Old Man An-zah-te didn't care about that. He rode over to the store, outside of which he found a pile of blue blankets—all brand new. He picked up as many as he could carry, brought them back, and gave one to each of us.

Day-nah-te tried it next. He went right into the store and began to help himself. Soon we all were crowding into the building, grabbing things off the shelves.

Another burst of gunfire put a stop to the looting. We rode back to the top of the bluff, where we met Chee-na-bony, a Comanche chief who had just arrived. At the same time some of us saw a group of soldiers sneaking up to our left and getting behind some rocks. We started to dismount and take cover.

"Don't bother to get down," said Chee-na-bony, who hadn't seen the soldiers. "I don't see any danger."

At that moment he spied the soldiers, who were now aiming at us. At once we all whirled about and started galloping away. A volley roared out, one of the bullets striking Chee-na-bony in the back of the head. He flopped to the ground. No one stopped to pick him up. We knew that the troops wouldn't scalp him, but would dig a nice grave for him.

Now the whole crowd started to shake up. Several of the *to-yop-kes* wanted to attack the soldiers who were in the trenches, but a Wichita chief named Buffalo Good objected. "Let's not have any more trouble," he said. "You Kiowas and Comanches go up the river. The rest of us will go down the river. That will stop the fighting."

We had begun to argue over this, when someone reminded us that there was a telegraph line, strung on iron poles, running from the agency to Fort Sill. The white men could send signals over it. We didn't know how, but they did it. They might ask Fort Sill to send more troops. We would be liable to get into serious trouble if we stayed around. So we agreed to scatter, like Buffalo Good had suggested.

All the Kiowas assembled first at Poor Buffalo's camp at Swan Lake. I don't know where the Comanches went, but I think they headed for the North Fork of Red River. Our Kiowa chiefs announced that we would ride west to Elk Creek. We would travel all night, not stopping to rest—not even the women and children—until we got there.

It was well after daybreak when we reached Elk Creek, somewhere on its headwaters. It was still fairly dark, because heavy rain clouds had gathered, settling right down on the breast of the prairie. We stopped to rest for a short time, letting our ponies graze and chewing some dried meat ourselves. Before we were ready to start again, it began to rain, coming down in sheets with great explosions of lightning. The very air turned sour with it, it was so close. We were soaked through and shivering. We knew that if the sun didn't come out that day, our blankets would still be wet for the night's camp.

Finally, as the mists lifted and the rain stopped, we could see the

186

plains all around us stretching away to the horizon. We went up Elk Creek to a low waterfall near its head. Nearby in a wide valley a large herd of buffalo grazed. We at once organized a chase. Thus we got warm, dried out again, and got enough meat to last for a long journey.

While the camp-movers were butchering the fallen buffalo a call came around: "If any member of Kicking Bird's band happens to go back to Fort Sill, he should tell Kicking Bird that we aren't going far out into the Staked Plains. We will come back if he wants us to."

At that time the peaceful half of our tribe was camped near the post, under Kicking Bird, who was keeping them quiet. The announcement reminded Satanta and Big Tree that they had promised to be good when Washington had persuaded Texas to let them out of prison last year. If they were now caught taking part in an outbreak, it would go hard with them. They began arguing whether they ought not to return to Fort Sill right away. Maman-ti and Lone Wolf persuaded them to stay with us for a while.

Maman-ti was in charge of the council by the waterfall. Lone Wolf was head chief of the tribe, but Maman-ti had the stronger medicine. Big Bow, who had joined us that day after travelling up from the breaks at the head of White River, had a suggestion. He urged that we turn back down Elk Creek and hide in a deep canyon. He said that he had seen troops scouting along the edge of the Staked Plains ahead of us, especially to the west.

Though Maman-ti and Lone Wolf weren't much in favor of Big Bow's plan, they gave in because all the other chiefs thought it was worth trying. Orders were given for the camp-movers to start south along the east bank of Elk Creek until they came to a deep canyon. They were to cross this at the first trail leading into the gorge.

My uncle Maman-ti called me aside and told me to stay behind to scout to the rear. "Blue Shield [Ke-soye-ke], here, will stay with you," he said. "I want you two young men to follow us after you are sure that no enemy is on our trail. But if you see danger, ride quickly to tell us about it. Here is some tobacco to keep you happy."

He ordered two other young men to scout to the north between the Washita and the Canadian.

After everyone had gone, I said to Blue Shield, "Let us go back to that ridge from which we can see far to the east." So we did.

We saw nothing, no sign of friend or foe. After waiting for a reasonable time we followed the trail of the moving village.

We saw where they had come to the deep canyon and had attempted the crossing at the first possible place. Failing there, they had gone to the sole remaining crossing, which they had traveled successfully. On the way they had dragged cedar trees to cover their tracks, but we had no trouble following them.

Late in the afternoon we saw a long line of people moving on the other side of the canyon. By the time we had gotten across, the lodges were already up.

At the council that night some of the leaders thought that we ought to stay in place. But Maman-ti got out his owl and made a prophecy that we would not meet soldiers if we went towards Palo Duro Canyon. It was decided to go near the head of the Washita, then turn southwest toward Palo Duro.

Next morning, Maman-ti again told Blue Shield and me to scout to the rear. We stayed near the old campsite until midmorning, carefully observing to the south and east. Then we followed the village. About noon, we overtook an Indian on foot. He was a tall, strong, young fellow but was feeble minded. His people had abandoned him like a dog. We stopped to give him some advice.

"Just follow the tracks of the village, and you will reach camp before dark," I told him.

He thanked us and said he would follow us along the trail.

During the afternoon, we came to a crowd of camp-movers who had stopped behind a hill because they had seen, in the distance, several men riding toward us.

Blue Shield and I rode to the top of the hill for a better look. "They are wearing hats," he said. "Maybe they are white men."

Just then the strangers saw us, got scared, and galloped off to the north. Since we now could see that they were Mexicans, probably traders, we didn't chase them.

Camp had been made that night near a big spring a little west of the head of the Washita. Immediately to the north were some sand hills. We scouts rode to the top of the highest hill, from which we could see the country for miles in every direction. To the west we could see the Cap Rock, an escarpment along the eastern edge of the Staked Plains. No one was in sight.

Early next morning I talked to my foster cousin, a white captive member of the tribe whom we called Tehan. He said that he was going out to look for some stock believed to have strayed from the previous campsite.

We didn't move that day. By nightfall Tehan had not returned, so some of us scattered to look for him. I was out all night. Early the next morning I saw from a hilltop some ten miles north of the camp what appeared to be a group of Indians on the next hill. When I came up to them, they told me that they had stopped looking for Tehan and were scouting for soldiers.

"Why?" I asked.

"Because we saw tracks of shod horses where Tehan's trail disappeared," one of them said. "Those tracks led north."

I went on till I came to more scouts looking for troops. They had seen nothing.

Still unwilling to give up the search for Tehan, I rode on until I caught up with Zontam and An-zah-te. They told me to go to the next hill, about two miles farther on. They didn't explain why they wanted me to do this, but I found out later that they had seen something moving in the distance. They wanted me to do their dangerous work for them by riding forward to find out what it was they had seen.

About halfway to the next rise in the plains, I met two other fellows, Sai-au-sain and Charley Buffalo. They agreed to go with me.

The next hill was grassy and had a few low mesquite trees on top. We could see from there without being seen. It was lucky for us that this was so, for there in front of us, about a mile and a half away, was a line of wagons guarded by soldiers! There were twenty or thirty white-topped wagons, each drawn by four mules, coming slowly in single file, preceded by ten to fifteen cavalrymen spread out ahead. About twenty-five walk-soldiers were marching in a single file on either side of the wagons. In the morning light we could plainly see the blue of their uniforms.[1]

Sai-au-sain said, "Botalye, you go back to the village with the news. We will stay here to watch the enemy. Tell the chiefs to bring up a big crowd of warriors."

I started back. On the way I met Kiowa Bill. When I told him what we had seen, he decided to go back with me. As we got closer to the village, which was moving, we began to see people. First a lone woman with a travois, then a little group with pack horses. Finally we saw the warriors, riding in a bunch, with the chiefs out in front.

As we approached them, we made our signal by riding in little circles. When we got close, they were waiting for us in line, Maman-ti and Lone Wolf standing behind an altar of buffalo chips. Kiowa Bill, who was the older, went forward and received the sage straw in his hair, after which he gave our report.

Every now and then, while he was talking, one of the young women would make her whoop.

"You women stand back!" shouted Maman-ti. "Keep quiet! You'll be the cause of some of these young men getting killed today."

He took out his owl and started to pray. Then he blew his eagle-bone whistle and invited everyone to come up and make an offering to the owl. He reminded the crowd that his medicine required that each man be barefoot when he came up with his present for the owl. I noticed that everyone except Big Bow and a few of his friends gave presents.

The *to-yop-kes* now got out their war bonnets from the bags in which they were packed and put them on. We all painted ourselves and tied up our horses' tails. We took off our shirts and wrapped our sheets around our waists in a tight roll. We made sure that our weapons were ready.

[1] This was a wagon train hauling rations and ammunition from Camp Supply to Colonel Nelson A. Miles's command which was operating against the hostile Indians. It was guarded by Captain Wyllys Lyman's Company I, Fifth Cavalry.

As the camp-movers rode back behind a hill, we went forward to meet the enemy. When I got to the high ground, some of the Indians were already riding across the front of the wagon train. Some were standing up on their horses' backs, others were hanging on the side and shooting under their ponies' necks. No one had yet made a charge.

The wagon train kept moving forward slowly, the soldiers shooting back at us. They crossed a deep ravine[2] and continued toward the southwest. Two or three soldiers who had been hit by our fire were loaded into wagons. By now the wagons were in double column about twenty yards apart. Suddenly some of our chiefs led a crowd of experienced warriors in a rush that took them closer to the wagons. At once the train stopped and formed a hollow square, with the soldiers in lines protecting the front, sides, and rear. None of our men were killed, but Sait-keen-te's horse was shot. Two other men took Sait-keen-te up as he ran along the ground, and he swung up behind one of them. The charge veered off and went back up the hill.

Now Pau-tape-te wanted to show his bravery. The chiefs told him not to get too close, but he went in anyway. He had hardly started down the slope when he was hit in the hand. He came back at once, crying like a little boy.

The walk-soldiers had guns with long straps which they fastened to their arms when they knelt down to fire. This gave them a steady aim. Their firing was so dangerous that we stayed well back on the high ground, riding rapidly in a great circle around them, yelling and enjoying the excitement. We kept this up until dark.

During the night we dug pits along the high ground from which we could fire in the direction of the enemy from time to time. In spite of this, some of them managed to go with canteens to a water hole. Tehan, who was with them, pretending to be friendly, offered to help get water. In the darkness he succeeded in getting away from the soldiers and coming back to us.

All the next day and the second night we kept the soldiers surrounded. There was some firing at long range by both sides, but our men didn't make any more charges. The chiefs said the enemy must

[2] Apparently Gageby Creek, about a mile from where it enters the Washita.

be getting short of water. Pretty soon they would make a break and run for it. Then we could ride them down.

But the third day came, and the soldiers hadn't gone for water. Some of our bravest men decided to stir things up. Yellow Wolf and Set-maun-te were behind the hill, getting ready to make a charge. They made their announcement as we all gathered to watch them make their preparations and pray to their medicine.

"Watch us now!" shouted Yellow Wolf. "See those trenches at the end of the wagons? You watch! We are going to ride between them and on out the other side!"

Set-maun-te got on his horse. His brother ran up, took away his war bonnet, and told him not to go; he said it was too dangerous.

Yellow Wolf put on his war bonnet and started to mount. His brother snatched the bonnet from Yellow Wolf's head, saying, "Don't be foolish! Cut it out!"

Meanwhile, I had been planning to go with them. No one was paying any attention to me. I was only an unrecognized young fellow. I was getting on my horse and was all ready when one of the buffalo medicine men noticed me. He asked what I was going to do.

"I'm going to make a run," I said.

He told me to go ahead, but only to make one and not to go too close to the soldiers.

I said to Yellow Wolf, "Brother, they stopped you, but I'm going. I shall ride right by that buffalo wallow to see how much water they have."

Yellow Wolf and the others looked at me in surprise. I dug my heels into my pony, and we were off! Over the crest we went at a dead run, down the slope, straight at the soldiers. Pai-kee-te, my partner, was coming along behind me. At first no one fired at me, but as I got halfway to the trenches, some of the enemy bobbed up and began shooting. The bullets were cracking past my ears.

Pai-kee-te turned back! I kept on going. As I got near the wagons, it was like in a hailstorm, with the slugs knocking up little spurts of sand all around me. Still I wasn't hit. My medicine must have been very strong!

I dashed between the trenches and the wagons. The soldiers

192

couldn't shoot at me for fear of hitting their own men. I raced on through and up the ridge on the far side. On top of the hill I rode in a little circle and tried to give my holler. I wanted to make it sound like the cry of a wild goose, but only a frightened squawk came out. I had had no experience.

I started down the hill again and headed back through the enemy to my starting point, where a big crowd of the Indians were watching. Instead of riding straight through, I made a dodging course like that of a jack rabbit chased by a coyote. The firing was so fierce that I thought I would surely fall. But I made it safely.

For my third run, I tied a loop of rope to my saddle so that I could get over on the side of my horse. In the middle of the charge I slipped down over his side like we had practiced so many times as boys. When I came out of the smoke on the far side of the wagons, the other Indians didn't see me; they thought I had been shot down. When I stopped and got off, they all came riding to where I was. I saw that bullets had cut off the stirrup on the opposite side of my horse and had creased his neck. Evidently the two feathers I wore in my hair had been sticking up over the horse's back, as had the knot in the sheet I had wrapped around my waist. There was a bullet hole through the latter, and the feathers had been shot off. But I hadn't been touched.

Maman-ti was the first to arrive where I was resting my horse. He told me to stop. But I was feeling great. I said that I would make a fourth run. I didn't tell them why, but my reason was this: When I was a young boy I used to play with two of Satanta's sons, Tsa'l-au-te and Sait-keen-te. One day while we were wrestling around inside the lodge, one of them knocked some coals against the walls and set the tipi on fire. It was Satanta's red tipi, the only one in the tribe. He came up just in time to keep it from burning entirely, but he blamed me for it. He said that if I was ever proved to be the coward he thought I was, he would whip me good. Since he was watching me now, I was going to show him that I was no coward.

So I mounted my pony again. Yellow Wolf and several of the other members of the Ko-eet-senko told me to stop; they said I had done enough to prove my bravery. But I wouldn't listen to them.

193

The fourth run was just like the others, except maybe there wasn't so much shooting. Some of the soldiers even stood up in the trenches to watch me dash past them. When I came back safely, Satanta came up to me and said, laughing, "If you hadn't done it, I was going to whip you."

"Go ahead and whip me anyway," I said.

"I wasn't really going to whip anyone as brave as you," he said, hugging me to his breast. "I couldn't have made four runs myself," he added. "No one ever comes back the fourth time! Once or twice is enough. I'm glad you came back alive."

Then Poor Buffalo, chief of our band, made an announcement: "Everyone listen! I'm going to give Botalye a new name. If any danger comes, we can depend on him! I name him *Eadle-tau-hain*— He Wouldn't Listen!" ☸

32 ✿ THE WRINKLED-HAND CHASE

BOTALYE CONTINUES HIS ACCOUNT of the flight of the Kiowas from Anadarko to Palo Duro Canyon and their return to the reservation. The Indians call this the Wrinkled-Hand Chase because of the condition of their hands after being constantly wet from rain water.

✿ On the fourth day of the wagon train fight our warriors began to return to the village because they thought that the women and children might be in danger. Other troops were reported coming in from the west and the north. For a day or two, however, most of them were delayed in getting back to camp because they became involved in fights with various small troop detachments.

With another Kiowa named Little Owl, I left the wagon train fight about midday and went directly back to the village, which was camped south of the Washita on the west bank of a little creek which flows north into the river. On the way we heard shooting break out again behind us, and we learned later that my friend Pai-kee-te had had his horse shot during an attack on several white men who had holed up in a buffalo wallow. They had put up a fierce fight, and those not killed were later rescued by the troops. The Indians captured their horses during the first attack. A Kiowa who got two of the animals nearly had a fight with some Comanches over them.

195

When Little Owl and I reached the creek near the village, he proposed that we take a swim. I objected, saying, "There is no time for that."

We were in camp eating lunch with the rest of the people when the camp sentinels warned us that some riders were approaching from the west.

"They are in a column of twos, so probably they are soldiers" was the report.

A Kiowa-Mexican named K'op-to-hau [Mountain Bluff] had just come in from Fort Sill with a paper signed by two officers and by Kicking Bird, which was to protect us from attacks by troops.[1] He had a white flag, too, so we tried to get him to go out to meet the troops and show them the safety paper.

The old fool refused, saying, "I want to smell some powder first." He had heard about the wagon train fight and wanted to get into it. We tried hard to get him to change his mind, but he wouldn't do so.

All the chiefs and nearly all the warriors were still skirmishing north of the river. Old Man An-zah-te had been left in charge of the village. Now it was up to him to organize some sort of defense, using the old men and boys, and to do it quickly. He called out Little Owl and me to join this small group. We formed a line in front of the camp, facing the troops. They had halted just out of range and were sitting on their horses looking at us.

A lone Indian came out of a draw to our right and started to ride across between us and the troops. It was Set-maunte, wearing his war bonnet. He had returned from the wagon train fight just in time to help us out. I think he was trying to attract the soldiers away from the village, which was now being packed up rapidly for flight toward the east. The soldiers fired at Set-maunte but missed him.

Since there were only a few soldiers, maybe ten or twelve, we made a plan to attack them from several directions and drive them away from the village. While we were discussing this, a larger enemy force appeared. With them was a small cannon. Both troops

[1] Probably a certificate of registration of this band as "friendly." Captain George Sanderson had registered all Kiowas except Lone Wolf's band and had given Kicking Bird the papers for delivery.

halted, each waiting for the other to begin the attack. We were getting excited, wanting to make our charges, but An-zah-te kept shouting, "Wait! Wait! They aren't close enough!"

A Comanche rode out of the draw where Set-maunte had appeared, about 350 yards from us, and went toward the enemy. Two officers, with drawn revolvers, were out in front. Apparently thinking that the lone Comanche was a chief coming out to parley with them, they put their guns back in their holsters. The Comanche shot at them, whereupon they again reached for their six-shooters.

This action of the Comanche caused firing to break out from both sides. The Comanche came back to where we were, his horse bleeding from a shoulder wound. We all rode behind a little hill off to the flank, from the shelter of which we began making our individual charges toward the enemy. By now the firing was continuous. Our spirits rose as our excitement grew stronger. This was a good fight, and so far none of us had been hurt.

Meantime, the women and children, with their pack horses and travois, had crossed the creek and were disappearing over the rolling prairie to the east. They had forded the stream just in time, for the water was rising rapidly from the recent heavy rains.

Late that afternoon our men began to break off the fight in order to follow the women and children. Little Owl and I were among the last to make a run toward the enemy. Suddenly we noticed that we were almost alone and that the sun was sinking in the red western sky. We turned and made our way back to the creek. A little group of Kiowas were there, trying to decide where was the best place to force their horses into the water. The creek was swirling nearly to the top of the bank. We could see that we would have to swim our horses.

Just then my horse began to choke. Thinking that the throat strap of his bridle was too tight, I started to dismount in order to loosen it. A little fellow named Haun-goon-pau [Silver Horn], seeing my trouble, rode up and said, "Don't get down! He is choking on a wad of grass." He gave my horse a couple of good belts with his quirt, which caused the horse to disgorge a big chunk of grass. In a moment he was all right and was nibbling more grass as if nothing had happened. A horse will eat anytime, even if he has just had a leg shot off.

197

While we were still arguing about the crossing, two soldiers appeared on the hill behind us. This cut short the conversation. We all jumped into the water and started struggling against the current, which was carrying us downstream. The two enemy scouts came closer, but very cautiously. Seeing us in the water they whipped about and galloped back to tell the troops. If all the soldiers had then come up promptly they could have slaughtered us in the water. But they were slow.

We all reached the east bank just as it was getting dark. Feeling safe now, sure that the soldiers could not or would not follow us across, we started cutting capers along the bank. A number of shots were fired at us out of the gathering gloom, which put a sudden end to the fun. We all took off to the eastward.

The village was camped on the upper waters of Elk Creek, about where Elk City, Oklahoma, is now. Although we felt safe for the time being, the chiefs held a council, trying to decide what to do next. While they were smoking and talking, Maman-ti got out his owl and got a message that we ought to head for Palo Duro. The next morning we packed up, ready to move, and were sitting on our horses while the chiefs smoked and continued to discuss what their next step should be. While we waited, it started to rain again. We waited most of the day for it to stop, but it continued to pour down. Suddenly the ground was covered with swarms of hairy black tarantulas, driven by the water from their holes. There was no place where we could sit safely on the ground, so we roosted on our horses during the rest of the day and all through the night. We were wet, hungry, cold, and in need of sleep. The Wrinkled-Hand Chase was becoming less fun.

Next morning the sky was clear, but the air was chilly. We moved westward for a day, then stopped to graze our horses. Locating a herd of buffalo, we had a good chase and resupplied the village with meat. But we didn't know what to do next. We knew that troops were moving about to the west of us. Maman-ti again talked to his owl, who insisted that we would not meet troops if we went southwestward toward Palo Duro. So we veered off in that direction.

There were only two places where you could get down into the canyon, one on the north bank and one on the south. We found the little narrow trail leading down from the north side and got down safely in spite of falling rocks. We felt safe in the canyon, but Maman-ti warned us that if we could find a way down, so could the troops. We would have to be watchful at all times. In spite of this warning we were all so tired that nearly everyone slept soundly, including the camp guards.

After camp had been made on the floor of the canyon, the leaders had another council inside the tipi of the medicine man. Poor Buffalo was a chief, but, not being invited to the council, he sat outside the lodge, trying to hear what was said. Inside the tipi were several of the chiefs, as well as Maman-ti and another medicine man named Tape-day-ah. The latter had a queer way of finding out what was going to happen. Today we would say that he received some kind of radio message from the spirits. He would sing a special song, which would bring a small whirlwind to strike the tipi. The whirlwind gave Tape-day-ah a message, which he interpreted. He reported that all was well, that we would be saved. The chiefs all thanked him.

Maman-ti then said, "I want to report what my owl has just told me."

"Go ahead," said the chiefs.

"Southeast from where Poor Buffalo is sitting, outside the lodge," said Maman-ti, "a tragedy is going to take place tomorrow."

The chiefs were surprised. They didn't know that Poor Buffalo was sitting outside. I have thought of this prophecy many times since then, and I realize that K'ya-been was killed the next day just where Maman-ti predicted the tragedy.

The leaders were uneasy. Not satisfied, in view of the medicine man's warning, with the present campsite, they had the village moved a little farther down the canyon where the chasm is nearly a mile wide, and there are high bluffs on both sides. We did not know it at the time, but at that very hour the Quahadi Comanches and the Cheyennes were searching along the south rim for the other trail, and they were being followed by Mackenzie's troops.

The next morning a few of the women were up early, cooking breakfast, but the most of us were still in bed. We heard two gunshots, but were not alarmed. We thought that it was some early-morning deer hunter getting meat. Soon there were four more shots. We still thought nothing of it. Later we found that the shots were fired by Chief K'ya-been [Red War Bonnet], who had seen soldiers coming single file down a trail from the south rim and had fired the shots to warn us.

Suddenly much firing broke out in the distance, like corn popping in a skillet. I got up and began putting on my war paint. The women and children started running toward the cliffs. They tried to climb up the bluffs to get away from any fighting which might occur in the bottom of the canyon. My oldest sister, and one of our cousins, Hoodle-tau-goodle, became afraid of the high cliffs and turned back.

The firing was coming closer. I was about ready, when a man outside the tipi called to me. It was K'ya-been. He told me to get on my horse and go see what was the matter with some woman who was crying. K'ya-been had on his buffalo horn cap and was just leaving to get into the fight. I wanted to join him, but did as he asked.

It was my sister, half crazed with panic. She had her baby in a carrier on her back. "Give me the baby," I said. "Then you can get away faster. I'll help you."

"No!" she cried. "Let's throw it away!"

"I'd rather throw you away!" I shouted. "Here. Hand me that baby. You get up behind." I took her and the child in the direction in which the other Indians had fled. We came to a place where those who were on foot were climbing the bluffs. I told her to get off, take her child, and join those who were climbing up a side canyon, where the cliffs weren't so high and steep.

Then I went back toward the firing. As I got closer, the gunfire slackened. I was afraid that I had missed out on the fight. As I went on past Indian saddles and blankets lying on the ground, I saw a gray Army horse lying on its side. An-zah-te, who was behind a tree, had shot the horse of the officer who was leading the troops. The soldiers had stopped and were rounding up the ponies abandoned by the Indians. With them were a few Wichita scouts, or maybe Tonkawas.

The guns started firing rapidly again. I heard an Indian singing

200

behind a pile of rocks. I stopped and looked. It was Poor Buffalo, singing the song of the Blackfoot Society.

"It is a great honor to be killed by an enemy," he said, "and K'ya-been is already asleep."

When I got to the place where K'ya-been had been shot, they already had his body across a horse. He had been hit in the head, but had not been scalped. The enemy had cut off his little finger to get a ring that he was wearing. We took him up the trail to the top of the canyon, where some of his band were waiting for us. They danced to honor K'ya-been's bravery. His little brother washed the blood from him, and the women dressed him in his finest clothing. In his hands they placed his eagle-feather medicine fan. They were afraid to tell his mother until several strong women held her. Then Haun-goon-pau called to the old woman.

"Your son has gone to sleep now," he said.

The mother said to the women who were holding her, "Turn me loose. And give me back my knife. I'm not going to kill myself."

She turned to Poor Buffalo, saying, "I want to say something about your Grandmother God. Don't pray to it when I get sick. Don't hunt for something to cure me. I would rather join my son. It was a great honor for him to be killed by an enemy, but"—she kissed K'ya-been—"my life is broken."

They carried the dead warrior to a hole in the cliff and piled rocks over him.

Off to one side were some Indians who were members of another band. They were laughing and shouting, having captured several Army mules loaded with sugar. They were helping themselves.

That night we had more hard rain. But the battle had stopped when the soldiers gathered up our horses and burned our lodges. Maman-ti made another prophecy, saying that we should go west on the Staked Plains and camp there for one moon. After that we would move back to Palo Duro. He called out Blue Shield and me to act as rear guards.

Later, as Blue Shield and I followed the village, we saw a big crowd ahead of us on a dark place in the prairie. At first we feared that the soldiers had surrounded our people and had massacred them. We decided to go on, anyway. Then Blue Shield wanted to turn back. I persuaded him to continue our advance. We agreed that we might as well die with our people.

When we got close, we saw that the dark mass was a train of pack burros that our people had captured from some traders. They were looting the packs.

The camp was moved west along the Prairie Dog Town Fork of Red River. That night the burros made so much noise with their braying that the chiefs were afraid that they would attract the attention of any troops who might be in the vicinity. So we turned them loose.

The next day we turned south to the Yellow House country. Blue Shield and I continued to act as rear guard. Occasionally we saw buffalo. Again we overtook the half-witted young man, who once more had been abandoned and was walking along in a forlorn way. We felt sorry for him, but couldn't offer him much except advice.

That evening we found the Indians camped on a sandy-bottomed creek, where they stayed for two days. The next move was to a place which Iron Shirt called Flint Cliff Creek. He said that the Cheyennes generally came there to get flints and that they rarely went any farther south. The place held a bad memory for Iron Shirt, because his brother had been killed there by Navahos while the two of them were hunting antelope. He showed us the place where he had buried his brother and said that the Navahos had come back later and stolen his brother's war bonnet from the grave.

For the next move, Poor Buffalo sent Poro, a Mexican member of the tribe, ahead to pick out the next campsite. Poro could talk to any Mexicans whom he might meet along the way.

During his journey, Poro saw two soldiers, who called to him in Mexican, inviting him to come up for a talk.[2] "We are on good terms with the Kiowas," they told Poro, "but we had better go and tell our officers that your village is coming, otherwise they might think you are hostile. If it is all right with them, we will let you bring your village here. We will also give you some hard bread."

[2] They must have been from the New Mexican militia, if they were indeed soldiers. No Mexican troops could have been that far inside United States territory at that time.

Meanwhile, the village had arrived nearby. The people were waiting for Poro's report. Blue Shield and I came up at this time. The two Mexican soldiers wanted some of us to go with them for the council at their camp, so several of us, including Maman-ti, went. At their camp we saw Mexican troops and a big blue wagon. At first we thought we had been trapped, but two officers came out and shook hands with us. They said they were friendly and would not fight us. They invited us to spend the night with them and have a feast. I was suspicious and urged our men to leave, but the idea of food was too much for them. The officer gave us some blankets and told us to make ourselves comfortable in the camp. I still advised our men against treachery, urging that we sit up all night, on the alert for attack.

Their captain must have understood something of what I was saying, for he tried to reassure us. Maman-ti then told him that he knew that a Navaho scout was with them. Since the Navahos were our deadly enemies, it was necessary as a proof of friendliness for the captain to bring the Navaho out to shake hands with us. The captain went to the blue wagon and woke up a Navaho who was asleep there. The Navaho undid his long hair, came over, and shook hands with us, smiling. We asked him what he was doing with the soldiers. He said that he was working with them.

Nearby was a band of Mexican buffalo hunters. They promised to bring us some coffee in the morning, also some sugar and tobacco. We took turns staying awake that night, but no one disturbed us. The buffalo hunters brought us the coffee, sugar, and tobacco in the morning, and we went back to our village.

Camp was moved south that day. In the evening one of our Kiowa-Mexicans named Mo-ha-te took his burro out to graze, as was his custom, and left it hobbled. As he was returning to camp, he saw a man approaching from a clump of trees. Although it was almost dark, Mo-ha-te could see that the man was carrying a gun. Mo-ha-te drew his pistol and in Spanish told the man to halt. They talked for a few minutes, but Mo-ha-te learned only that the stranger was the Navaho whom some of us had seen at the Mexican camp the night before. The Navaho's manner convinced Mo-ha-te that the Mexicans were planning to attack us and that the Navaho was scouting our camp.

That night half of our horse herd was stolen. Tracks of shod horses were found right beside one of our tipis. Those of us on the east side of camp did not lose our horses, but those on the west side lost all of theirs. This put us in bad shape, especially since we had lost much spare stock and a lot of our camp gear in Palo Duro. We began to doubt that we could stay away from the reservation much longer.

We turned eastward toward the Wichita Mountains and camped the first night at Gyprock Creek, or Trading River.[3] Big Bow, who had been with the Comanches since the wagon train fight, rejoined us here. Tehan had been with him, but had disappeared. Big Bow remarked that some of us now seemed to be on foot, like Pawnees.

Our next move took us to a big round lake, where there was a large camp of Quahadi Comanches. One of them, a man named O-ha-ma-tai, recognized me. He and my grandmother were relatives. He asked why some of us were traveling on foot. I explained that the Mexicans had stolen our stock. He then said that he had heard that I had turned out to be quite a warrior. This made me feel pretty good.

While we were camped at this place with the Quahadis, a Kiowa woman named O-ma-tay died during a choking spell. A Comanche medicine man doctored her without success. It was the custom to move from any campsite in which someone had died, so on the following day we moved to the place where the stones had moved. I cannot explain how those stones had moved on that old lake bed. They must have moved by themselves, for no one could have done it.[4]

---

[3] Trading River was either White River or Duck Creek.

[4] This refers to a mysterious terrain feature, described by many old Indians, which was apparently located somewhere northwest of Lubbock, Texas. From the accounts of Kiowas and Comanches who had been there while on the warpath in the 1860's, it was a dry lake bed where at one time huge boulders had slid across the surface in straight lines. Photographs of a like phenomenon in the Far West have been published recently, but no satisfactory explanation has been offered. The Indians, of course, attributed such things to supernatural causes.

Next we came to the place where recently some troops had attacked a Comanche village and had captured the women and children. We saw the tracks going southwest from there. It was part of the same band we had seen on Trading River, who had fallen behind during the move to the lake and had been overtaken by the soldiers.

At sundown, Poor Buffalo made an announcement. He said that An-zah-te, Ay-pay-yah, and I should saddle up, follow the troops, and find out what they were doing. We thought he was the biggest fool to suggest such a reckless move, but we did it. We followed the trail through the evening shadows until we came to the top of a hill. The fires of a soldier camp were burning brightly in the valley beyond. I told the other two men to hold my horse while I crept closer to find out if any Indian scouts were with the troops. But they wouldn't let me, saying that it was too risky for one man. All three of us sneaked up to the camp. The soldiers had gone.

On our return trip to the village, my horse's hoof struck some metal object. I dismounted to see what it was and found a new revolver and a belt full of cartridges. Some soldier had dropped it in the darkness. My happiness over this find did not last, because one of my companions asked me for the gun and belt. It was a Kiowa custom that if a fellow tribesman asked us for anything we had to give it to him.

Soon after we reached the camp, I heard some one singing in An-zah-te's tipi, which was next to mine. Presently Little Owl came to my tipi to say that they were getting up a raid. He invited me to join. I said I would.

Next morning eight of us started on this raid. Ai-yah-te was the *to-yop-ke*. On the second day a snowstorm blew up. The leader evidently had been expecting this, for he was dragging along with him a lodge pole. We broke this in half for firewood and used the other half for a tipi pole. Fortunately the storm was a mild one, and the weather was still fairly warm for that time of the year.

The following night we came to a spring dug by Apaches. It was a free-flowing artesian spring, which made a lake. The Apaches had abandoned it because of some superstition about artesian springs. Though this was not our superstition, we had been warned against using any of the water, so we went thirsty that night.

We now turned back to a place near the Pecos River where there was a trading post of which we had heard. It was deserted, having been raided by the Apaches. Two Comanches who were with us found some tobacco in the store which the Apaches had overlooked.

I now decided that I had had enough traveling, having been on the move for several weeks. But when I told the leader that I was going to turn back, he said, "You might get lost. You don't know this country."

But I started riding east by myself, traveling at night. After riding steadily for two nights and two days, with only short stops to rest, I came to our village. The rest of the raiding party came in two days later, much surprised to find that I had not gotten lost.

The Comanche chief, Esa Rosa, and another Comanche named Frank Maltby came to the camps. They wanted the Quahadis to go in to Fort Sill and surrender. They had a white flag and a message signed by Colonel Mackenzie, Chief Black Beard, and Kicking Bird. Many of the Indians now decided to go in and give themselves up.

I left the party at Navaho Mountain and went on in alone. When I reached Signal Mountain, at about sunset, some Indians came at me as if they were charging. I got out my bow and arrows and made ready. As they came closer, I saw that they were Kiowas wearing soldier uniforms. I recognized Sai-au-san, Kau-goo, and a Comanche. They had become army scouts. They didn't bother me.

I left my horse by a spring and threw my bow and arrows into the creek, then footed it on in to the military post. My heart was beating faster as I drew near the barracks, for I didn't know what they would do with me.

It was now dark. I heard Indian drums beating and Indians singing the song of the Blackfoot Society. That club was having a dance in Kicking Bird's camp. I went there, just as though I belonged to their camp. A fellow named Bo-tone recognized me and asked what I was doing there. He told me that my own band had surrendered and were prisoners. They were counted every day. He didn't think that I could join them. He told me where my mother's tipi was, but doubted that I could get into it.

Seeing two men at the dance who were from the prisoner camp,

I went up to them and told them that I was ready to become a prisoner. They said, "You'll get your head cut off!"

I replied, "All right. But at least I'll get a good meal first."

The prisoner camp was along Medicine Bluff Creek east of the present highway bridge. The Indian scout's camp was between that and the ice house where the prisoners were held. Lieutenant R. H. Pratt, in charge of the prisoners, counted them every day.

That same night Sankey-doty and several other members of the raiding party came in also. They said that they were not going to be put in the guardhouse, but they didn't know about me. They told me to go up and report to H. P. Jones, the post interpreter, before I went to bed. They took me to his house and knocked on the door. Jones, who spoke Comanche, came to the door and asked me what I wanted. He invited me inside and told me to sit down. He felt me all over, then said, "You're pretty young to be thrown in with these other prisoners, all of whom are older warriors. What have you been doing?"

"Been on a raid," I said.

He asked me how I managed, at my age, to get into a raiding party. I gave him a big story about how I had been out with the Apaches during the recent outbreak. Some report had to be made to Kicking Bird so that he could decide what to do with me.

"You ought to go to school," said Jones. I agreed.

The next morning they took me up to post headquarters to put me in the guardhouse. The sentry said, "You'll have to see Kicking Bird first."

When I saw Kicking Bird, he told me that I would only have to be in the guardhouse for four days.

My stepfather was in there. At the time I was released, they told me that I could pick out five other men to be turned loose at the same time. I chose Quitan, Tsa'l-au-te, Sait-keen-te, Aun-bodle, and a Navaho captive named To-ya-kee.

But in my excitement I forgot to include my own stepfather. ✿

207

33 ✿ THE MYSTERY OF TEHAN

IN THE KIOWA TRIBE were at least two white captives, each of whom the Indians called "Tehan." The name is simply the Mexican pronunciation of *Texan* (*Tejan*) and indicates that they were captured in Texas. One was the woman, Mary Hamleton, whose story has already been related. The other was a tall, powerfully-built, young man with blond or reddish hair and a red neck. The Indians say he "looked like an Irishman." At the time of the Wrinkled-Hand Chase (fall of 1874), Tehan was thought to be about eighteen years old. Since he still remembered his mother tongue, I would judge that he was eight to ten years of age when taken; it was the common experience that children kidnaped while young eventually forgot all their English or Spanish.

Such captives usually retained vague recollections of their parents and the circumstances of their capture, but when adopted by an Indian family lost all desire to leave the tribe. Those recaptured by the troops and forcibly restored to their white relatives returned to the Indians at the first opportunity.

We do not know Tehan's real name or his origin. Possibly it could be worked out even at this late date by obtaining information from the Kiowas about the probable sun dance year in which he was captured and the area. This information, compared with frontier

and Indian Bureau records of captives not recovered, or those sup-
posedly killed, might produce clues to his identity. So far as I know,
no one has undertaken such a study in the case of Tehan.

The following account of Tehan's activities in late 1874 was furnished by Hoodle-tau-goodle (Red Dress), daughter of Maman-ti
and foster sister of Tehan.

☼ Just before the wagon train fight we made camp one evening on
the west side of a two-pronged creek that ran northeast into the upper Washita. After we had put up our tipi, Mother said, "Three colts
are missing from our herd. We are going back to see about it."

My brother, Ai-pay-an, said, "Please do not go—either you or
Father. Let Tehan go." He was afraid for Mother and Father to
go. Tehan was our foster brother.

So Mother asked Tehan if he would go, and he said he would.
He had just started to saddle his dun mule when our cousin, Botalye, rode up and asked Tehan what he was getting ready to do.

"Going back to last night's campsite to look for some lost stock,"
said Tehan.

"Don't do it; or if you must go, be careful," said Botalye. "Our
scouts have seen fresh tracks of shod horses not far to the north and
west. It is dangerous to be separated from the village at this time
when troops are probably looking for us."

Tehan laughed. "I'm a white man. I still understand their language. I can talk my way out of any trouble if they catch me."

Our father gave him an old muzzle-loader and told him to go
ahead to look for the stock, but to wait until morning before starting
out. "It is too dark to leave now," he advised Tehan. "You won't be
able to find the animals."

Early next morning, Tehan took a bag of dried meat that Mother
gave him, mounted his mule, and rode off to the east. My sister and
I cried when he left. We were afraid for him.

As Tehan told us later, he found the stray colts grazing near our
former camping place and started to drive them to the village. On
the way he saw a buffalo, which he shot. While he was butchering
the carcass, the ponies which he had been herding continued on

toward camp, which was visible in the distance. It was near sunset, and the thin wisps of smoke from our tipis were rising in the orange sky to the west.

After Tehan had packed the meat behind his saddle, he mounted his mule and rode on, following the colts. He started to look for a ford a little upstream from the camp because the water had risen from the recent heavy rains. Suddenly he heard a clicking noise to his right and looked up. Four soldiers had just come around a clump of trees and were sitting on their horses only a few paces away, staring at him. Their guns were in their hands, ready for instant use.

Tehan snatched his gun from the scabbard and jumped to the ground. The soldiers didn't move, but they had him covered. Their leader said, "You are a white boy! What are you doing here? Are you living with the Indians?"

Tehan had to think for a minute before he found the English words with which to reply. "Yes. They treat me good."

They took his gun and his mule, made him take off his moccasins so that he wouldn't run away, then put him up behind one of the soldiers and rode off toward the Canadian River. They took him to a soldier camp where there were a lot of wagons. The officer in charge of the camp came out of his tent and said, "Why, this is a young white man, dressed as an Indian! Where did you find him? Why do you bring him here?" The leader of the patrol explained that they had snatched up Tehan when they were scouting an Indian village and that since they were hurrying with dispatches for General Miles, they had to turn him over to the nearest troops. They told the officer to watch Tehan, lest he try to escape. They said that he seemed to be thoroughly Indianized.

The white officer shook hands with Tehan and told him to sit down. The soldiers asked him many questions about his life with the Indians.

The next day, Sai-au-san and his wife were following Tehan's tracks, which they saw when they were on their way to the village. First they came to the place where he had butchered the buffalo. Going farther west, they came to where he had been captured. They saw his barefoot tracks and the tracks of the shod horses. Looking around in the grass, they found his rifle scabbard and one moccasin. Sai-au-san decided that some Indian had been captured by soldiers and probably taken elsewhere to be killed.

"Take this moccasin to camp," he said to his wife. "Maybe some one will know whose it is. I am going to follow the tracks to see where they killed him."

That evening we were having a victory dance over the killing of some soldiers during our first day's attack on the wagon train. None of our family's people had been killed or even hurt, but some of their horses had been shot from under them, which was an honor. So my mother, sister, and I were dancing to do them honor. During the dance the camp crier made an announcement:

"Listen! Attention! Up against the sand hill on the other side of the creek, someone has been caught and taken captive. Sai-au-san's wife has the moccasin. Everyone come here to see if we can tell whose it is."

When we saw the moccasin, we burst out crying. We knew right away that it was Tehan's and that the soldiers had caught him. It was terrible.

Quite a few of us started out to hunt for the body. I was with those who went to the ford where the moccasin had been found. It was dark, but we lit some wisps of dry grass and saw Tehan's barefoot tracks in the mud. Some of the men followed the soldiers' trail. Next morning they brought word that Tehan had been taken to some soldier camp on the Canadian.

During the wagon train fight, while the troops and the wagons were still moving toward the Washita, some of the Kiowas had seen someone whom they now realized must have been Tehan. He was walking along under guard of two soldiers.

A large number of Indians took part in the attack on the wagon train. Nearly the whole tribe was there. It was dangerous to get close, but I was young, curious, and didn't mind the danger. I saw most of the fight, including the preparations made by our men before they charged. All the men were getting ready in a little valley on the other side of the ridge from the wagons. Each man was putting up his medicine and praying to it. Old Man Frizzlehead [Ai-mo-tai] called for attention.

"I pray that the enemies' guns will shoot dust instead of bullets," he cried.

The *Tai-me* keeper was there too. A lot of people were making offerings to his medicine.

When the shooting started, I went up on the ridge. There below us were the big canvas-topped wagons, with soldiers going along on foot on both sides. Our men scattered out as they got closer. Once in a while one of the Indians would make a horseback charge. I still don't see why they didn't get hit. I saw my cousin Botalye making dashes on his chestnut horse. He became famous on the third day for making more charges than any other warrior. Ke-so-yay-ke was also there. He made a target of himself but wasn't hit.

We learned later that during the fight Tehan was in one of the wagons making plans to escape. Finally the soldiers got short of water. The Indians shot at them each time they tried to go to the water hole. They made another try for it on the third night. Tehan volunteered to go with them. When the Indians shot at them, one of the soldiers was hit and fell down. Tehan fell too, pretending that he was hit. But in the darkness he rolled and crawled to where the Indians were. In this way he rejoined our people.[1]

When Tehan came back to us, he had on a uniform and a new pair of pants. When my father heard that Tehan had returned, he gave a victory dance for him. I saw Tehan dancing with the other men that night. After the dance he told us what had happened when

[1] Captain Wyllys Lyman, Fifth Infantry, commander of the wagon train, describes this episode in his detailed report of the engagement: "On the 9th of September at Oasis Creek, Lieut. Frank Baldwin turned over to me a young white man who had been brought up with the Kiowas, and with Indian instincts and ideas, and whom he had made prisoner the day before while the man was on picket, mounted on a mule, near an Indian camp on the Washita River. Lieut. Baldwin, moving with three scouts, had fallen unexpectedly on this camp, and snatching the picket, made off." Lyman stated that he had placed the prisoner under guard and had cautioned the sentries to watch him. During the fight he had forbidden his men to go to the water hole, but some of them had slipped away, accompanied by the captive, who had thus escaped. This, of course, was Tehan.

he was captured, and later. He said that now the soldiers were getting weak from lack of water. The next morning he said that he was going to fight them.

"What's the matter?" we asked. "They are your own people."

"I like to eat raw liver so much that I am going to stay with the Indians and fight on their side," said Tehan.[2]

On the fourth day of the fight our scouts reported that another column of troops was coming from the northwest. We began to break off the fight and moved south a few miles. As we came out of the fight, we met six soldiers and killed them.[3] The Indians trapped them in a little hollow in the prairie south of the river. We camp-movers gathered at a little distance and watched the fight. While this was going on, some messengers came from Kicking Bird inviting us to go back to Fort Sill. They had some safety papers for us and a white flag. But none of our bands were willing to go back at that time. Our men were too "hot" from the fight, too excited.

It began to rain again. Our scouts told us that troops were now coming from still another direction. One of our camp criers announced that it should be possible to find a gap somewhere between the advancing bodies of troops and that we should be able to escape. We turned and headed northeast toward the Canadian. Most of my time during those days was spent on the run.

One of our men, Tai-keep-te, was now so sick that he had to be carried on a travois. Big Bow ordered several of the warriors to guard the sick man at all times and under no conditions to abandon him.

That night it was still raining. We didn't try to fight any more, we now were only trying to get away. It was a miserable journey. We would get sleepy, get down on the ground, and try to sleep in the mud while holding to the reins of our horses' bridles. Then the

[2] This expression concerning "eating raw liver" was the Kiowa way of saying that a man was a true Indian.

[3] This was the famous Buffalo Wallow Fight. The six men were civilian scouts Billy Dixon and Amos Chapman and four soldiers. One soldier was killed, and all but one of the other men were wounded. They were rescued by some of Miles's command.

chiefs would get us started again. At one of those times a boy named Luther Sah-maunt said, "No. I'm not going to get up. I've just got my puddle of water warmed up, and I'm not going to leave it." But they kicked him out of it.

When daylight came, we were heading for the Canadian once more. Some other messengers arrived from Fort Sill to ask us to turn back to the Wichita Mountains. Some of the Kiowas accepted this offer, but the band I was with refused. The men said they preferred to have some more fighting. The biggest part of this group scattered out, but soon reassembled. Some of us now started back toward Fort Sill, ready to give ourselves up.

My oldest sister's husband said to Tehan, "Let's go out on the Staked Plains. We don't want to become prisoners at Fort Sill."

Tehan wanted to go, but he was worried about the old folks. "Who will take care of Mother?" he asked. Mother wanted him to stay with her, and he agreed. But some of the other men, including my father, wanted to head west and stay out with Poor Buffalo and Lone Wolf. Therefore part of the Kiowas headed for Palo Duro, while the rest of us went to Fort Sill. When we crossed the Salt Fork of Red River, about where the town of Mangum now is, we felt safe. Tehan thought that he could safely leave the band now and join Big Bow and Kia-pooh-ke, who were planning to join the Quahadi Comanches on the Staked Plains. So he packed up and went with them.

It was still raining. The clouds hung low over the prairie. The last time I ever saw Tehan he was riding into the mists and silences of the Staked Plains. He never came back.

Later we had reports that Big Bow, suspicious of anyone with white blood, had killed him. I believe that to be false, for a Comanche later known as George Maddox told me that Tehan had come to their camp, which some of our family verified by talking to other Comanches. Maddox gave me this story:

"After the Indians fled from Palo Duro, Tehan and I became partners and went on several raids. We lived for some time with some friendly Apaches in the Mescalero country. Finally Tehan heard that his foster father had been taken, with other Indians, to a prison in Florida and had died there. He told me that he must go back to take care of his mother. I said that I would go part way toward Fort Sill with him, but was afraid to go on to the post. I thought they might put me in jail. After we parted, I did not see Tehan again."

I do not know what happened to Tehan, whether he was killed by an enemy or starved for water in the desert. He may have lived for a long time with Indians who stayed out. Many years later I was called to Anadarko to talk to a white man named Joe Griffis who said that he was Tehan and wanted to see some of his old Kiowa friends. I did not recognize him as my foster brother, but he may have been some other Tehan. He did know some Kiowa and something of our customs. But no Kiowa ever learned the final end of our Tehan. ✿

As a postscript, it might be added that in May, 1875, a Comanche named Aycufty, which means Red Hair, was killed on the Loving Ranch, in Texas, by some rangers under Lieutenant Ira Long. This red-headed Indian may have been Tehan, but the evidence of that is very slim. It must be concluded that Tehan's fate remains as much a mystery as his origin.

34 ✤ FROM TULE CANYON
TO PALO DURO

SHORTLY AFTER BIG BOW, accompanied by Tehan, disappeared into the Staked Plains, he reappeared with Black Horse's band of Quahadi Comanches, somewhere in the vicinity of Tule Canyon, or about halfway between the site of the present Plainview, Texas, and Palo Duro. He was accompanied by another Kiowa, whom Mumsukawa calls "Stick Game Man." Whether this was Tehan, we probably will never know.

Mumsukawa, who told me this story, was a Quahadi and brother of Co-hay-yah, another Comanche informant. His account of the happenings during the few days immediately preceding the Battle of Palo Duro Canyon is like many Indian fragments of history—it has no beginning, no end, and no plot. But it illustrates the spirit in which the Indians conducted many of their "battles." They were simply having a good time.

✤ After the fight at the Wichita agency at Anadarko, some of us ran off to the west. One day a few of us were moving our camps along a stream which we called the Indian Perfume River. This may have been the Prairie Dog Fork of Red River, but more likely was Tule Creek. I am not sure of this. It was the first branch that ran south of the Goodnight Ranch.

216

We tried to hide our tracks at first, but soon forgot about that and went up on a hill to look for buffalo. This was in an area where there was a two-forked creek. As I galloped up the hill, I saw a great herd of buffalo on the other side. Near them rode a lone soldier whose sorrel horse was shying at the buffalo. I hurried back to report to our party what I had seen. As I approached them, I shouted that there was a white man on the other side of the hill—an *eks-a-pana* [soldier]. They all got out their horses and started to mount up. My partner and I dashed off without waiting for the rest; we wanted to make first coup.

When we got to the top of the hill, the white man had disappeared into the buffalo herd. We started to track him, but at first saw nothing but buffalo tracks. As we were preparing to cross the creek, another Comanche came up. He asked us what we were doing. We told him. He doubted our story, saying, "I don't see anything."

But in a muddy spot on the other side of the stream we saw a few fresh tracks of a shod horse, going away from us. Just then Chief Black Horse came up. Together, we followed the tracks. Other Indians were coming along close behind us. At the crest of the next hill we saw the soldier again. He saw us too and stopped. Then he galloped off over a low rise.

When we got to the place where the man had been, we saw in the distance the white tents of a large soldier camp. In order to get a closer view of it, we went up the branch that came from the camp. Soon we saw lots of soldiers herding horses. They outnumbered us, and in addition we saw some Tonkawa scouts with them. On a little hill nearer us was a lone man, probably acting as a sentinel.

Big Bow, who with another Kiowa had joined us, yelled, "Let's stop and shoot that tai-bo!"

Big Bow raised his sights and shot at the man, but missed. He spurred his horse to get a better shot, then stopped. It was still quite a distance to the man. We all stopped. Maybe the man was an Indian. We weren't sure. We wanted to have a smoke and discuss the great number of soldiers we had seen and what we should do about it. One of our bunch said, "I see two soldiers driving horses away from the camp, one a sorrel and the other a white horse."

A Comanche and Big Bow started toward these soldiers. At first we only watched. Then Black Horse said, "I'm going up there and get those horses away from them!" He started out, came up a hill, and shot at the two enemies. The two soldiers jumped on their horses and started back toward their camp. We chased after them. The man who was riding the white horse was thrown to the ground. Big Bow and the other Kiowa were on foot too, but Black Horse, being mounted, caught up rapidly. Big Bow shot the soldier who was on the sorrel horse. As he fell slowly from his horse, Big Bow caught him in his arms and scalped him. The other man ran into the brush along the branch and disappeared.

Hearing the shooting, the soldiers who were herding the horses began to run around and catch up their stock. We withdrew slowly in the direction from which we had come. In a moment we stopped and looked back. Here came Black Horse, leading the big sorrel of the soldier killed by Big Bow. It was limping from a wound in the ankle.

The soldiers hadn't seen us. They went chasing off in the wrong direction. We saw their dust cloud going through the hills and saw little groups on the high ground looking for us.

Toward sundown, as we approached our camp, two of us stayed behind as rear guards. We saw nothing except a single white man who rode across in front of us. He didn't see us, and we didn't bother him, but continued on toward camp. That evening the village moved again, the movement continuing all through the night. By climbing up the Cap Rocks we got on to the Staked Plains, where we made our camp. The following day we moved again, preceded by Big Bow, who acted as scout for us because he was very familiar with this part of the country. Our camp was now on a little branch that we called Cedar Creek, the source of which was far out to the west.

The next morning, while chasing buffalo, we were joined by a large number of Cheyennes. We took them to our camp and held a big dance and feast in their honor. Everyone sang the Warpath Journey Song.

About noon the next day the Cheyennes came in to tell us that they had seen some soldiers very near us. Several Comanches got on their horses and rode out to investigate. They met Big Bow, who also reported soldiers coming our way. No troops appeared, so we decided that these reports were not true, that Big Bow and the Cheyennes had seen something else moving on the plains. It is not always easy to tell what distant moving objects may be.

In this case we were wrong. That night we saw lights on the plains. When we came up to them, we found that the troops had built campfires, then had moved away from them in order to fool us. It was a clear moonlit night, and there was no timber in that area. It was light enough so that the enemy tracks could be followed. Three Comanches and three Cheyennes started to follow them; I was one of this group. We dropped off a man to listen, while the rest of us moved on a little. Then we dropped off another man, within hearing distance of the first. The night was so quiet that anything moving on the prairie could be heard for a long distance. In this way we covered a broad front as we advanced. But we failed to locate the enemy.

After a time I saw a bright light to the west. Going up to it with my partner I found Big Bow and the other men assembled. From that point on we all dismounted and continued to search the prairie on foot. Presently we saw some horses in the bright moonlight. They were near a water hole on the creek. From the sounds, the troops were just arriving at their camping place. I saw no wagons and did not hear the usual "Whoa, whoa" of the mule drivers.

The three Cheyennes in our party, who had their guns ready, began to fire at the soldiers, who promptly fired back. The night was lighted up by the red flashes. From the sound, these must have been the long rifles of the walk-soldiers rather than the Spencer repeaters of the cavalry. The Spencers had a lighter sound.

By this time a few more Comanches and many Cheyennes had joined us, but after firing for a few more minutes we all decided to withdraw a little and wait for daylight. In the morning we could hear bugles and voice commands in the soldier camp. I decided to play a joke on one of the other young Indians. I proposed that the two of us ride out in the open toward the soldiers and let them shoot at us. To my dismay he took me up on it. I couldn't back out, so we went up behind a hill and started to paint ourselves and decorate our ponies. But before we were ready to make our run, some Cheyennes beat us to it. This spoiled our plan, in fact spoiled the attack of the Comanches. Everyone scattered, while the firing broke out in all directions.

I saw some soldiers ride down and shoot a Cheyenne who was retreating on foot. Then, while the soldiers charged some other Cheyennes, we went in the opposite direction down a small creek. It was becoming quite exciting, and we were enjoying being chased.

Then everything quieted down. Six Comanches, some men and women, came along, asking what had happened. We told them about the Cheyenne who had been shot, whereupon they wanted to go over and have a look at the body. We pointed out where he was lying on the side of a hill and went with them. After satisfying our curiosity, we all rode off over the hill.

The question now came up of how we should assemble all the scattered Indians. Early that same morning some of us went to a waterfall in a side canyon that ran north into Palo Duro. Black Horse went in another direction to round up others of our band. The Cheyennes, who knew that soldiers were coming, had already gone down into Palo Duro Canyon. When we Comanches got to the rim the troops had already arrived, had worked their way down the cliffs, and were attacking the Indian camps.

Most of our party had not yet arrived, but four of us went toward the sound of the gunfire. On the way we met Chief Mow-way and his nephew. He told us to clear out.

"You had better escape from the troops while you are able to," he said. "The soldiers have already driven the Indians out of the main canyon and are rounding up their horses and shooting them."

We went back to a rocky branch, where we found Black Horse. He asked us who had been attacked. We replied that according to Mow-way it was the band of a Kiowa named Red War Bonnet. Soon after this we met some Indians who were trying to get out of a side canyon by climbing the cliffs. The soldiers still held the only trail which led into the canyon from the south rim. They told us that the only Comanches who had been in the canyon at the time of the attack were Tabananica's brother, named Roan Girl, and a few of his people. Only one Kiowa had been killed, Red War Bonnet, and no Cheyennes nor Comanches.

The troops had driven the horses they had not shot into a side canyon. After we were sure that the soldiers had withdrawn, we went down there and helped ourselves to them. I caught one which had a scalp and a war bonnet tied to the saddle. When we had gone back to the plains, I asked some Cheyennes whom we met whether they knew who owned the horse, the scalp, and the war bonnet. They took these things.

That's all I saw. ☼

35 ❂ DEAD MAN'S MEDICINE

THE OFFICERS AT FORT SILL and the officials at the Indian agency
had heard little or nothing of the man who, other than Kicking Bird,
was the most powerful and clever Kiowa leader. This man, who did
not make himself known to the white men, was Maman-ti, a medicine man and war chief who took a leading part in most of the raids
conducted by the warriors of the tribe during the period 1864–74.
He was wise in planning, skillful in leadership, and above all he
could foretell whether an expedition would be successful, for he was
an owl prophet.

When the wars ended in 1875, he was one of the leaders nomi-
nated by Kicking Bird for imprisonment in Florida, together with
the nominal head chief, Lone Wolf, and a number of other prominent raiders. The Kiowas of that day claim that because of Kicking
Bird's role as agent for the white men and his naming of those who
were to be punished, Maman-ti promised to cause his death by
witchcraft. Shortly after the prisoners departed from Fort Sill on
their way to St. Augustine, Kicking Bird did die suddenly. The post
surgeon listed the cause as "poison," though he performed no au-
topsy. Meanwhile, Maman-ti declared that his own life would soon
be forfeited because he had used his power to cause the death of a
fellow tribesman. Not long after the prisoners reached old Fort

Marion, where they were confined, the following telegram was received from Lieutenant Richard H. Pratt, officer in charge of the Indian prisoners:

FORT MARION, ST. AUGUSTINE, FLORIDA, July 29, 1875.
To the Adjutant General: I have the honor to report that at 8 o'clock A.M. the Kiowa Chief Mah Mante died in the hospital at St. Francis Barracks. . . .

Born about 1835, Maman-ti, whose name means Sky Walker or Man-On-A-Cloud, was about the same age as Kicking Bird and his rival for top leadership or position of chief influence among the Kiowas. He was married twice. By his first wife he had three children, the oldest being a girl named Hoodle-tau-goodle. By his second wife he also had several children, one of whom was in later years known as Rainy Mountain Charlie. Hoodle-tau-goodle said that Charlie looked exactly like his father. She described Maman-ti as being a tall, slim man, slightly bowlegged. He had straight, shiny black hair and a slender face. She emphasized that he was a famous man in the tribe and that he was friendly, sociable, and popular.

Originally Maman-ti was a buffalo medicine man, perhaps one of the earliest members of that cult. One day he went down to the creek to cool off and while there fell to studying the whimpering cry of a screech owl which was in a nearby tree. Presently he realized that he understood what the creature was saying. The Kiowas believed that the owl was the embodied spirit of a dead relative. From the owl Maman-ti received new medicine power, and thus he became an owl prophet. In addition to this experience, he had an even more interesting adventure in which he died, traveled to the village of the dead men, and thus gained increased knowledge of the spirit world. Iseeo, who was one of Maman-ti's friends, tells this story.

☼ There are some things that I saw myself, but I can't explain them. When I was a young man the greatest medicine man among the Kiowas was Maman-ti, whom we usually called Do-ha-te.[1] He

[1] *Do-ha* means "medicine man." The final syllable *te* might be a familiar ending

223

died once, visited the dead men's village, but came back. After that he had the dead man's medicine. He did wonderful things, some of which I saw myself.

Once, many years ago, the Kiowas were camped where the cattle trail later crossed the Washita River. Do-ha-te, who had a bad fever, died at sundown. He died all over, except his heart, which had a slight movement. Because of this he was not rolled up for burial. He remained dead until sundown the next day, when he moved a little, opened his eyes, and looked around. Within a week he was well enough to sit up, and from then on he got better fast.

For a year Do-ha-te said nothing about the time when he was dead, and he did not tell anyone what he saw while he was dead. Then one day while the Kiowas were camped on the North Fork of Red River he sent for his friends to come to his lodge. He wanted to talk to them. I went with the others.

Do-ha-te said, "A year ago I was very sick with fever. I lost most of the meat from my bones, and my face was so poor that I looked like a dead man. Finally one evening I died, and my breath [soul] went out of my mouth and right on up.

"I saw the dead man's road, which I followed afar off to the top of a smooth ridge. From the summit I could see a clear, sparkling stream in the valley beyond. Beside the timber along the stream was a very big village. The lodges were as numerous as the blades of grass in the field. Many people were moving about in the village, while off to the side were grazing thousands of horses.

"Some one called out in Kiowa, whereupon the other people looked up and saw me. Quite a few came to meet me, including my father, mother, brothers, sisters, and other relatives who had died long ago. They took me into the village and said, 'We left you when you were a little boy down there. Now you are big. Up here we have put away the poverty and hunger and sickness that overtake people down there.'

"Even the Cheyennes and Arapahoes in the dead men's village,

---

of personal names, like the *y* in *Charley*, for *Charles*. Probably, however, it is simply a masculine ending to a proper name, meaning "man."

whom I had never seen before, knew me. The first time the dead people took me into their lodges everyone crowded in to see me. They all stared at me—people I had known before and others who were strangers.

"They all said, 'So you died down there below!'

"After a while I became frightened and started to go out of the lodge. But all the dead people said, 'Hold up! Wait! Do not go out. Sit down.'

"But I bolted out of the lodge. At that moment my eyes opened and I saw my live relatives looking at me anxiously. Then I knew what had happened. I said to myself, 'I have been in the dead men's village. But I got away!' Now that I was alive again, and had gotten over my big scare, I began to remember how good it was up there. They had horses and everything else that we have. I remembered that when I looked inside their lodges I saw things that were lying around on the ground the same as we have. Actually we are worse off than they are. Their country is better. They live better than we do. I now am homesick for that land. I do not want to live here. I want to go back to the land of the dead men!"

Some time afterward, the Kiowas were made prisoners [1875] and were moved in to Fort Sill. Some of the chiefs were chosen to be sent east to prison. Do-ha-te was one of these, for he had been a great war chief and had led many war raids. A few days after they arrived at the prison, according to what one of them told me later, Do-ha-te said, "Call in all my friends."

The other Kiowa prisoners went into his room and sat down.

Do-ha-te said, "My friends, I am sick. Not very sick, but I do not live well here. I had a bad journey coming here. About three hours after sunrise tomorrow I am going to die. I want to go back to that land above, where I was before."

The next morning he said, "Call my friends quickly!"

We went into the room where he was sitting on an army cot. We looked at him without saying anything.

"I am going above this morning," he told us again.

He did not appear to be sick, but he got up, walked around our group, and shook hands with each of us. Then he went back to his bed, lay down, and pulled the blanket up over his head as if he were going to sleep. We talked quietly for a long time. He did not move again.

After a while one of the men went over and pulled the blanket off Do-ha-te's face.

"He isn't breathing," said the man. "I think he has been dead for an hour or more, for he is getting cold."

This time Do-ha-te had gone to the dead men's village to stay, for later that day Lieutenant Pratt sent a man who put him in a black box, and they buried him in the post cemetery.

If one stays only a little while in the village of the dead men, then he may get well and come back; at least a few have done so. But if he stays a long time there, he is truly dead and will not recover. I have heard our old people tell about some who had died but came back after a day or two. This was when the Kiowas were in the far north where boiling water and steam shoots out of the ground. These people, when they came back from the village of the dead, said the same things that Do-ha-te told us. So I think they must be true. ☼

36 ✸ WOMAN ON THE WARPATH

By the summer of 1875, the Kiowas and Comanches had been subdued by the military campaigns conducted during the previous winter. The leaders thought to be guilty of causing the outbreak had been sent to prison in Florida, and the others were required to camp on the reservation near Fort Sill, where they could be watched. The rations allotted them by the Indian Bureau were insufficient, being based on the theory that the Indians could support themselves by hunting and by raising crops. Unfortunately, the nomadic Indians could not instantly become proficient in agriculture, while at the same time most of the game had either been driven away or killed by the white buffalo hunters. Consequently, by 1878 the Indians were starving.

These deplorable conditions did not cause the Indians to go to war, but they did result in two killings, both of which could have been prevented by issuing adequate food. Some of the officers, moved by the pitiable condition of the Indians, were buying beef for them out of their own pockets, but the post commander discouraged this, saying that the Indian agent either could not or would not reimburse them for such expenditures. He gave the Indians permission to go beyond the western limits of the reservation to hunt buffalo and furnished a troop of Negro cavalrymen as escort. The soldiers went along more to keep the Indians from becoming involved in fighting the Texans than to supervise the hunt. In this they were not entirely successful for, as stated, two men were killed, an Indian and a Texan. The following story of these tragic episodes is based on material furnished by Ay-tah, whose first husband was Set-maunte, Gui-tone, Hunting Horse, and his wife, Peah-to-mah.

❁ The Indians left their camps near Mount Scott and traveled west to the vicinity of the Goodnight Ranch in the Staked Plains. Not finding any game in that area, they were about to turn back, when Iseeo encountered a Comanche who told the Kiowas that his people had gone south of Red River in the neighborhood of where the town of Quanah was later established and that they had found buffalo there. He said that his father's camp was well supplied with meat.

At once the Kiowas headed in that direction. They found the Comanche camp, but the Comanches advised them to get back across Red River at once because Texas Rangers might attack them. They explained that they had avoided danger so far by remaining concealed in the timbered hills during the day and venturing out to hunt buffalo only at dusk.

The Kiowas recrossed the river, but Sun Boy refused to go farther. He made his camp on the north bank. Iseeo and his band then separated from Sun Boy's group and continued north to about the site of Granite, Oklahoma. Iseeo felt that it was unlucky to remain with Sun Boy who, having killed a fellow tribesman in a drunken brawl a few years before, was regarded by most of the Kiowas as being a murderer even though he was a chief.

There was deep snow on the ground, and Iseeo's people were very hungry. The day after they made camp on a tributary of the North Fork, Ay-tah gave birth to her first child, a daughter. In desperation they killed and ate one of their horses, and they didn't have many. They stayed in this area for several days.

Meanwhile, at the camp on Red River, A-to-tain slipped out early one morning, crossed the river, and killed two deer with his bow and arrows. To his disappointment he found them to be fawns born the previous spring. They would not furnish meat for the whole camp, but he brought them in and invited a blind man named Sone-pau-pah to share the meal. The blind man prophesied that bad luck would befall them on account of killing fawns. This cast a gloom over the entire camp, already in a state of low morale because of the severe hunger.

A-to-tain ordered his youngest wife to go to the camp of the soldiers nearby and to borrow a gun and some ammunition. He wanted to cross the river again and continue hunting for game in the cedar-covered hills. The woman brought the gun. A-to-tain prepared for an extended hunt. He took with him a man named Buffalo Calf Tongue, to help locate the game and to assist in packing back to camp any game that they might kill. They crossed the deep canyon through which the river flowed at that point and went up a tributary ravine. There was a heavy growth of cedar trees on both banks. A-to-tain went up one side and his companion up the other.

A party of Texas Rangers was trailing the Comanche who had notified the Kiowas that there was good hunting in that area. A-to-tain and Buffalo Calf Tongue had not gone far up the canyon when they saw the Texans approaching. A-to-tain was on top of a bluff, his companion at the bottom. The Texans saw A-to-tain and started to ride toward him. The Indian knew that they were going to attack. He was mounted on a weak horse and realized that it was useless to try to escape. Therefore he dismounted and prepared to die fighting. He was a warrior, a *to-yop-ke*, had many coups to his credit, and had an honored name in his tribe.

A-to-tain had only four rounds of ammunition, which he intended to save until the enemy came closer. But the Texans started firing right away. A-to-tain fell dead.

Buffalo Calf Tongue, hearing the firing, fled back to camp, where he reported that A-to-tain had been killed. He said that the Texans were coming to attack the village. Captain Nicholas Nolan, commanding the troop escort, assembled his men and had them start to dig trenches to use for the defense of the camp. He told the women and children to conceal themselves behind the earthworks and urged the men to take up their weapons and join the soldiers. But the Indians, thoroughly cowed, were afraid of getting into trouble later if they fired on the rangers. They merely hid behind the troops.

Soon they saw the Texans picking their way down the bluffs on the far side of the river. As they drew near the camp it was seen that the leader was wearing a leopard-skin vest. The Indians were sure that there was going to be a fight, and they were not at all sure that the Negro troopers would get the best of it.

The ranger captain halted his men and rode into camp. Captain Nolan met him, waving in the air his orders from Fort Sill and the written permission from the agent for the Indians to go on the hunt. The ranger read the papers, then hurled them in Nolan's face, berating him for allowing any of the Indians to cross the border into Texas. Nolan knew that his case was weak in that respect, but he demanded the return of the carbine which A-to-tain had carried, since it was government property. The Texans produced it and threw it on the ground. It had a bullet hole through the stock. Following this, the ranger turned abruptly and rode away, followed by his detachment. On seeing this, one of the Kiowa women inadvisably emitted one of their peculiar tremolo whoops to honor Nolan. He didn't appreciate it.

As the Texans passed over the bluff on the opposite side of the river, they pointed to A-to-tain's body. In a few minutes some of the Indians went to recover it. A-to-tain had not been scalped, but his ring finger had been cut off and the red wrappings of his braids removed. The Kiowas buried him in the trench which had been dug by the soldiers.

By Nolan's direction the band now started for home. Messengers were sent to the other bands telling them to return to Fort Sill.

Those who knew the Indians realized that some of A-to-tain's relatives would organize a revenge raid. But this was handled so secretly by the Indians that no word of it leaked out until some time after the war party had returned from their grisly task. Vengeance being a family matter, one of A-to-tain's brothers carried the pipe. This was Pago-to-goodle, at that time not very well known to the whites, but nevertheless one of the most formidable war leaders and fighters in the whole tribe.

"We have to go and get even with the Texans," said Pago-to-goodle. "We will move our camp to Rainy Mountain Creek, just below Rainy Mountain. Any young man who wants to join the raid can meet us there."

Thirty-seven men and one woman, Ay-tah, joined the expedition. Some of those who went were Chaddle-kongey, Tsa'l-au-te, Little Bow, Quitan, Set-bo-hone, Bau-dai, Yee-ah-goo, Lone Bear (Set-pah-go), and Set-maunte. Five or six of these were still living in 1938.

Pago-to-goodle led the party southeast past Teepee Mountain and on toward Red River near where A-to-tain had been killed. North of the site of Quanah there is a lone hill in the prairie which the Indians call Prairie Dog Hill. It was a well-known landmark on their war trail leading south, and for years they had been accustomed to make their raid headquarters in the vicinity. They waited behind this hill all night, and in the council at which plans were completed they agreed that they would be satisfied by killing one white man.

Little Bow, a medicine man of sorts, made a prophecy of success. The next day, Saturday, April 12, 1879, Little Bow, one of the scouts, went to the top of the hill to watch for the approach of prospective victims. The Indians knew that this was a route frequently used by emigrants headed for Leadville, Colorado, and by men going to and from cattle camps. They knew that sooner or later some one would appear.

About midmorning Little Bow signaled that white men were coming along the road. There was a lone horseman followed at a little distance by a wagon with two men on the front seat. They were moving at a walk along the cattle trail, apparently headed for some cattle camp. The Indians remained concealed behind the hill until the white men were opposite them. Then they raced up a little draw which ran parallel to the road and concealed them from the whites. They were riding to head off the leading man.

Ay-tah said that she was riding an old roan horse, too slow to keep up with the rest of the crowd, but she made an effort to stay with the charge. The white man did not see or hear the Indians until they whooped over the little ridge to his left. He was at once surrounded

231

and had no chance to save himself. Pago-to-goodle grabbed the bridle of his horse on one side, Set-bo-hone on the other, and one of the others—probably Bau-dai—shot the man off his horse.

When Ay-tah came galloping up, she saw the white man lying on the ground with a bullet hole in his head. The front of his clothing was on fire, but she did not know whether this was from the flash of the gun or some Indian had set it deliberately. The two men riding in the wagon stopped when they saw the horseman being killed. They quickly unhitched their team, vaulted on to the horses' backs and rode off to the east. In accordance with their agreement, the Indians did not bother these men.

The Indians scalped the dead man, whose name was Joe Earle, and looted the wagon. It was loaded with flour and other groceries and evidently was destined to resupply some chuck wagon. Ay-tah got a coffee grinder for her share of the loot. Quitan got a cheese box which he later made into a tom-tom. The Indians kept the coffee and sugar but spilled the flour on the ground. After robbing the wagon, they departed in considerable haste. When they had ridden less than a mile, they looked back to see four horsemen following their trail. They resumed their flight with greater speed. They also endeavored unsuccessfully to hide their tracks. The pursuers still followed, and from the smoke of signal fires the Indians thought that other white men were gathering to join the chase. When they reached Red River, a big sand storm blew up, in the midst of which they succeeded in throwing off pursuit.

No one was arrested for the killing of Earle. The authorities at Fort Sill got wind of the incident and made an investigation without learning anything definite. The Indians held their usual victory dance secretly and kept the whole affair very quiet. It was supposed at Fort Sill that the Texans took no action because they had insufficient identification of the guilty Indians to enable them to get an indictment in the courts. Joe Earle was the first man buried in the cemetery at Quanah. ☸

37 ✿ A PRAIRIE DERBY

GEORGE HUNT GAVE ME THE FACTS concerning the events in this story of sport on the Plains.

✿ Most Indian ponies were of a cold-blooded strain, being descendants of wild mustangs and domestic animals taken in Texas or Mexico. Though the Indian horse had less lung power and staying quality than the Thoroughbred, occasionally he showed surprising speed over short distances. Perhaps this was at least partly the result of selective breeding. A brave always chose as his favorite war pony the fastest pony in his herd. Several generations of such a line would eventually produce some excellent racers.

Two chief forms of Indian entertainment were horse racing and gambling. Since the two went hand in hand, a race meet generally attracted large crowds. An Indian would wager his most prized possessions, sometimes all that he owned, on the result of a race. If he lost, he was apt to take it very hard. If in addition he thought he had been the victim of trickery or given the short end of a doubtful decision in a close race, he was sometimes given to violent reaction.

The Kiowas and Comanches were subdued by military force in 1874–75, following which their weapons and most of their horses were taken away from them. Not long afterward it was seen that

233

they had to have some mounts, as well as a few weapons, if they were to support themselves, or at least supplement their rations, by hunting. So they gradually built up some small herds. But their stock was never as plentiful nor as good as in the old days when the tribesmen were wild and free. Despite this, horse racing was resumed, if indeed it had ever been interrupted.

In the summer of 1888, the Kiowas, having been forced by the agent to give up their annual sun dance, were turning to a new prophet named P'oinkia, who was trying to keep the tribe on the old road so far as religion was concerned. That summer he summoned the tribe to a favorite camping ground on Elk Creek near its junction with the North Fork of Red River. Here, relatively free from the influence of the missionaries, P'oinkia was staging a medicine show designed to interest the tribesmen anew in the old gods and, incidentally, in a few new ones of his own devising. It is to be feared that he had in the back of his mind a sordid commercial motive.

Some of the Kiowas, notably skeptics Big Tree and Gotebo, saw through P'oinkia's schemes. They drifted away from the revival gatherings and turned to horse racing for entertainment. Gradually a substantial number of other Indians, tiring of P'oinkia's nonsense, joined them. Some exciting times were had until by late fall it became evident that one horse was much faster than the rest and that the average man stood to lose all that he owned if he bet on any other nag. Big Tree and Gotebo cast about for some outside competition. Below the North Fork, in what later became Greer County, Oklahoma, were some new ranches and cattle camps operated by Texans. They too were addicted to horse racing. Big Tree and his partner rode south a mile and a half to a trading store run by Charley and Will Cleveland, where they met some cowboys and arranged to hold a race between the champion horse of the punchers and that of the Kiowas.

On the appointed day over a hundred and fifty Indians, all armed, showed up as spectators. There was an even greater number of whites, likewise wearing shooting irons. Before the race, every man began betting with someone on the other side, and as the stakes increased, so did the tension. There seemed to be a good chance that

234

the race would bring on a general shooting match, with live targets. In placing their bets, the Indians and the whites paired off, one of each to a wager. The bets consisted of cash, horses, saddles, bridles, blankets, firearms—in fact anything of value that the men brought with them. The horses were tied neck to neck and placed in a corral. The articles were also tied together and piled on the grass. The Cleveland brothers and their employees were the stake holders. A trio of soldiers from a nearby cavalry detachment camped at Soldier Spring were the officials—a starter and two judges.

The Kiowa entrant, owned by Podal-doan, was a very fast horse which had cleaned up in all the Indian races that summer. The cowboy entrant was unknown to the Kiowas, but he looked like a dangerous competitor, being long limbed and in fine condition.

The race was run when excitement was at a peak. It ended in so close a finish that each side claimed a victory, and each pair of betters began to grab for the stakes. But the judges fired a pistol in the air to command attention, then announced that the cowboy horse had won. Some Indians who could not accept this decision resumed their snatching at the prizes. The cowboys joined in the grab-bag contest, so that there was a confused melee of small tugs of war in the corral and at the pile of bets. Eonah-pah, Tape-day-ah, and Tone-yai-ai-te each got away with his horse and that of his opponent by cutting the animal loose and galloping away bareback.

The cowboys, taken by surprise, did nothing for a moment, then with increased vigor resumed tussling. Fortunately, a real fight was averted by the action of Big Tree, Gotebo, and several other leaders who aided the Clevelands and the three soldiers in restoring order. After a brief consultation between the opposing leaders and the officials, it was agreed that the race would be run over again, and that all bets would stand. The announcement of this decision was well received. The Indians were even more satisfied when a cowboy named Phil Hutchison got up on the stand and said, "One of those Indians [Tape-day-ah] ran off with my horse. If we win, tell him to bring it back together with his own. If you win, he can keep the horse, and also you take him this money besides." This more-than-fair offer made a good impression.

After half an hour devoted to straightening out the tangle in the corral and letting the horses rest, the race was run once more. The Kiowa jockey was Dom-ai-te, a son of old Big Bow. He was a very tricky rider, who tried several times to cut in front of his opponent and cause the latter to pull up. In spite of this the white man's horse came in ahead, though the race was again fairly close.

Most of the Indians admitted they had lost. Not Blue Jay. He hung onto his old plug, while his white rival was jerking at the rein on the other side. Similarly a Navaho captive member of the Kiowa tribe, an adopted son of Big Bow, tried to run off with his horse. The cowboy with whom he had bet pulled a gun. The Indian let go the reins. Seeing this, Blue Jay drew his revolver and waved it at his antagonist. But another Kiowa stepped between them to prevent bloodshed.

"Let it go," he told Blue Jay. "A man's life isn't worth a horse."

The excitement gradually died down, and the disgruntled Indians went back to their camp. Big Tree and Gotebo remained on the scene for some further talk with the representatives of the cowboys. The two chiefs proposed that the white men give the Indians a

chance to get even by holding another race in the spring of the following year. The white men agreed, but insisted on a change of the rules. They reminded the Indians of the illegal riding of Dom-ai-te and stated that the course would have to be a straightaway, with lanes staked off in which each horse must run. If a horse moved out of his lane, he would be disqualified and the other declared the winner. Big Tree and Gotebo accepted these conditions, albeit reluctantly.

During the winter, the Kiowas held a series of tryouts to select their entry in the meet. The winner was a previously unknown gray colt which showed amazing speed over short courses. It had been bred from Chief Au-soant-sai-mah's war pony. Since the warpath days were over forever, he had given the horse to his adopted daughter, the white captive Millie Durgan. Later the chief had fallen seriously ill. Millie appealed to the next most influential member of the family, Toyebo. The latter urged that a medicine woman, the mother of Yellow Wolf and several other former warriors, be called in to treat the patient. The old woman was an owl prophet. Her therapy, consisting of the usual incantations, was effective. Au-soant-sai-mah got well—perhaps he couldn't stand the treatments.

In deep gratitude Toyebo gave the medicine woman Millie's gray horse. The medicine woman, not aware of its possible value, in turn presented it to her youngest son, Ai-sah.

Ai-sah idly entered the gray colt in the race elimination contests. To his great delight it won every heat quite handily. All the Kiowas were pleased with the colt's spectacular performance, except a man named Ai-au-te, with whom Ai-sah had had a falling out. Unfortunately the Kiowas could not keep the good news to themselves. Through the prairie grapevine the cowboys in Greer County learned that a mysterious horse had been developed by the Indians. They countered by chipping in their pay to buy the current champion of southwest Texas.

When the great day was only two weeks off, a dreadful thing happened. The quarrel between Ai-sah and Ai-au-te had come to blows, in which Ai-sah had the better of it. Ai-au-te was a half-crazed man, having had an evil spell cast over him by the sinister witch doctor,

Tone-a-koy. Burning with revenge, he went secretly to Greer County, where he traded his horse for a Winchester and a box of ammunition. Then he headed for Ai-sah's small frame house at the foot of Rainy Mountain.

Ai-sah, his wife, and two friends, Ah-tape-ty and Toyebo, had gone to ration issue that day at Anadarko agency. Ai-sah had let his wife ride the gray horse. On their return they had unsaddled and were just turning their horses loose in the corral when Ai-au-te came up.

"I'm going to shoot your gray horse!" shouted Ai-au-te. Before the others could interfere he raised his rifle and shot the colt. It sank to its knees and rolled over. Ai-au-te then whipped about and scurried up the west side of Rainy Mountain, where he sat down on a rock and stared at the sunset. Ah-tape-ty followed him and took the gun out of his unresisting hands.

Meanwhile, the other Indians were examining the horse to see if anything could be done for it. But its eyes were glazing over. Ai-sah rushed into the house and came out with his gun.

"I'm going to kill that man," he cried furiously, throwing a shell into the chamber.

Toyebo promptly seized and held Ai-sah while Ah-tape-ty disarmed him. They continued to hold him tightly until he breathed more normally, then released him. They kept the two rifles.

Ai-sah shook himself, then started up the hill toward his enemy. His heavy rawhide quirt dangled by its thong from his wrist. He came up to Ai-au-te, who took no notice of him. Ai-sah aimed a tremendous blow at the demented man, knocking him prostrate. Using his whip, he gave Ai-au-te a brutal beating about the head and chest.

After it was all over, Ai-au-te got up with a smile on his face. "The first chance I get, I am going to kill you," he said. He turned his back on Ai-sah and started to walk away. Ai-sah took up a big rock and hit him a terrific blow between the shoulder blades.

Ai-au-te was not killed, but he was a long time recovering from the effects of the beating he had received. His cause was taken up by his brother, Komalty, a former warrior and formidable fighter. Ai-sah was forced to go into hiding until the trouble blew over.

The Kiowas were aghast over this affair. The fight between Ai-sah and Ai-au-te gave them no concern, for that was a personal matter to be settled, according to custom, between the families involved. But the loss of the gray horse was a disaster to the whole tribe. There was no chance to find a suitable replacement during the short time remaining. They could not ask to have the race canceled, for that would involve too much loss of face. Everyone was in despair.

At that critical juncture, Big Tree had a happy inspiration. "I will go to Caddo Bill and borrow one of his horses," he said.

Caddo Bill Williams was a white man who had married into the Caddo tribe and had lived among the Indians for many years. At his ranch near Verden he kept several fine horses, including a few Thoroughbreds purchased in Kentucky. He had raced them in the Bluegrass region as well as in the prairie country, and with considerable success.

Big Tree placed the problem of the Kiowas before Caddo Bill and asked his help. "We would like to borrow one of your race horses," he said. Bill promised to consider the matter and give the chief an early reply.

Upon making inquiry among the racing fraternity, Caddo Bill learned that the cowboy entry in the forthcoming race was Corn Stalk, the champion of southwest Texas. He was familiar with Corn Stalk's record and best time for the half-mile. He realized that no ordinary race horse could insure victory for the Kiowas and that they stood to lose most of their personal possessions. It so happened that Bill owned a horse that he felt sure could do the trick, a Thoroughbred named Tom Thumb. This bay colt came from the Steel Dust line, which Bill's stable featured. The horse had already won many races in the Middle West and was in prime condition. Unfortunately he was so well known that the Texans, if they discovered they were faced with so formidable a contender, might call off the race, or at least would not place any bets.

Caddo Bill summoned Big Tree and told him, "Chief, I am going to let you enter my horse Tom Thumb in that race. But he is well known in Texas. You must keep this a secret, even from the Kiowas. Keep the horse covered right up to the start of the race. Don't let any come near him, except two handlers you can trust. Don't even tell your rider about him, or let that man see him before the race. If you do not do this, some Indian will forget himself and will get to bragging. The news will get to the white people."

Big Tree agreed.

"Here is something else," Caddo Bill added. "I'm giving you $25.00 to buy grain for the horse. He needs more than prairie grass. Also here is some money which I want you to bet for me." He handed Big Tree a wad of bills.

Then he took out some more money. "Here is $50.00 which you can bet for the Kiowas. If you win, you can pay me back. If you lose, just forget about it."

Big Tree was properly grateful.

On his return to his camp on Rainy Mountain Creek, Big Tree sent word to all the Kiowas that a substitute horse had been found. He said that he thought they had a chance to win, but that the new entry was by no means as good as the one that had been killed. This falsehood, carefully spread in Greer County, as though by accident, encouraged the whites. Betting began even before the gathering for the race. The Indians, advised by Big Tree, in whom they had confidence, sold most of their livestock to get money to bet on the race.

When the time came to assemble at the place selected for the contest, Big Tree cautioned all the men to go armed. "If you don't have a gun, at least take a knife," he said. "There may be trouble. The whole tribe must be well prepared." Then he changed his former line of talk by saying, "We have a good horse, and we have a good chance. But keep quiet about it." Everyone promised to do as Big Tree asked.

Bill Williams' brand was a new moon. Under Big Tree's supervision the two handlers carefully altered this symbol by plucking out hair until the crescent became two concentric circles with a dot in the center. They tied some deer-hoof rattles around Tom Thumb's neck for good medicine and a skunk's tail at the root of his tail. This was believed to bring good luck and, anyway, it would make Tom Thumb look more like an Indian horse. They wisely didn't try to change his color, for that would be evident and would arouse suspicion.

Big Tree was satisfied that the horse looked pretty much like an Indian nag, but to further strengthen the deception he kept a sheet over the animal as he was led to the paddock at the end of the course, even pulling it over the horse's head. The handlers were told to keep all white men at a distance and not let them examine the horse.

The cavalry detachment was still camped at Soldier Spring to watch the cattle trail and prevent unauthorized grazing within the Indian reservation while the great herds were driven north to the railheads in Kansas. Half the detachment was from Fort Sill and half from Camp Supply. The commander was Lieutenant "Squid" Rice. The Indians asked Rice and his sergeants to act as officials at the race.

"If a fight starts," said Big Tree, "you may join either side, as you like. Or you may get into the fight as a third party and shoot at both sides."

In addition to Lieutenant Rice, the affair was attended by a number of prominent civilians from west Texas and the Territory, including sheriffs, marshals, judges, and traders. These, together with the ranchers, cowboys, and Indians, formed a much larger crowd than had been present in the fall.

Once more the bets were made, recorded by the Clevelands and their clerks, then tied together and piled on the grass in an enclosure. The horses were tied neck to neck and placed in a corral. In some cases horses and cows were paired. There was a considerable amount of currency in the hands of the stake holders, and a conglomeration of weapons of all sorts. The betting went right on, up to the very start of the race.

Big Tree again passed the word to the Kiowas to be on the watch for signs of trouble.

A straight course, half a mile in length, had been laid out on a smooth part of the prairie, free from rocks and prairie dog holes. At one end was the starting line, and back of that was a small corral which served as paddock.

The white man's entry, Corn Stalk, a beautiful sorrel stallion, was already there, dancing around in the hands of his groom, lunging and rearing—very spirited and hard to handle. Tom Thumb, still covered with his sheet, was standing quietly in a corner. Whenever someone came up to look him over, the handlers said, "No, no! Medicine man say very bad luck. No can see!" The white men would grin tolerantly and move away.

The Kiowa jockey, a middle-aged man named He-at-keah, stood nearby. He was a pint-sized fellow, weighing less than a hundred pounds, and certainly not at all impressive. Nevertheless he was the best horseman in the tribe, a trick acrobatic rider and a noted buffalo chaser. If he was foremost of a people who were the best equestrians the world has ever seen, he was indeed good. He was wiry and muscular, reckless and resourceful. But he had never even seen his mount before, so he was trembling slightly as he stood there awaiting the signal to mount. He had stripped to his G string, tied a black bandana around his hair, and in his hand he carried a heavy rawhide quirt. He wore no spurs, only moccasins, and was going to ride bareback, guiding his mount with a light racing bridle with a snaffle bit, furnished by Caddo Bill.

Bill Williams stayed away from the race, lest his presence excite suspicion and remind some well-informed Texan that he had seen that Indian horse before. He had sent word to the Indian jockey to use the quirt sparingly and then only on Tom Thumb's forequarters.

The white jockey was in striking contrast to the Indian. He was only a youth, but he had a hard, wise face, and he was a professional racing jockey. He was dressed in the conventional racing costume, with a silk shirt, long-billed cap, breeches, black boots, and small spurs. Corn Stalk had been fitted with a light, flat racing saddle with short stirrups. As the jockey mounted his restless horse, he seemed completely confident, and even wore a slight, contemptuous smile.

The Indians took the sheet off Tom Thumb. He-at-keah took hold of his mane and vaulted easily to his back. He rode out of the corral and trotted down his lane slowly to test out the track. He saw that the white men had gotten away with some trickery of their own. During the night they had carried water from a nearby tank and had softened up the ground in his lane. But he said nothing. He had been told to avoid a quarrel before the race because it might draw too much attention to his mount.

When both horses were lined up at the starting point, "Squid"

Rice came up with a revolver in his hand. "I'm going to count *one, two, three, four*. When I say *four*, I'll fire the gun, which is the signal to start."

The white jockey began to edge his mount forward. The two handlers were having a hard time holding it. He-at-keah's bay was standing quietly, but the Indian could feel him trembling.

Rice counted, fired the gun, and they were off!

You should have seen Corn Stalk leap forward! Tom Thumb was a fraction of a second late in starting, but his first jump jerked He-at-keah clear back to his rump. The Indian edged forward as quickly as possible. He was already several lengths behind, and the white boy was still gaining. Dirt flew up in He-at-keah's face.

By the time he had reached the quarter-mile mark, He-at-keah was holding his own, though still well behind. Now he began using the quirt. Tom Thumb fairly flew. He drew even, passed Corn Stalk. He continued to gain. At the finish he was out in front by at least ten lengths. He-at-keah easily checked him and brought him down to a trot, then a walk.

The Indians went wild. They whooped exultantly and fired their guns in the air. Then they raced to claim the wagers. But there was no need for haste. The decision of the judges wasn't required. The cowboys wandered away disconsolately. Some of them flocked to see the Indian racing wonder. But his handlers threw the sheet back over the horse and whisked him away.

When the white men returned to their ranches, they continued to marvel about how an unknown Indian pony could best the champion of southwest Texas. They never could figure it out. Only Charley Cleveland seemed to have gotten wise. He kept his thoughts to himself, except for a knowing grin when he met Caddo Bill. The rest of the whites wondered if maybe there wasn't something to Kiowa medicine after all! ☼

38 ✸ BIG BOW'S LAST WARPATH

THIS STORY of a great war chief's last fight closely follows material furnished by George Hunt.

✸ In 1886, the Indians were living peacefully on their reservation. A few lived in small frame houses built by the government, but most of them still used tipis. The Kiowas were north of the Wichita Mountains, generally in the Rainy Mountain area. But in the summer of that year many of them were camped along the cattle trail on Elk Creek in order to supplement their meager rations by negotiating with the cattlemen for a few steers. Big Bow's band was at Sheep Mountain, east of the confluence of Elk Creek and the North Fork of Red River. Lone Wolf [Mamay-day-te] was a little farther north at Scratching Rock.

One day a well-dressed white man appeared at Lone Wolf's camp. The fellow had a fancy vest, two big revolvers in silver-studded holsters, a waxed black mustache, and altogether he presented the appearance of the typical professional gambler of that period. He played several games of monte with the Kiowas, permitting them to win modest sums from him.

Little Bow took the gambler down to his father's camp at Sheep Mountain, where he induced the man to spend the night so that Big

244

Bow's group could win some money. They did win a few dollars, and in the morning the white man took his departure. The Indians did not know that their guest was a notorious horse thief and was locating their herds.

Ah-lay-te [Loud-talker] owned a trick horse which was trained to run into camp if anyone tried to rope him. That night after the visit of the white man this horse came dashing into the village. Ah-lay-te, going out to investigate, discovered that his herd and that of Big Bow had vanished. Tracks showed that the horses had been stolen and driven northwest.

Big Bow at once mounted his horse and started for the agency at Anadarko, a distance of seventy-five miles. He intended to consult the authorities and obtain a pass to pursue the horse thieves. Leaving Elk Creek at four in the afternoon, he rode all night, arriving at the agency at daylight the next morning. As soon as the office opened, he went in to see Agent Lee Hall. He wanted to know how he should act if any trouble arose when he tried to recover his property. Hall told him that if the thieves shot at him he could shoot back to defend himself, but under no other circumstances.

Big Bow departed from Anadarko at once and arrived back at his camp that same evening. Though he was 53, he had ridden 150 miles in 24 hours. He rested that night and set forth early in the morning, accompanied by three volunteers: Pay-kee, the son of Ah-lay-te, Henry Gee-oy, nephew of Iseeo, and Tah-baye. They followed the trail of the stolen herd up the North Fork, west of the present town of Lone Wolf. Before they reached the boundary of the Texas panhandle, Gee-oy and Tah-baye dropped out, giving various flimsy excuses.

Big Bow and his companion, Pay-kee, went on. They had little food with them and were poorly armed. Big Bow had an old carbine, but only one cartridge; Pay-kee had a worn-out Winchester .44 and six shells. Realizing that they would have to conserve their ammunition for emergencies, they did not dare use it to kill game for food.

The trail of the stolen horses went near Mobeetie, Texas, then headed northeast toward the Canadian River, near Antelope Hills. The Indians, hungry and out of food, were tired after their almost continuous pursuit of 130 miles. They stopped at a rancher's house, where they were given a good meal and some information. The rancher said that he had seen strangers driving a herd of horses northward on the previous day. The Indians were sure, from his description of the animals, that they were on the right trail. The friendly white rancher gave them some biscuits to take with them as provisions.

That night they found where the thieves had camped the previous evening. About an hour after sunrise the next day, as they came over a low crest, they saw their horses grazing peacefully on the side of a distant knoll. A thin wisp of smoke rising from a nearby campfire indicated where the robbers had bivouacked. No doubt they thought that they had outdistanced any pursuit by the Indians.

Old Big Bow began to feel in his bones a familiar sensation that used to warn him, when he was on the warpath, that fighting was imminent. Nevertheless, he intended to observe, to the best of his ability, the injunction of the Indian agent to avoid giving provocation which would lead to shooting. Therefore, he and Pay-kee went peacefully toward the white men, carrying in their hands only the paper which Agent Hall had given them. They hoped that the white men would surrender the stock which they had stolen.

There was a gully between them and the rustlers' camp, near which they could see two saddled horses tied to a small mesquite tree. As they approached, they were met by gunfire. At once the Kiowas rushed forward and took cover in the gully. The thieves kept on shooting with their pistols. Big Bow told the younger Indian to conserve his ammunition until he was sure of getting a hit. Pay-kee waited a moment, took careful aim, missed the advancing thieves and shot one of the stolen ponies. His second shot was better placed —it hit one of the white men in the arm. The whites at once ducked down and began wrapping a bandanna around the arm of the wounded man.

This gave the Indians a few moments to plan their next move. They decided that while Big Bow kept the enemy occupied, Pay-kee would slip around the flank and drive away the horse herd. This scheme required considerable courage, for the Indians, having so little ammunition, stood a good chance of being killed if they separated. Pay-kee stripped himself of all his clothing, in the usual warpath procedure, and unbraided his hair. He told Big Bow to bring the clothing to a distant point where they would meet as soon as he had driven away the horses.

While Pay-kee was stealthily carrying out his part of the plan, Big Bow kept up a clamor of whoops and catcalls to divert the attention of the white men. Presently he saw Pay-kee dashing over the hills in wake of the horses. He mounted and went in the same direction. Looking back, he saw that the thieves were charging after them.

The Indians saw at once that the white men would soon overtake them unless they abandoned their effort to drive away the horses. This they would not do. They halted, therefore, and prepared to defend themselves and their property. The white men galloped forward, pistols raised ready to fire. Pay-kee, standing behind his horse, rested his gun over the saddle and took aim. Big Bow drew his knife and made ready. Then he took out the papers which the agent had furnished him and waved them at the approaching white men. But the robbers came straight on. Big Bow now recognized one as being the gambler who had visited their camps on Elk Creek.

There followed a bit of dodging about on the part of the Indians, the whites trying to get into position to shoot the Indians without having to fire through their horses. Big Bow kept waving his pass in the air and calling out that he had a "safety paper" from the agent. The robbers paid no heed.

The leader of the thieves was now aiming his pistol at Big Bow at point-blank range, trying to steady his horse so that he would not miss.

"I'm going to shoot him!" growled Pay-kee.

"Go ahead!" Big Bow replied.

Pay-kee fired one shot, striking the robber in the chest and knocking him from his horse. His back was broken, but as he lay on his face in the grass, the man's arms were extended up into the air behind him, and in his convulsive struggles he emptied his pistol into the air. When the flurry was over, Big Bow stepped up and, using his single cartridge, finished the man off. The other robber was disappearing over the hills.

"All right," said Pay-kee. "Where are my clothes?"

Big Bow began to laugh. "I forgot to bring them with me. I was too excited. But here, take this fellow's clothes."

Pay-kee refused. They were soaked with blood. It was bad luck to wear the blood-stained garments of a fallen enemy. They did not hesitate, however, to appropriate the white man's guns.

Pay-kee was forced to ride naked for many miles. He was so embarrassed and annoyed over this that he wouldn't speak to Big Bow for the rest of the day. Finally they came to the camp of a Cheyenne, located on Custer's old Washita battleground near Antelope Hills. Here they obtained food and some garments for Pay-kee. The latter was still mad at Big Bow, however, when they reached their own camp on Elk Creek. Here the shooting of guns and the whooping of the women to announce their triumphant return mollified him somewhat.

Big Bow was later brought before a magistrate to explain the killing of the white man. Agent Hall quickly obtained his release. The evidence showed that the Indians had acted in self-defense. Furthermore it was known that the dead robber had a long criminal record.

Big Bow tied another knot in the fringe on his leggings to represent another enemy vanquished without the aid of medicine. ✿

248

39 ❋ MEAT FOR GENERAL MILES

THIS INCIDENT, reflecting life at Fort Sill after peace had been made with the Kiowas, was recalled for me by George Hunt.

❋ In 1893, General Nelson A. Miles was department commander with headquarters at Chicago. In November, he sent word to the Seventh Cavalry at Fort Sill, Oklahoma, that he wanted some wild game for his Thanksgiving dinner. The colonel told the troop commanders to get busy.

It was a rush order. Only a few days remained before the holiday. Each cavalry troop made different plans to accomplish the mission, for the problem was a tough one. All game had become scarce on the reservation.

At Troop L, the Indian troop, there was a council of war among Captain Hugh L. Scott, Lieutenant Ernest Stecker, and First Sergeant Iseeo. The latter was told to pick three men who had had much experience in hunting. He chose Sergeant Kicking Bird, nephew of the late chief, Sergeant Jim To-done, and Mark Auchia, youngest son of Satanta. Each white troop also picked its best huntsmen.

The Indians left before daylight and rode west towards Jones Ridge. When they got to Four-Mile Crossing they split up. Auchia, on the right, went along Medicine Bluff Creek toward Mount Hinds. Kicking Bird, in the center, went due west, while on the left, To-done rode just to the north of Signal Mountain.

The Indians knew that deer always go to the high ground at daylight. Just as Kicking Bird peeped up over a hill, he saw five deer coming toward him. In his excitement he failed to tie his horse. He lay down, took aim, and fired, hitting one of the deer. As the animals ran, he hit another. Then a third. Two of the deer he had shot were crippled, but ran. He followed the trail of blood. Shortly afterward he found one of the deer he had wounded. That made two for certain.

Presently he heard a shot from the direction To-done had gone. Since his horse had run away, he called to To-done to ride after it and bring it back.

Now the sun was rising. Auchia, who had followed the creek, flushed five turkeys. One lit in a tree. Auchia sneaked up close enough for a shot and hit the turkey in the neck.

Therefore, the three Kiowas were able to return to the post an hour after sunrise packing two deer and a fat gobbler. They were met by Captain Scott who grinned broadly when he saw what they had. He was proud of his men.

The white soldiers brought in a few quail and prairie chickens.

The post quartermaster boxed the game, packed it in ice, and took it in a buckboard to the railroad station.

A few days later a telegram came from General Miles expressing his thanks and congratulations to the huntsmen.

The following year Miles decided to come to Fort Sill and get his own meat.

The post commander sent Captain Scott with a large troop detachment to Cobb Creek to establish a hunting camp before General Miles should arrive. Scott took his own Troop L and one of the white troops, as well as the regimental band. The Indians could see that this was going to be a very luxurious hunting camp and that everyone was going to have a big time.

Scott had nearly established his camp when Iseeo came in from Fort Sill with the mail and some messages from the post. Some of the officers from the post had just come in from Beaver Creek, reporting that there was far more game on Big Beaver Creek, south-west of Duncan. Scott decided to move camp to that locality.

The camp consisted of conical Sibley tents for the men and wall tents for the officers. For General Miles they erected a hospital tent, with a fly out in front as an awning.

While waiting for General Miles to arrive, the Indians spent their time playing monte. The game was in full swing one day in the big mess tent, which was made of two or three wall-tent flies. One of the gamblers was Hau-nai-te, an accomplished braggart. During the game Hau-nai-te was boasting about how he was respected as a boy and how his father and mother always fixed him a fine soft bed. He finally talked himself into building an exceptionally luxurious bed for himself in his squad tent, while the rest of his comrades slept on the ground.

Hau-nai-te left the monte game, went out into the timber along the creek, and cut four stout forked stakes and some crosspieces. He lashed these together with willow strips and bark to construct a frame, supported by the forked stakes sunk in the ground. After all this labor he was dripping with sweat, for it was a hot day in late October. Then he returned to the woods for moss, leaves, and brush for his mattress and pillow.

While Hau-nai-te was engaged in all this labor, several practical jokers in the monte game made plans to destroy the fancy bed about the time it was completed. The idea was that they would start a fake fight and that the other men would try and stop it but would fail. One man was to chase the other out of the mess tent and into the tent where Hau-nai-te was finishing his bed. Everyone would rush in to stop the fight, and in the confusion the bed would be smashed. Hau-nai-te couldn't blame anyone—it would be an "accident."

The fight came off as planned, and Hau-nai-te's bed was duly destroyed. The only trouble was, the fight turned into a real one. Even the sergeants couldn't stop it, and finally the camp guard had to be called out to quell the rumpus.

As the ring leaders were brought before the troop commander for company punishment, they wondered if maybe Hau-nai-te wasn't having the last laugh.

Finally General Miles arrived, very handsome in a tweed hunting jacket, a jaeger hat with a feather, and sporting curled mustachios. He and Scott, accompanied by the latter's three pointers, went hunting for several days, bagging an escort-wagon-load of turkeys. The hunt was a great success. ☸

40 ✦ THE RED NOSE

I HAVE ALWAYS REGARDED other people's superstitions with an amused contempt. Nevertheless, there are certain tunes which I will not whistle or hum because I have noticed that they invariably bring me bad luck. I never deliberately subject myself to the sure peril of untoward events by putting on my right shoe before my left one. These controls have been firmly established over the years, and I heed them.

It is now time to confess that a curious thing once happened to me that compromised, at least in part, the superior attitude which I formerly held toward other peoples' whimseys.

One hazy October day in 1936, my wife and I drove up through the Wichita Mountains to visit some of our Kiowa friends. They persuaded us to take them to an Indian trading post north of the Washita in the Cheyenne country. I think it was somewhere near Cloud Chief, Oklahoma. We found the store worth the trip, being stocked with a wide variety of Indian curios. It is true that some of them were made by machine in Chicago and designed chiefly for the undiscriminating tourist, but this establishment, being well removed from the routes of the ordinary sight-seer and catering mostly to the Kiowas, Cheyennes and Arapahoes, had some authentic collector's items. Most of the articles on the shelves were, of course, trade goods which have always appealed to the Indian—bright blankets, shawls, and calicoes, small colored beads used in decorating garments and moccasins, and soft doeskin, either white or yellow. There were also bracelets, arm bands, earrings, and other ornaments, usually set with turquoise, which have been made in New Mexico by Mexicans and Indians and sold to the Plains tribes for two centuries or more.

Our Kiowa friends also pointed out to us a number of rare articles which had been made several generations ago when the tribes were nomadic and "wild." Among these were pipes carved from a red stone found in the far north, and fans and war bonnets beautifully made from eagle feathers. These were genuine museum pieces, quite costly. In fact most of them were beyond my means, but I was no collector.

Some of these Indian heirlooms were recognized by our Kiowa friends. They knew the families from which they had come and in some cases gave us a short history of the article and its old-time owner. They told us that an old Indian would not part with such a keepsake unless his need for cash was acute, and even then he only pawned it, hoping at a later date to redeem the article. Usually the trader would not sell the piece without consulting the Indian who had brought it to the store.

We noticed then and at other times that the Indians, like rural people of the white race, are interested primarily in displays featuring things which pertain to their own life. When they later visited us in Washington, D.C., from time to time, and we took them to the Smithsonian Institution, they always headed straight for the Indian exhibits and could not be diverted by Lindbergh's plane or the replica of Mount Vernon made of Japanese cultured pearls.

While we were browsing around the trader's store, I noticed hanging on the wall what appeared to be a taxidermist's skunk. When I took it down to examine it more closely, I noticed with surprise that our Kiowas scurried off to the other end of the store and devoted close attention to some Navaho rugs.

"This is a pouch made of the entire skin of a skunk," I said to my wife. "But it is odorless. Our friends needn't have been so alarmed."

"I wonder what it was used for?" mused Elleane.

254

"Perhaps to hold small articles," I said. "Or maybe kinnikinnick. See, here are some little pieces of cloth, with something tied up in them. Either tobacco or herbs. At least I hope so!"

I looked at the price tag with some astonishment. Polecats came high. Besides, it wouldn't quite harmonize with the decor of our living room. And it wouldn't be entirely appropriate in the dining room.

"I don't see how they managed to peel off the entire hide from the head, body, legs, feet, and tail without making more than this small incision in the underside. It is expertly tanned, too; it's soft and pliable."

Holding up the pouch I called to one of the Kiowas, "Look at this, Jim! A whole skunk skin made into some kind of a pouch or handbag. What's it for?"

Jim and his wife did not appear to have heard me. Again I called to them. Other Indians in the store looked up, saw what I had in my hand, and began to edge away from me. One or two couples hurriedly left the store.

Jim and his wife glanced at me with little smiles of embarrassment and walked still farther away. I followed, holding out the black-and-white fur bag for them to see.

They drew back in horror. "Please put it down! Don't handle it! Don't touch us with it!" they cried.

My curiosity was now fully aroused. "For heaven's sake, why?" I asked. "It's harmless, absolutely odorless, and clean."

"Put it down right away," Jim insisted. "You'll get Red Nose."

I wondered what they meant by that. Their distress was so evident that I didn't want to press them for an explanation, since I seemed to have created some kind of a crisis among the other customers. So I decided to question them on our way home.

Later, while driving our friends back to Rainy Mountain, I asked what they meant by "Red Nose." No explanation was vouchsafed, but they did say that the bag was the medicine pouch of some Arapaho witch doctor and that anyone else who handled it would get Red Nose. I saw that they were unwilling to discuss the matter further.

At home that night I remarked to my wife, "I still don't know what they meant by Red Nose. It is beginning to bother me."

Elleane seemed unconcerned. "Just relax," she said. "You'll probably find out in due time."

A few days later our Kiowa friends came down to Fort Sill to see us. When I went to the door, they stared at me for a fraction of a second without speaking. Their faces were expressionless. Tactful as always, they forebore to comment on my appearance. I couldn't help but wonder if they weren't laughing inside.

For, as surely as my name is not Rudolf, I had a red nose—a beautiful, ruby, glowing, Red Nose!

Sure, it must have come from an infected hair follicle in the nostril. No doubt about it at all. Yet sometimes I wonder. . . .

41 ✸ UNDERWATER MEDICINE

DOCTI WAS THE KIOWA EFFORT to say "doctor," and they gave the nickname to a witch doctor who served an enlistment at Fort Sill as a member of the Indian scouts—Troop L, Seventh Cavalry. Iseeo, a sergeant in this unit, once told the story of where Docti got his special power.

✸ Docti had a bewitch medicine he told me about himself. A long time ago he started with six other Kiowas on a raid to get horses in Texas. The first day they camped in a canyon of Red River where there is a wide and deep pool. When the Indians drove their horses down to drink, they saw many turtles in the water.

Docti decided to bathe himself in the pool. The warm water made him feel drowsy. While lying in the shallow water eating tubers of cattail rushes, he went to sleep. He awoke to find himself in the green depth of the pool, in the center of an underwater lodge. On each side of the door and facing each other with their wide mouths open, were huge fish. The opening itself was in the shape of a big turtle. Around the lodge sat underwater medicine men in the forms of frogs, snakes, water dogs, turtles, and other weird creatures.

Then the Sun god, streaking down through the dark green water in a shaft of light, ordered the water witches to give Docti whatever part of their medicine he should request. So Docti went around the circle and asked each one for a piece of his medicine. In this way he not only got bewitch medicine but medicine to make bewitch fail— unbewitch medicine. He also got medicine to cure sickness and still other medicine to give success with women. Any kind of medicine— he has it.

When Docti went to cure a sick man he would sit on the foot of the sick man's bed and sing and shake his rattle. The sick man liked to hear that; it made him feel good. Then Docti would give him something to swallow—I don't know what. In his medicine pouch he had different things, one medicine for stomach hurt, other medicine for other trouble. He also slapped the sick person gently with a fan made of five or six eagle feathers. Sometimes he sucked the sore place, or scratched it with a flint knife. Then he sucked out the blood, and with it the sickness, which he spat out on the ground. At other times he only sang and danced a little. Or he blew on the sickness, and the man got well and paid him for it.

Docti's medicine was all the things that lived under the water. But his special medicine was a turtle with a back and tail having rough, sharp points on it. So he took the name *Tone-a-koy*, which means "Snap Turtle."

Many Indians say he was a bad man and that he killed people with his bewitch medicine. They say that the two Comanche chiefs, Tabananica and Cheevers, died from being bewitched. They were not sick. But suddenly they dropped dead. ✿

Tone-a-koy denied that he bewitched anybody when he was reported to the Indian Bureau for killing people twenty miles away. The case was investigated by the officials, but nothing was learned. Captain Scott testified that the Indian had been a reliable soldier during his period of military service.

42 ☼ THE POWER
OF THE WITCH DOCTOR

HUNTING HORSE, who was related to Tone-a-koy by marriage, had numerous occasions to observe the power of the medicine man. He combined several of these in the following account.

☼ Tone-a-koy frequently renewed his medicine power by making visits to the underwater gods who had given him that power in the first place. On hot summer days he used to go under the water of Medicine Bluff Creek near Fort Sill to sleep. Once I saw him lie on his back and sink slowly below the surface. I stayed there for an hour, but he didn't come up. I went to the scout camp to tell his wife what I had seen and that I feared that her husband had drowned. But when we returned to the creek to pull out his body, Tone-a-koy was standing up in the water shouting strange things at it.

Once a small child named Clyde Koko fell sick with a high fever. Tone-a-koy lifted the boy in his arms and walked into the deep blue pool now called Heyl's Hole, above Medicine Bluffs. He kept the child under water for an hour. When he finally came up, with Clyde sleeping peacefully in his arms, the fever was gone.

On another occasion four Comanches came to Tone-a-koy's tent in the scout camp. They had been drinking and were bragging that they were better medicine men than the Kiowa. One of them,

Saddey-taker, said, "We came here to find out who has the most power, the Comanches or the Kiowas. Let me show what I can do." He took a soft white eagle feather from his hair. He passed it around the circle to let everyone inspect it. Then he opened his large mouth and shoved the feather down his throat. In a moment, when he pulled the feather out, it was bright blue. "Now let us see what you can do," he said to Tone-a-koy.

Tone-a-koy untied a string of black and white beads from around his forehead. He laid them in his open hand and began to rub them. When he took his upper hand away, only a few wisps of grass were in his palm. He threw these into the fire. Then he thrust his hand into the blaze and took out the beads unharmed.

"It's your turn," he remarked to Saddey-taker.

The Comanche simply repeated his trick with the feather.

Tone-a-koy removed the black handkerchief which he wore around his neck. He rolled it into a ball, put it in his mouth, and swallowed it. Then he jerked it out of his side.

The Comanche desperately did his feather trick again.

Tone-a-koy now smoothed off a place on the ground in front of him and made a little mound of dirt. Over this he spread his black handkerchief and blew on it four times. The pile of dirt turned into a string of beads. These he threw into the fire and took them out again unharmed, as before. He leaned over backwards, thrust his fingers far down into his throat, and began to tremble. In a moment he pulled out a ball of ice, which he passed around for inspection. He tossed the ball into the fire. After it certainly was melted, as we all could see, he reached in, took it out again, and swallowed it.

Saddey-taker sheepishly went through his one trick with the feather once more.

Now for the final test! Tone-a-koy belched loudly, coughing up seven army carbine cartridges. Everyone was permitted to handle them. He threw them into the fire. We all tried to get out of the tent, expecting them to explode. But they did not. Tone-a-koy took them out of the fire, one at a time, and swallowed them.

Guy Ware told me that he once saw Tone-a-koy let one of his helpers shoot him in the mouth with a rifle at eight paces. The bullet went through his neck, for when he fell over unconscious there was blood coming from behind his head. But when they went up to him, the blood had turned to Indian paint, and Tone-a-koy got up unhurt.

I had a bad time with him once when I was a young man. As I grew up, I wanted to be friendly with everyone and live at peace. One of my nieces was married to Tone-a-koy. All the Kiowas knew that he was very cruel to her. But his medicine was so strong that we were afraid to do anything to him. Finally I couldn't stand it any longer. Though he was older than I, I told him that he would have to quit mistreating my niece. He didn't pay any attention to me.

I got to brooding over this. Finally I said to myself, "This is a very bad man. He has a crazy heart. I want to kill him." When I had thus made up my mind, I was very decided about it. I loaded my Winchester and called to my friend Yellow Hair. I wanted him for a witness.

Tone-a-koy was asleep in the next tipi. I gave Yellow Hair a smoke and told him, "Tonight I am going to kill Tone-a-koy. I am going to walk right up to him and shoot his brains out!"

Yellow Hair, taking me by the hand, said earnestly, "Wait, wait."

"I'm going to do it now," I insisted.

"No, no! Put your heart back! I love you. Everyone likes you. You are a good man. If you do this thing, it will be evil. Don't let the bad spirit lead you to do this awful thing!"

By this time I was sort of shivering with excitement. As my friend talked to me, I trembled harder than ever. Meantime my enemy was sleeping all unaware in the next tipi.

Finally I said, "All right. Let me go now. I won't hurt him." We were outside under the arbor. The moon was streaming down on us. I fired my gun in the air, thus saving Tone-a-koy's life. He heard the shot. In the morning he asked me who shot the gun. I told him that it was I, that I was saving his life by shooting the gun in the air after I had loaded it to kill him.

Instead of being grateful to me for saving his life, the medicine man was angry at me. He said that he was going to use his medicine against me. A few days later I started to the agency at Anadarko. The ground was dazzling white with snow. After awhile a scum started to grow over my eyes, dimming my sight. The Indian doctors at Anadarko and the elders of the tribe smoked and discussed my case. They suspected that Tone-a-koy was the cause of it.

That summer we were camped near Saddle Mountain. The council of old men advised me that the treatment of the Indian doctors wasn't going to do me any good. They suggested that I go up into the mountains and fast. It had always been the custom of our people to go to a high place and fast for four days and nights as a cure for various troubles. By this time I was almost blind, so I agreed to do it.

First I went to the creek for a good bath. Iseeo's son, Spotted Horse, saddled up his mount and started for the mountains, with me going behind, holding to a rope. We went to a rocky hill several miles west of Mount Sheridan. At the foot of the hill we left the horse and climbed the hill on foot. Since it was in July, the rocks were hot and dangerous with snakes.

Spotted Horse said, "We can't make it."

I told him to go on back. I would continue alone, and I would return in four days. "Or maybe," I added, "I will be eaten by wolves or bears."

The rocks were scorching. I began to cry with pain. I cried to the spirit—any spirit—to have mercy upon me. Then I lay down on the rocks. Toward evening, as I lay there sweating, it began to rain. The air was filled with a terrible roar. The rain turned to hail. It seemed that I could hear a tremendous swishing noise overhead, like a flock of giant birds. This passed right over me and went on toward the Medicine Bluffs. Then I heard sounds like several cannon shots. I covered my head with my robe. The awful storm was all around me. A pile of hailstones grew larger on my chest and I became very cold. I didn't know whether I was dead or alive.

Suddenly I heard a voice saying, "You are going to get well!"

Maybe it was God. That is all I heard. No more.

Toward daylight I woke up shivering. I was still covered with hail. As the skies got brighter, I could see! It was a great joy to me. I got up, turned to the sunrise, and said aloud, "Oh, thank you, thank you!" Then I took up my robe and walked toward my home.

The old people were gathered there smoking. When they saw me coming, two of them ran to meet me. I cried, "I can see! My eye-sight came back. I didn't have to stay on the mountain top any longer."

How happy we all were! ❁

43 ✸ EVIL MEDICINE

HERE IS ANOTHER STORY about Tone-a-koy, which George Hunt obtained from Big Tree and Gotebo many years ago. The events described took place some time after 1890.

✸ On ration day for the Kiowas and Comanches, the Caddoes and Wichitas also used to hang around the agency to trade watermelons for beef. The Kiowas and Comanches, remembering that the Caddoes and Wichitas had aided the troops during the fighting in 1874–75, still regarded them with a certain amount of distaste. But this did not prevent all four tribes from getting together for gambling and horse racing.

During a monte game, a former Wichita scout irritated Tone-a-koy by mocking the Kiowas and otherwise making fun of them. Finally Tone-a-koy smacked the Wichita across the face with his quirt.

"I've got it in for you," snarled the Kiowa medicine man, "because you are acting smart and also because you helped the soldiers when they were fighting us."

The Wichita wiped the blood from his face. "Just because you are Poha-Kiowa [Kiowa medicine man], you think you can do anything. You are going to find out that someone else is more Poha-Kiowa than you!"

264

Snapped Tone-a-koy, "Go the limit!"

Each then threatened the other with deadly witchcraft, for both were witch doctors.

With his kinsmen Big Tree and Gotebo, Tone-a-koy returned to his camp on Saddle Mountain Creek. He asked them to remain there until his contest with the Wichita was settled. He needed some witnesses, in case anyone else should challenge his power.

Thereafter, for several successive nights, Tone-a-koy, before he went to bed, painted his face, neck, and chest green and yellow. He explained that this was to make him look like a bullfrog, source of some of his most effective underwater power. He said that it was a shield against the evil magic of the Wichita medicine man.

After several days had gone by, Tone-a-koy told Big Tree and Gotebo that for several successive nights he had had a bad dream. In this dream the Wichita man was continually threatening his life. Each time his heart had almost stopped. He knew that some kind of power was working against him.

"Tonight I am going to strike back," he said. "I want you to come to my lodge to watch."

After dark, Big Tree and Gotebo went to Tone-a-koy's tipi to see the promised incantation ceremony. Big Tree later said that he was afraid to stay there, all the more so because at the climax of the magic demonstration, Tone-a-koy had produced a gun and said that he was going to shoot. But he had assured them that he wasn't going to shoot them. The Kiowas who were outside the lodge said that they heard this shot fired, then they heard water poured on a fire, which hissed. Then the door opened and Big Tree and Gotebo came rushing out. Later they would not tell exactly what happened. But they said that the ashes rising from the fire, when the water was poured on it, represented something falling to hide their tracks.

Gotebo and Big Tree were obviously badly shaken by what they had seen in the medicine lodge. They agreed that they didn't want to see another such performance. They were even more disturbed to hear, a day or two later, that the Wichita man, while going home from a trip to a store in Anadarko, had suddenly dropped dead.

This was reported as being from heart failure, but the Kiowas knew better. As nearly as could be determined, the death had occurred at the very time that Tone-a-koy had fired the shot. This was at the climax of the death prayer offered in the medicine lodge. Big Tree did tell some of his people that the shot was fired at a drawing on the ground of the Wichita man.

Some complaints were made to the agent by the relatives of the Wichita man. An investigation was held, but nothing could be proved against Tone-a-koy. Since he was still an army scout, the authorities at Fort Sill testified in his behalf at the investigation, saying that he had given no trouble during his enlistment.

Tone-a-koy's sinister reputation grew and spread. ❁

44 ❁ THE STRONGER GOD

CATHOLIC PRIESTS, notably Father Isidore, and missionaries from several Protestant churches began their evangelistic work among the Indians not long after the wars were over. For a time the Indians were unresponsive, and even as late as 1895, Christianity had made little impression on them. In the Rainy Mountain area the Baptists had built a small mission where Miss Reeside and Miss Ballew were in charge. Their interpreter and assistant was Julia Given, a full-blooded Kiowa girl, the daughter of the late chief, Satank. These three young women lived in a small white cottage near the mission. Nearby was Toyebo's home, while across Rainy Mountain Creek were the camps of Big Tree, Gotebo, and Bo-yeadle. Other Kiowas lived in the immediate vicinity.

Tone-a-koy, still an active medicine man, who had also taken up the peyote cult, rode over from Saddle Mountain Creek one afternoon to visit his brother Gotebo and his brother-in-law, Bo-yeadle. They all planned to attend an all-night peyote session. At that time the peyote religion had not embraced any part of Christianity, which it did later. Big Tree was still a pagan, though his wife had been baptized and had joined the Baptist church. Nearly all the other Indians in that area also still followed the old beliefs.

Recently one of the younger members of the peyote circle, Sanko,

267

had become converted to Christianity. Previously he had been one of Tone-a-koy's assistants and understudies, though he had never taken part in one of the death-prayer ceremonies and did not share the witch doctor's malevolent nature.

Tone-a-koy had been enraged when he learned that one of his apprentices had deserted him. Several times he warned Sanko that he would not stand for this and that Sanko had better return to the old religion, and do so at once. Finally the matter came to a show-down. The dramatic story of how this came about has been told to me several times by different Kiowas. Each version differed slightly in detail, though agreeing in all essentials. The one which I repeat here, supplied by George Hunt, has the greatest impact and contains a wonderful lesson.

☼ One afternoon the Kiowas at Rainy Mountain Creek were butchering a steer for the feast which would follow their all-night peyote worship. Among those present were Big Tree, Gotebo, Bo-yeadle, Tone-keah-baw, Goom-dah, and Sanko. The latter was no longer a member of the peyote group, but doubtless hoped to participate in the refreshments. They were standing around the carcass enjoying some gossip and eating chunks of raw liver on which gall had been sprinkled, when Tone-a-koy rode up. Big Tree invited the medicine man to dismount and have a piece of liver.

Tone-a-koy rudely refused. He addressed the Christian convert: "Sanko, I am going to warn you for the last time. Give up the white man's god! Quit that business entirely. Return to the Indian way. Do you get what I mean?"

Sanko replied, steadily, "I have taken the Jesus Road. It is a good road. When I take up a new road, I keep it!"

Tone-a-koy's scowl deepened. "You are doing a very dangerous thing. Jesus is only the white man's god. He is not for the Indians. I am telling you, you had better give up this foolishness!"

"Tone-a-koy," said Sanko, "I have looked all through the old Kiowa religion. I have listened to Pau-tape-ty, who promised to bring back the buffalo. I threw away the lying words of Eadle-tau-hain, who was going to call down the sun to destroy all the white men. I have danced the Ghost Dance and seen it fade away. I have been a faithful worshiper at the peyote altar. There is nothing in any of these medicines.

"But the Jesus Road is kindness. It says to love your brothers, which we Indians have always known was good. The white God is the Great Spirit. He loves us all. I believe in his medicine. I have taken it close to my heart, and I will hold it fast."

"Give it up!" growled Tone-a-koy.

"I cannot," Sanko insisted.

The other Indians had broken off their conversation and were listening intently.

"Do you want to live long?" asked Tone-a-koy.

Sanko wet his lips. "I do. But I am not afraid to die. I am not afraid of your medicine."

"In that case," said Tone-a-koy, furiously, "you had better dig your grave. You are not going to live more than two days. I'll see to that!"

Though badly frightened, Sanko stood firm. "I'm not going to follow your gods," he said. "They promise no salvation."

Tone-a-koy turned to the other men. "Tomorrow my women will build my medicine lodge at the foot of Rainy Mountain. After sundown I will work my power. I will dispose of Sanko. I want all the people to see it, so that they will know whose god is the strongest. Announce it through all the camps, I want all the Kiowas to be there. In the meantime, this poor little Sanko had better get busy and pray!"

Sanko went home. He was terrified. That night he couldn't sleep. By morning he was fairly quivering. He got up, saddled his horse, and rode over to the missionary cabin. Miss Reeside met him at the door.

"Why Sanko!" she cried, "What is wrong? You look sick."

"Me got big trouble," Sanko replied brokenly, "Want help."

"Come in and tell us about it," said the missionary.

Sanko poured out the whole story. When the women tried to reassure him, Sanko insisted that the medicine man had always succeeded in harming his enemies. He told how the Wichita man had recently been prayed to death. He cited other cases known to the whole tribe, wherein Tone-a-koy had used his power for evil.

"What shall I do, so that my God's power will stand against that of Tone-a-koy's god?" he asked.

The women were still inclined to make light of the problem. They assured Sanko that superstition could not harm him, that a Christian was above such things.

Julia Given took the part of Sanko. "You do not understand these things, Miss Reeside. You cannot break the power of the witch doctor by simply saying that such power does not exist. To the Indian it is very real. I have seen some of these things myself, and they are hard to explain."

"Then we must pray," said the white woman. "God will help us."

They all knelt down and prayed for a long time. Their prayers were earnest and sincere. They asked for divine help for Sanko in this, his time of trial. When they were finished, the tears were running down their cheeks—including Sanko's.

For a time Sanko felt better. He went home, lay down on his bed, and tried to make up some of his lost sleep. But his eyes wouldn't close. He couldn't banish the anxiety which was now returning. He felt that his heart was gripped by a pair of icy hands.

Meanwhile Tone-a-koy had awakened from an undisturbed sleep. At breakfast he was still talking about what he was going to do to Sanko. Feeling that a stimulant would be helpful to him in the test of strength that was going to take place that evening, he decided to go to Cloud Chief and buy some whisky. He harnessed a team to his buckboard and drove to the frontier town, some eight miles distant to the north. He took along Dag-o-moi to drive on the way home, in case the stimulant proved to be too powerful. They visited a little saloon where liquor was sold to the Indians clandestinely. Tone-a-koy bought a bottle of whisky. He took a couple of swigs before he left, which made him quite talkative. He also had a few more on the way home, but Dag-o-moi said later that they "went light" on it because Tone-a-koy wanted to be able to act and talk straight at the incantation ceremonies that night.

During the day he had several sharp pains in his belly, and spent

270

a good deal of the time lying on his bunk, softly shaking his gourd rattle and practicing his medicine songs. His women went quietly about their work in the lodge, but about midafternoon he directed them to put up the big medicine tipi on a little rise near Rainy Mountain. Working under his supervision, they also laid a bonfire near the tipi entrance and erected a smaller tipi at the rear, which he would use for his properties for the performance and as a dressing room.

Late in the day Tone-a-koy went to the medicine lodge and, with the flaps closed, prepared the scenery for the big act. Then he went into the smaller tent where he devoted an hour or more to painting himself and donning his costume.

By this time the sun had set and the people were beginning to gather in a semicircle, seated on the ground some twenty to thirty paces in front of the door. There wasn't much talking, and that only in whispers. The spectators were filled with superstitious fear, but couldn't stay away. Even Sanko, the intended victim, came at the last moment and hovered on the back edge of the crowd, no one noticing him in the gathering darkness.

Finally Tone-a-koy's wives lighted the fire, which illumined the tent with a wavering light. They stood on either side of the door and at a sign from within pulled back the flaps, exposing the full interior to view.

"T-t-t-t-t-t-t!" A long drawn expression of amazement and wonder ran through the crowd. On the ground on one side of the lodge was a fire hole filled with glowing embers. On the other side was a miniature lake or pond, realistically constructed with moss in the center, willow twigs around the edge to represent trees, and filled with water. In the water and on the banks were several turtles—live ones with their heads up like serpents, staring unblinkingly at the crowd. Between the pond and the fire hole was the effigy of a man lying on his back with his arms outstretched. The figure was fashioned from earth, and in the chest, over the heart, was a heart-shaped hole about six inches deep. Every person there knew who was represented by that figure.

Suddenly the booming of a bullfrog was heard, first low, then

growing louder. Through a slit in the rear wall of the tipi a gro-
tesque figure entered, leaped to the front, and stood full in the light
of the fire. It was a giant frog. Tone-a-koy had very cleverly painted
his entire body green with yellow splotches. Over his head he had
slipped a realistic mask made of leather and painted to represent
the head of a frog, with its bulbous eyes and wide, gaping mouth.
No doubt the adults present knew this was the medicine man. But
the children did not, and even some of the elders were badly frightened. There were some choked-off cries of fear and a good deal of
whimpering.

Never had the Kiowas seen anything so fearsome!

After a short pause in order to allow the full effect of his appearance to take hold, Tone-a-koy began his dance. He squatted, he
leaped, he waddled like a frog. Then he began to gyrate, shaking
his rattle and chanting his special, sinister songs.

Now and then he pointed to various objects in the lodge, while
in his chant he explained which underwater medicine they represented and boasted of the power which they gave him. He was doing
very well indeed, and the effect on the crowd was all that he could
wish for, especially on the hapless Sanko.

At length he stopped, took up a metal dipper, and scooped up
some live coals from the fire hole. With a flourish and a wicked
grin he poured these into the heart of the effigy. At that moment
Sanko felt an agonizing pain in his chest. Cold sweat stood out all
over him.

Now Tone-a-koy began the dread death prayer. With his arms
outstretched and upward and the leather flaps which he had fastened
to his hands and feet in imitation of the web feet of the frog beating
a tattoo, he prayed to the south, west, north, and east in turn.
The prayers were loud, clear, and completely understandable. They
called on the underwater devils to strike Sanko dead at a certain
signal which he was about to give. As he alternately drew near the
bonfire, then back, Tone-a-koy's shadow on the back of the tipi
looked first like a misshapen dwarf, then blew up to that of a monster, its claws outstretched menacingly.

Sanko was choking, his knees buckling.

The crowd was transfixed. Every man, woman, and child was holding his breath.

Quickly the tempo of the dance increased. The weird chant rose to a screech. At the very climax, Tone-a-koy seized a loaded rifle, pointed it at the heart of the effigy, and fired.

Sanko saw no more. He had fallen to the ground unconscious.

But the crowd witnessed a miracle. As the reverberations of the shot died away, the witch doctor suddenly clutched his midsection. He tore off his mask, disclosing an agonized expression. He swayed for a moment, then fell heavily on his face.

Before anyone else could move, the two wives rushed in and turned the man over. Foam was appearing on his blue lips. He was breathing stertorously. The gasps came more and more slowly. Then they stopped. Tone-a-koy was dead.

The people remained in place, staring at the body of the vanquished shaman. Clear in the evening air rose the wails of his wives. Soon they were joined by his sister, who came running forward. Knives appeared. The mourners began to gash themselves—on their arms, breasts, and faces. The blood flowed copiously over the front of their garments. The wailing grew louder. Miss Reeside and Miss Ballew, who had refrained from attending the gathering, though they knew what was taking place, heard the crying. They came across the creek to comfort Tone-a-koy's women. Soon their dresses too were covered with blood.

Someone threw water on Sanko, who during the commotion had lain unnoticed. He sat up, blinked his eyes, and arose unsteadily. He was filled with wonder. He was alive, not a spirit! Gradually he realized that the wailing was not for him, but for his enemy who was lying dead in the light of the fire.

Sanko pushed through the crowd. He strode up the little slope to the side of the women. He looked down at Tone-a-koy. Then he faced the people. His eyes were shining. He lifted his arms to the heavens and shouted, "My God win! My God win!" ❁

Though a bit anticlimactic, the sequel to this story is of interest too.

Nothing could have impressed the Indians more than this convincing demonstration of power. Within a few days it was learned that Big Tree had asked to be baptized. Here and there other families began to come to the missionaries to learn about Christianity. Before long, the Baptist mission filled up at every Sunday service. Little by little the membership grew. In a surprisingly short time a substantial part of the tribe were members of the church. They have remained devout throughout the succeeding years.

Tone-a-koy was rolled up in a canvas sheet a short time after he died. He had said to his followers, "If I should die, take my body under the water in a deep hole in the Washita River. Let me stay there for four days and four nights. If I remain the full time, and do not come out of the water of my own accord, take me up and bury me."

But his sister would not agree to this. She didn't want him to lie in the water all that time. So they buried him on a nearby hill.

About 1925, they were exhuming some bodies from Indian graves to rebury them in the Rainy Mountain Baptist Church cemetery. A white man had been hired to do this. At length he came to the grave of Tone-a-koy. There was a small hole in the top of the mound. The Indians who were there told me that out of this hole crawled a small turtle, with a red feather in its mouth. As it came into view, it died. They put it in the water over night and it came to life. They sold it to Corwin Boake, at the town of Gotebo, who put it in a goldfish bowl. The next day it was gone.

When the undertaker dug into the grave he found no bones, only a little cluster of rifle cartridges which Tone-a-koy had once swallowed during one of his medicine shows. But the undertaker took up the dark earth where Tone-a-koy had been, placed it in a coffin, and reburied it in the cemetery. When the Indians pointed out his grave, they showed me also a little hole in the top where, they said, a snapping turtle crawls out occasionally.

It is said that the undertaker was bothered by bad dreams for a year after he had disturbed Tone-a-koy's remains.

Sanko lived to a good old age, dying on October 13, 1936. His faith had never wavered. He too was buried in the Rainy Mountain cemetery, where his grave and that of his enemy's may be seen to this day, a perpetual reminder of bad medicine and good.

Chief Characters
and Principal Informants

ADDO-EETTE (Big Tree). Born in 1847, Chief Big Tree was an outstanding warrior before he was twenty. After an active career as a raider, he was arrested in 1871, together with Satank and Satanta, for crimes committed in Texas. Sentenced to hang, he was later paroled, then pardoned. An early convert to Christianity, the Chief became an elder in the Rainy Mountain Baptist Church and taught a Bible class there for many years. He died in 1927.

ANDREW STUMBLING BEAR. Son of old Chief Stumbling Bear and a valued informant.

AN-PAY-KAU-TE. Son of Satank. Known to the whites as Frank Given, he had several other names, including in his last years, Set-ankia (his father's name). He was registered at the Indian agency as Au-kaunt. Old enough to have been on several raids during the years 1866–74, he was both participant and storyteller. He inherited from his father one of the Grandmother gods. He died in the late 1930's at about age eighty-five.

AN-ZAH-TE (An-zai-te, or Buffalo Udder). Grandfather of Jimmy Gui-tone. Prior to 1833, he was a chief of the highest rank, one of those authorized to wear scalp-hair fringes on his leggings. He went into battle riding a pure-white horse and wearing a scarlet cape, and thus was recognized by his enemies as well as his friends. Another tribe made him a "prince." But he was demoted after the Cutthroat Massacre for failure to rescue his shield and other trappings when the Osages attacked. Apparently, too, he had been in charge of the village and had failed to provide for its security. In later years he was an inveterate storyteller.

A-TO-TAINTE. A war leader who chose to die fighting rather than run or creep past his enemies. A brother of Chiefs Sun Boy and Pago-to-goodle, he was the owner of a sacred medicine lance presented to him in 1874 by Satanta.

AY-TAH. Wife of Chief Set-maunte. She accompanied her husband on several war expeditions, and thus was a participant as well as an informant. She later married Toyebo.

BOTALYE (later known as Eadle-tau-hain, or He Wouldn't Listen). A seventeen-year-old apprentice warrior who performed unusual feats of bravery during his first experience on the warpath. A member of Maman-ti's band, he may have had Mexican blood—perhaps he was half Mexican. In the 1880's, he became a fake medicine man, but was finally discredited. He was a voluble talker and a good informant.

DO-HAUSON (Little Bluff). Not the chief character of any story presented here, he was, nevertheless, one of the most prominent figures in Kiowa history. He was principal chief of all the Kiowa bands from 1834 till his death in 1866.

GUADAL-ONTE (Painted Red). Leader of an expedition into the Southwest in 1837 that was defeated by Mexican dragoons north of El Paso.

GUI-PAH-GO (Lone Wolf). Successor to Do-hauson as principal chief. Stepped down in favor of Mamay-day-te in 1874, but actually was superseded by Kicking Bird, who had more influence in the tribe and was superior in character. After his son was killed in Texas, Lone Wolf became a hostile, and was imprisoned in 1875. Shortly after his release in 1879, he died and was buried secretly on the north side of Mount Scott.

GUI-TONE (Que-tone or Wolf Tail, known as Jimmy). Grandson of
An-zah-te and father of George Hunt and Guy Queo-tone, the latter
a present-day Kiowa leader and Methodist minister. Too young to
go on the warpath before the end of the wars, he was, nevertheless,
widely acquainted with the participants in exciting events and well
informed on Kiowa history. An excellent informant.

HONE-ZEP-TAI (On Top of the Gun). War chief or raid leader killed
in 1864 while attempting to find a new route home from Mexico.

HOODLE-TAU-GOODLE (Hodle-to-guadal, or Red Dress). Daughter
of Maman-ti, cousin of Botalye, and foster sister of Tehan. Gave a
detailed description of the last outbreak during the period 1874–75.

ISEEO. An old-time warrior who died as a result of wounds. He was
the uncle of Tape-day-ah and Tah-bone-mah, who later took the
name Iseeo.

KOM-PAI-TE. Young brother of Chief White Horse. He went on several raids and eventually was killed while a member of Long Horn's
war party.

KONE-AU-BEAH. Survivor of Guadal-onte's disastrous fight with the
Mexicans at Hueco Tanks who, after a miraculous escape, found a
tribal medicine called the *T'au*.

LONG HORN. Yaqui Indian captured deep in Mexico while a small
boy and raised as a Comanche. Later, through marriage, he became
a Kiowa. Popular leader of a number of war parties. A limestone
ridge northwest of the Wichita Mountains is named for him. His
daughter, a college graduate, married a Sioux. (This is typical of
young western Indians who meet members of other tribes while at
school.)

MA-MAN-TI (Walking on a Cloud, Sky-Walker, or Do-ha-te). Except for Kicking Bird, this medicine man and owl prophet was the
most powerful leader of the Kiowas during the 1860's and 1870's.
Yet he was virtually unknown to the whites. The Indians selected by
Kicking Bird for imprisonment in 1875 persuaded Maman-ti to

cause the death of this chief by witchcraft. In agreeing, he stated that his own life would thus become forfeit, and he died shortly after reaching Fort Marion.

MARY BUFFALO. A descendant of Chief Poor Buffalo, she furnished data on the early tribal history.

MUMSUKAWA. A Comanche warrior who in later years furnished information to students of Indian life and history.

NAH-GOEY. A leader whose obstinate optimism in the face of unfavorable omens brought about the almost total destruction of his party.

PAGO-TO-GOODLE (One Young Man, or Solitary Young Man). A hereditary name, the first holder of which helped bring about the lasting peace between the Kiowas and Comanches. In the 1860's and 1870's, a Pago-to-goodle was again a very active and respected war chief.

PAH-GIA-GOODLE. One of two sisters captured in 1839 by the Cheyennes, then rescued by and married to a white trader. Her descendants are the Botones, Moses Botone being the present *Tai-me* keeper.

PAU-TSO-HAIN. Originator of the medicine of the buffalo cult.

PEAH-TO-MAH. Wife of Hunting Horse and an excellent informant.

QUANAH (Fragrant, also known as Quanah Parker). Outstanding young war chief of the western Comanche bands who became famous when it was discovered that he was the son of a white captive named Cynthia Ann Parker. After the Indian wars he rose, through ability, to the predominant position of leadership in the Comanche tribe. He has many descendants in Oklahoma who are prominent and respected citizens.

QUITAN (Queton, not to be confused with Gui-tone or Queo-tone). Born about 1852 in the city of Chihuahua, son of a Mexican soldier. Captured when a small boy by Comanches who later sold him to the Kiowas. Became a popular warrior on account of his unfailing good humor, energy, and helpfulness. Married a sister of Big Bow.

SET-ANKIA (Set-an-gia, or Sitting Bear, commonly called Satank). Known to the whites as a dangerous fighter from as early as 1845. A leader of many war parties and a member of the Ko-eet-senko, warrior order composed of the ten bravest members of the tribe. Killed at Fort Sill in 1871 after having been arrested by order of General Sherman. He has many descendants, some of them college graduates and ministers.

SET-IMKIA (Stumbling Bear, or Bear that Pushes You Down). Prominent chief, born in 1832. Cousin of Kicking Bird and member of that chief's peace faction. A signer of the Medicine Lodge Treaty.

SET-KONE-KIA (Black Bear). A young warrior who won the title of *to-yop-ke* through bravery and high qualities of leadership.

SET-MAUNTE (Bear Paw). The original holder of this name appears in several of the stories in the role of warrior. His namesake, better known as George Hunt, was the principal informant, not only for the author, but for several other writers and investigators. Hunt was born in 1878 and died in 1942. He was a nephew of Tah-bone-mah, in whose tipi he was raised. He was educated in the Fort Sill grammar school and learned Comanche and the sign language from his uncle and from General Scott. His English was quite good, and he even wrote a number of accounts in that tongue, one of which was published in the *Chronicles of Oklahoma*. He ranks as the chief Kiowa historian. He was a devoted Baptist and active in that church for many years. His first wife was the daughter of Satank; after her death he married Lillian Goombi, daughter of the white captive Millie Durgan. His character was of the highest, and he is mourned by the author and many other close friends.

SET-TAINTE (White Bear, commonly called Satanta). The "Orator of the Plains," well known to government officials and others on the frontier during the troubled times because of his raiding and kidnaping propensities, but even more for his genial effrontery. Arrested at Fort Sill in 1871, together with Satank and Big Tree, he spent several years in the penitentiary at Huntsville, Texas, finally committing suicide when he learned that release would never be granted.

His descendants, like those of several other famous chiefs, are law-abiding and respected citizens.

SET-TOI-YOI-TE (Many Bears, or Heap of Bears). The name of a succession of war leaders and *Tai-me* priests.

TAH-BONE-MAH. Well known at Fort Sill for many years under the name Iseeo. General Scott, when chief of staff, had Iseeo made a permanent sergeant in the army. An experienced warrior and skilled storyteller.

TAPE-DAY-AH (Standing Sweat House). Older brother of Tah-bone-mah. Warrior, medicine man, and owl prophet. One of the heroes in the story of the long journey north through the Rocky Mountains in the period 1863–64.

TAY-BODAL (T'e-bodal, or One Who Carries the Meat from a Buffalo's Lower Leg). Born about 1816, he was a survivor of the Cutthroat Massacre. In 1896, he was one of Mooney's informants and the oldest man in the tribe. He was a warrior and amateur surgeon of some note.

TAY-NAY-ANGOPTE (Eagle Striking with Talons, known as Kicking Bird). One of the most distinguished Kiowas of all times. His grandfather was a Crow, and he came from a line of chiefs. His eminence in the tribe came from his superior intellect, courage, and force of character. He was influential among the whites, too, because he favored peace. He probably suffered martyrdom for this cause, since, in 1875, he died mysteriously, likely murdered by the disaffected elements of the tribe. He is buried at Fort Sill.

TEHAN (Texan). A white captive whose origin and death are still a mystery. Near the end of the Wrinkled-Hand Chase he disappeared into the Staked Plains. He was a big fellow with a red neck and red hair.

TO-GOAM. A white girl captured in Texas in 1867 and never recovered by her relatives. Married a Mexican member of the Kiowa tribe named Calisay. There is strong evidence that her name was

Mary Hamleton. Her many descendants regard themselves as Indians, but have no Indian blood.

TONE-A-KOY (Snapping Turtle, also called Docti). Witch doctor who used his powers for evil, but finally succumbed to his own "medicine"—bad whisky.

T'ON-ZAU-TE. First of the buffalo medicine men.

TSEN-TAINTE (White Horse). An active, athletic war chief, noted as a raider in Texas. Imprisoned in Florida after the wars, he was soon released and lived many years, still "unreconstructed."

TSEN-TONKE (Hunting for a Horse, known as Hunting Horse, or Old Man Horse). Went on his first raid in 1874, but was revolted by the brutality and bloodshed. Devoted the rest of his life, he said, to "being a friend of everyone." In this he succeeded admirably, dying at the age of 107 with a host of friends, many of them high-ranking army officers, and a large number of descendants. As an Indian scout, he had veteran's status, and lies buried at Fort Sill. At least two of his sons have been Methodist ministers. Hunting Horse was half Spanish and had gray eyes. He said that his mother, who remained a captive all her life, was named Sevilla.

ZEPKO-EETTE (Big Bow). A war chief whose high rank is indicated by the fact that he wore leggings with fringe of scalp hair. More or less a lone operator because his skepticism concerning "medicine" alienated him from the tribe. He stayed on the Staked Plains and associated with the Comanches. In his later years, he became a Christian.

Index

283

Fort Marion: 223, 225, 226
Fort Richardson: 137n.
Fort Sill: xvi, xviii, xix, 3, 81, 186, 206, 213, 214, 215, 222, 227, 230, 241, 249
Fort Supply: xi
Four-Mile Crossing: 249
Fizzlehead (A-mo-tai, or Ai-mo-tai): 104, 212

Gageby Creek: 191n.
Gail, Tex.: 175n.
Gambler steals Big Bow's horses: 244–48
Gee-oy: 245
Geysers: vii
Ghost Dance: 269
Gia-gi-hodle: 147
Given, Julia: 267, 270
Gold convoys during Civil War: 117
Goodnight Ranch, Tex.: 216, 228
Goombi, Mrs. (Millie Durgan): xiv, 237
Goom-dah: 268
Gotebo: xix, 107, 234, 235, 236, 237, 265, 267, 268
Gotebo, Okla.: 133
Gourd Society: 58
Graham, Tex.: 137
Grandmother gods: vii, 30, 31, 45, 49–51, 172, 201
Granite, Okla.: 228
Great Stinking Lake: 174
Great White Father: xv
Greer County, Okla.: 234, 240
Griffis, Joseph: 214
Guadal-onte: 36
Gui-ka-te (Wolf Lying Down): xi, 11–13
Gui-tone, Jimmy: xix, 30, 132–34, 228
Gyprock Creek: 204

Hah-bay-te: 138
Hail storms: 155
Hair braids: 165

Half-witted man abandoned: 188, 202
Hall, Lee: 245, 248
Hamleton family killed: 135–36
Hamleton Mary: 135–42, 208; see also To-goam-gat-ty
Hansford Land and Cattle Co.: 179
Harrington, John P.: 156n.
Haumpo: 51
Haun-goon-pau (Silver Horn): 51, 197
Hau-nai-te: 251–52
Hau-vah-te: 153–54, 172–77
Haworth, James: 81
Heap of Bears (Set-toi-yo-te): 54, 148, 149
He-at-keah: 241–43
Heraldry: 95
He Wouldn't Listen: see Eadle-tau-hain and Botalye
Hone-a-bone: 81
Hone-geah-tau-he (Silver Head-Plate): 41
Hone-zep-tia (Kills With A Gun): 97–99, 115–19
Hoodle-tau-goodle, or Hoddle-to-goodle (Red Dress): 151, 209–15, 223
Horsehead Crossing: ix
Horse racing: 233–43
Horses: viii
Horse stealing: 152, 168–69
Ho-to-yeah: 137
Hoyu-ke-ta: xx
Hueco Tanks, Tex.: 36
Humming Bird: 46
Hunt, George: vii, xix, xx, 36, 46, 48, 51, 57, 70, 73, 77, 81, 83, 105, 115, 123, 138, 157, 164, 167, 233, 244, 249, 264, 268
Hunting Horse (Tsen-tonke): vii, xix, 36, 228, 259–67
Hutchison, Philip, 235

Indian Bureau: 227
Indian Perfume River: 216
Iron Shirt: 202

Maunte-pah-hodal (Kills-It-With-A-Gun): 105–107
Maxwell's trading post: 85
McCusker, Philip: 138
Medicine, personal: 49
Medicine Bluff Creek, Okla.: xiii, xvi, 207, 250, 259
Medicine dance: *see* sun dance
Medicine horse (tornado): 155–56
Medicine Lodge Treaty: xvi, 137
Mescalero Apaches: ix, 5, 114, 174–75, 205, 214
Messenger-announcing custom: 33, 190
Messenger-Announcing Song: 33
Mexican lancers: 36–40, 96–101
Mexicans: 10, 104
Mexicans from New Mexico: 188, 202, 203, 204
Mexico: xi, xiii, 115; *see also* Chihuahua
Miles, Col. Nelson A.: 190n., 210, 213n., 249–52
Missionaries: 267
Mobeetie, Tex.: 245
Mo-ha-te: 203
Mokeen: 55, 66
Mon-ka-yee (tornado): 156
Montague County, Tex.: 55
Mooney, James: xix, 10, 49, 50n., 52, 54, 81
Mountain View, Okla.: 140
Mount Hinds: 250
Mount Scott: 51, 184, 228
Mount Sheridan: 262
Mow-way: 220
Muchaque, Tex.: 28, 175
Mumsukuwa: 216–21
Myres family killed: 135–36

Navaho captive of White Horse (To-ya-ke): 145, 147, 207, 236
Navaho Mountain: 206
Navahos: ix, xiv, 5, 10, 20, 22, 24, 83–88, 117, 143–47, 202, 203, 204
New Mexicans: ix, 84–85, 88–89

New Mexico: xiv, 11, 20, 104, 114
New route through mountains: 116
New Spain: 11
Nokoni (Wanderer) Comanches: 13, 14, 180
Nolan, Capt. Nicholas: 229–30
North Fork of Red River: ix, x, xviii, xx, 129, 137, 186, 224, 244, 245
Nudity deplored: 157, 162, 248
Nye, Elleane: 253–56

Oak Creek Sun Dance: 76
O-ha-ma-tai: 204
Old Women's Society: 65
O-ma-tay: 204
Onde: 95
Osages: ix, x, xi, 53, 113
Otter Belt: 180–81
Otter Creek: ix, xiii
Owl prophets: 83, 151–54, 190
Owls, superstition: 151

Pago-to-goodle (One Young Man): 3–9, 158, 172, 230–32, 175–76, 230–32
Pah-gia-goodle: 77–80
Pai-kee-te (Pay-kee): 192, 195, 245–48
Palo Duro Canyon: 188, 198, 201, 204, 214, 216, 220
Parfleche: viii
Parker, Cynthia Ann: 141
Parra-o-coom (He Bear): 180-82
Paso del Norte, Tex.: 36
Pau-tape-te: 191, 268
Pau-tso-hain: 47
Pawnees: ix, 47, 104, 204
Peah-to-mah: vii, 20, 228
Pecan Creek: 174
Pecos River (Pau-aidle-san): ix, 20, 21, 27, 30, 32, 83, 84, 114, 115, 205
Penateka Comanches: xii, xiii, 13
Peninsular Sun Dance: 110
Peyote cult: 267, 268
Pipe men: *see* to-yop-ke

289

Bad Medicine & Good has been set in Linotype Caslon Old Face of 11½ points, with 1½ points of leading between lines. The Caslon face was originated by William Caslon in England in the eighteenth century, was transplanted to American print shops in the Colonial period, and has since been one of the most popular of this country's type faces.

UNIVERSITY OF OKLAHOMA PRESS

NORMAN